MW01622081

WHY *Old Places* MATTER

For Carolyn and Jay,
With great appreciation — and thanks for saving Wild Goose —
Thompson M. Mayes

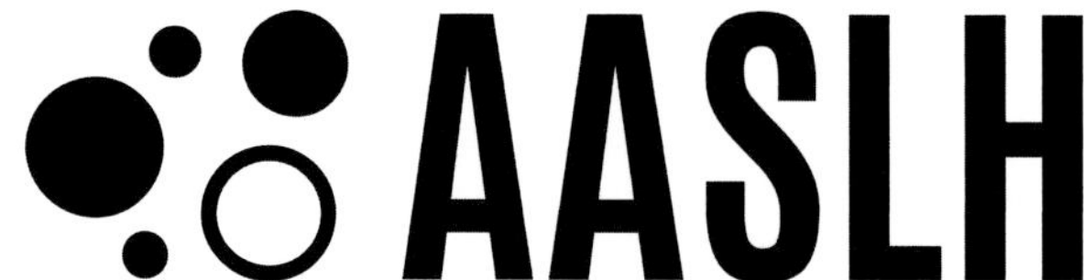

AMERICAN ASSOCIATION FOR STATE AND LOCAL HISTORY BOOK SERIES

ABOUT THE SERIES

The American Association for State and Local History Book Series addresses issues critical to the field of state and local history through interpretive, intellectual, scholarly, and educational texts. To submit a proposal or manuscript to the series, please request proposal guidelines from AASLH headquarters: AASLH Editorial Board, 2021 21st Ave. South, Suite 320, Nashville, Tennessee 37212. Telephone: (615) 320-3203. Website: www.aaslh.org.

ABOUT THE ORGANIZATION

The American Association for State and Local History (AASLH) is a national history membership association headquartered in Nashville, Tennessee, that provides leadership and support for its members who preserve and interpret state and local history in order to make the past more meaningful to all people. AASLH members are leaders in preserving, researching, and interpreting traces of the American past to connect the people, thoughts, and events of yesterday with the creative memories and abiding concerns of people, communities, and our nation today. In addition to sponsorship of this book series, AASLH publishes *History News* magazine, a newsletter, technical leaflets and reports, and other materials; confers prizes and awards in recognition of outstanding achievement in the field; supports a broad education program and other activities designed to help members work more effectively; and advocates on behalf of the discipline of history. To join AASLH, go to www.aaslh.org or contact Membership Services, AASLH, 2021 21st Ave. South, Suite 320, Nashville, TN 37212.

WHY *Old Places* MATTER

HOW HISTORIC PLACES AFFECT OUR IDENTITY AND WELL-BEING

THOMPSON M. MAYES

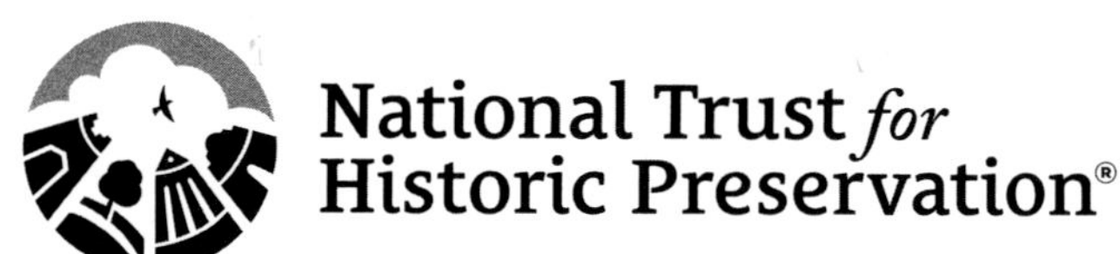

Washington, DC

ROWMAN & LITTLEFIELD
Lanham • Boulder • New York • London

Published by Rowman & Littlefield
An imprint of The Rowman & Littlefield Publishing Group, Inc.
4501 Forbes Boulevard, Suite 200, Lanham, Maryland 20706
www.rowman.com

Unit A, Whitacre Mews, 26-34 Stannary Street, London SE11 4AB

British Library Cataloguing in Publication Information Available

Library of Congress Cataloging-in-Publication Data

Library of Congress Control Number: 2018949402
ISBN: 978-1-5381-1768-2 (cloth: alk. paper)
ISBN: 978-1-5381-1769-9 (electronic)

∞™ The paper used in this publication meets the minimum requirements of American National Standard for Information Sciences—Permanence of Paper for Printed Library Materials, ANSI/NISO Z39.48-1992.

Printed in the United States of America

In memory of my sister,
Carol Harris Mayes,
and my mother,
Elizabeth McCord Mayes

We do not only inhabit space, we also dwell in time.

—Juhani Pallasmaa

Contents

Acknowledgments

Why Old Places Matter could not have been written without the many people who kindly shared their ideas with me over the course of years, as well as the institutions that supported my research and the publication of these essays. First and foremost, the National Trust for Historic Preservation unhesitatingly supported the project from the beginning, providing me with a sabbatical to research the ideas, publishing the essays as blog posts through *Preservation Forum*, and supporting the publication of the essays as a book. The American Academy in Rome awarded me not only the National Endowment for the Arts Rome Prize in Historic Preservation, but more importantly, gave me access to the city of Rome and the astonishingly generous and thoughtful community of fellows, fellow travelers, scholars, and artists at the American Academy. The American Association for State and Local History (AASLH) championed the publication of the essays as part of its book series shortly after I returned from Rome and pursued it through completion.

At the National Trust, a special heartfelt expression of gratitude to Paul Edmondson and particular thanks to Stephanie Meeks, David Brown, Katherine Malone-France, and Lyn Moriarity for their unstinting support of the project. Susan West-Montgomery, Priya Chhaya, Byrd Wood, Julia Rocchi, Germonique Ulmer, Rebecca Bice, Lisa Thompson, and Alison Yue worked with me with thoughtfulness and good humor on the blog posts, articles, communications, and a host of other support; Ross Bradford, Anne Nelson, Sharee Williamson, William Cook, Betsy Merritt, Shantia Anderheggen, and Paul Edmondson took over my regular work while I was in Rome and did it so well and with such pleasure that most of it stayed with them. Thanks also to Raina Regan, Latoya Livingston, Moira Nadal, Elaine Chang, and Georgiana Hale of the law department for their support and goodwill.

Many other present and past colleagues at the National Trust, its sites, and related organizations shared their thoughts, ideas, and support, including Kevin Murphy, Margaret O'Neal, James Lindberg, Tabitha Almquist, Mike Powe, Robert Nieweg, Roberta Lane, Rhonda Sincavage, Joseph McGill, Barbara Pahl, John Hildreth, Sheri Freemuth, Kelly Schindler, Brent Leggs, Anthony Veerkamp, Chris Morris, Laurie Ossman, Donna Hassler, Jenny Buddenborg, Rosemarie Rae, Carolyn Brackett, Nancy Tinker, Alicia Leuba, Dennis Hockman, Ashley Wilson, Callie Hawkins, Erin Carlson Mast, David Young, James Schwartz, George McDaniel, Judy Clark, Irv Henderson, Kevin and Mary Daniels, Tim Whalen, Marita Rivero, Jim and Janet Vaughan, Frank Sanchis, Carl Wolf, Tom Cassidy, Marianna Knight, David Field, and Theresa Pasqual. Mary Butler found images and created designs on an impossibly short deadline. Ann Thornton, Kimberly Skelly, and Hilary Baar sought or identified funding for the book.

At the American Academy, I was inspired to understand more about old places through experiencing Rome, but I was even more inspired by the generous interdisciplinary cross-fertilization that the academy fosters. I thank Adele Chatfield-Taylor for her friendship and her unwavering support for historic preservation as a discipline at the academy, Cristina Puglisi for understanding the soul of the academy as a preservation philosophy, Christopher and Anna Celenza for their thoughtful leadership and kindness, Kim Bose for the walks and talks, Peter Benson Miller for his intellect, Sebastian Hierl for always helping me obtain articles and books, Mark Robbins for his continuing engagement, Shawn Miller, Gianpaolo Battaglia, and Giulia Barra for all of their help and good cheer, Alessandro Lima, Tiziana Del Grosso, Chris Behr, Christopher Boswell, Gabriel Soare, and the interns of the Rome Sustainable Food Project for the astonishing food and drinks, as well as the late Pina Pasquontonio, whose persistence surpassed many hurdles.

The fellows, fellow travelers, residents, visiting scholars, artists, and other visitors to the American Academy in Rome during 2013 and 2014 are a continuing joy. People generously shared their ideas through interviews, conversations, videos, recordings, and writing, including Thomas Leslie, Max Page, C. M. Chin, Dan Hurlin, Ruth Lo, Hamlett Dobbins, Yoko Hara, Catie Newell, Thomas Kelley, Irene San Pietro, Andrew Ollett, Peter Bognanni, Junita Bognanni, Lindsay Harris, Stephanie Frampton, Cotton Seed, Jessica Nowlin, Jonathan MacLellan, Nicolas de Monchaux, Brad Cantrell, Eric Nathan, Dan Visconti, Ruth Noyes, Gabrielle Ponce, Elizabeth and John LaBombard, Ryan Bailey, Sheramy Bundrick, Peter Streckfus, Heather Green, Catherine Wagner, Loretta Gargan, Anna Betbeze, Reynold Reynolds, Saskia Reynolds, Patrick Nold, Maya Maskarinec, Cesare Santus, Leigh Ann Lieberman, Tracey Watts, Martin Eisner, Matt King, Sarah Bainter Cunningham, Katherine Whipple, Joseph Farrell, Ann De Forest, Alice Waters, Lucille Tenazas, Patricia Cronin, Frederick Steiner, Arianna Gullo, Juhani Pallasmaa, Laurie Olin, Joel Katz, Bunny Harvey, Cynthia Altman, Chas Miller, Birch Coffey, Geoffrey Symcox, Petra Nordcamp, Paul Bray, Jonathan Reynolds, Heidi Ettinger, Deanna Marchulina, John Kamisuka, James Packer, Billy Hayes, Harvey Goldblatt, Walter Hood, Sara James, and John Taylor. I am eternally grateful to have shared memories with them all in the Eternal City.

Other people in Rome and in the United States shared interviews, speeches, writings, videos, and other information, including Guiseppe Albano, Luigi Prisco, Cinzia Abbate, Carlo Vigevano, Sofia Bosco, Peter Gould, Jeffrey Blanchard, Rita Rivelli, John Coates, Ed Perlman, Didier Repellin, Jorge Hernandez, Brock Bierman, Anthony Wood, Joel Gilman, Paul Goldberger, Myrick Howard, Donovan Rypkema, Andrew Potts, David Schon, Randall Mason, Robert Jaeger, Stephen Callcott, Charles Wolfe, Jeremy Wells, Ned Kaufman, Luca Zevi, Simone Quillici, Stefano de Caro, and Jukka Jokilehto.

The idea for these essays arose from teaching preservation law, and I gratefully acknowledge Donald Linebaugh and David Fogle at the University of Maryland, Randall Mason, now at the University of Pennsylvania, who was particularly generous with his time, knowledge, and experience in Rome, as well as Brown Morton at Mary Washington University, and the late Dorothy Miner at Columbia University for encouraging my teaching.

One of the remarkable consequences of being at the academy with such talented and generous people was that I returned with a greater appreciation of my community of creative and thoughtful friends and colleagues, many of whom have been helpful in thinking about these ideas and supportive of writing and creative work. Without naming all of you, I thank you.

I am particularly thankful for three individuals who supported the project at the beginning and who fought tirelessly for the preservation and understanding of places that matter: Charles Granquist, Dan Jordan, and Richard Moe. I am also thankful for the Historic Preservation and Conservation panel for the American Academy in Rome, Mark Rabinowitz, T. Gunny Harboe, and Michele Marincola.

For identifying and sharing photographs, I thank Michael Green, Sam Kittner, Peter Krogh, Stewart Gray, Michael Mayes, Michael Pollock, Catie Newell, Frank Vagnone, Gary Albert, Kelly Schindler, Melani Hom, Meryle Cawley, Erin Carlson Mast, and Theresa Pasqual. For help with the bibliography, Phoebe Walsh.

For asking me to propose the book as part of the AASLH series, I thank Bob Beatty. For publishing the book and guiding me through the publishing process, Charles Harmon, Michael Tan, and Della Vache at Rowman & Littlefield, and for careful and thoughtful copyediting, Erin McGarvey.

I would also like to acknowledge the many organizations and individuals who have invited me to speak about why old places matter, including Lisa Craig at the City of Annapolis, Myra Best from the Cleveland Park Historical Society, Jeremy Wells and Lynne Manzo at the Environmental Design Research Association, Kim Trent at Knox Heritage, Heath Fox and Judy Haxo at La Jolla Historical Society, Nancy Finegood at Michigan Historic Preservation Network, Judy Clark and Susanne Pandich at the Pocantico Conference Center of the Rockefeller Brothers Fund, Danielle LaPresta Parker at the Preservation Alliance of West Virginia, Alexander Ives at the Preservation Foundation of Palm Beach, Paula Mohr and Michael Morain at Preservation Iowa, Myrick Howard at Preservation North Carolina, John Hurzan, Charlotte Rea, Barbara Lamb, and Susan Godshall at the New Haven Preservation Trust, Ashley and George Wilson at the Athenaeum Salon in Alexandria, Ken and Dottie Woodcock at Matunuck Preservation Society/South Kingstown Land Trust, Richard Tower at the Miami Design Preservation League, Mike Koop at the Minnesota Historical Society, Kristine Gerber, Nicole Malone, and Cindy Tooker at Restore Omaha, the Smartgrowth Network, Jana Shafajog at Morven Park, Katie Spencer, Mary Fitch, and Kathy Adams at the American Institute of Architects, Washington, D.C., Patrice Frey at National Main Street Center, Jo Leimenstoll at University of North Carolina, Greensboro, Amy Munson and Fern Swenson of State Historical Society of North Dakota, Don Linebaugh for the Marvin Breckinridge Patterson Lecture at the University of Maryland, Randall Mason at University of Pennsylvania, Joel Katz at University of the Arts, Philadelphia, Pennsylvania, Karelia Carbonell and Becky Matkov at the Historic Preservation Association of Coral Gables, as well as David and Tessie Doheny.

This book is in memory of my sister, Carol Harris Mayes, and my mother, Elizabeth McCord Mayes, who shared and enabled my love of old places. I am also deeply grateful for the love and support from my brothers and their families, Dan, Eric, Glenn, Betsy, Elisa, Matt, David, Jess, Colton, and Libby, as well as Chris, Susan, Miranda, and Marissa, and my extended family, and family of friends. The deepest thank-you to my husband Rod, for being on this journey with me. Home is where he is (but it's almost always an old place).

Finally, I am deeply grateful for all the people throughout America and the world who work tirelessly to save places that matter.

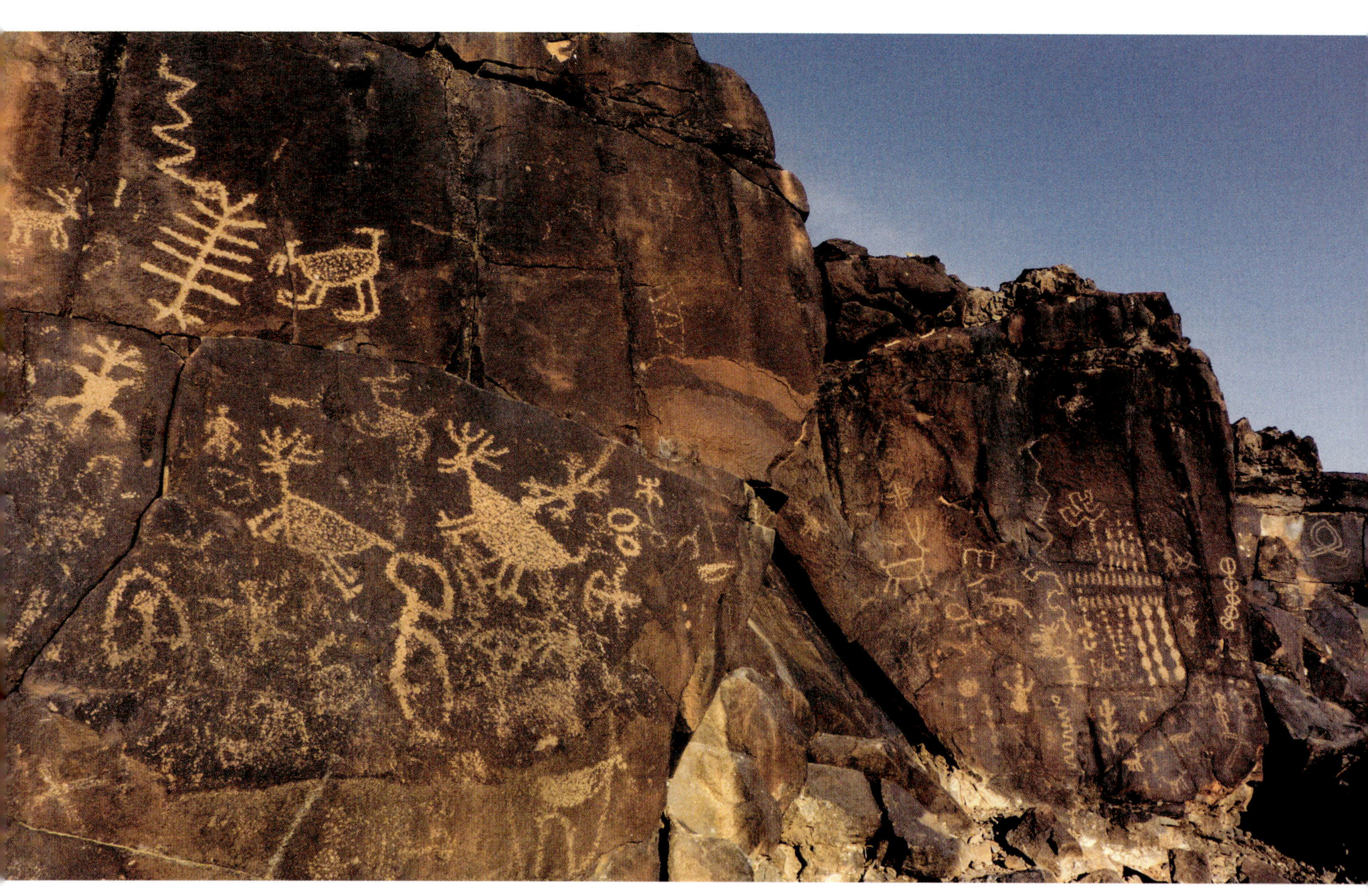

Ancient petroglyphs at Sears Point, in the Great Bend of the Gila, a National Treasure
ANDY LAURENZI

Foreword

THE POWER OF OLD PLACES

Stephanie Meeks

Why do old places matter so much to us? What is the essence of their enduring pull? How do they continue to hold such a power over us long after they were formed or built? These are questions we have been pondering since the dawn of recorded history.

Just as the Romans marveled at the ruins of Troy, many over the years have noted the role of old places in bringing to life, across millennia, the long continuity of the past. "From the heights of these pyramids," Napoleon Bonaparte once told his troops at Giza, "forty centuries look down on us." Whereas Napoleon saw his vast ambition reflected in the stones of Egypt, another Frenchman, Gustave Flaubert, drew the opposite lesson from them. "All this ancient dust," he shrugged, "makes one indifferent to fame."

Other writers have highlighted how places help us to establish a sense of identity—to recall who we are and where we come from. "How hard it is to escape from places," observed the modernist writer Katherine Mansfield, early in the twentieth century.

“However carefully one goes they hold you—you leave little bits of yourself fluttering on the fences like rags and shreds of your very life.”

A similar sentiment was famously crooned by four lads from Liverpool: “There are places I’ll remember all my life,” the Beatles told us, full of “moments of loves and friends I still can recall.” By contrast, losing the places that tell our story can be traumatic. “How will we know it’s us without our past?” John Steinbeck’s displaced families ask in *The Grapes of Wrath.*

For several years, Tom Mayes, vice president and senior counsel at the National Trust for Historic Preservation and winner of the 2013 Rome Prize in Historic Preservation from the American Academy in Rome, delved deeply into these questions about place—questions that are fundamental not just to our work as preservationists, but to our basic understanding of ourselves and our communities.

After intensive research and many discussions with his colleagues in Rome and elsewhere, Tom composed a wonderful series of essays about why old places matter for Forum Blog, our preservation leadership blog. In these powerful, thought-provoking essays, now gathered here into one volume, Tom reflects on continuity, memory, identity, beauty, sustainability, and other compelling reasons that old places continue to move us.

Ultimately, I hope these remarkable essays encourage you to ponder this same age-old query: why do old places matter to you?

For my part, I think of the houses in Colorado where I grew up, the schools that shaped who I am. And I think of a sod-roofed dugout on the Kansas prairie where my father’s ancestors lived more than a century ago. This is not a landmark or a monument; it is an earthen home sculpted from the tallgrass prairie. It is a place where, to escape from poverty, my great-great-grandparents and their eight children lived a hardscrabble existence, so that they and later generations could live a better life.

My family’s American story begins in that Kansas dugout. That unremarkable place—unlikely to be added to the National Register anytime soon—nonetheless connects me across the generations to my great-grandmother, who left Norway with four children to follow her husband in search of a new start amid America’s Great Plains.

One of the most evocative portrayals of that particular pioneer experience is the author Willa Cather, best remembered for her prairie trilogy—*O Pioneers! The Song of the Lark*, and *My Antonia.* In the second of these novels, Cather’s heroine, Thea Kronborg, a young, aspiring artist from Colorado, visits ancient Native American dwellings above Flagstaff, Arizona, and imagines herself living among them centuries earlier:

> On the first day that Thea climbed the water trail she began to have intuitions about the women who had worn the path, and who had spent so great a part of their lives going up and down it. She found herself trying to walk as they must have walked, with a feeling in her feet and knees and loins which she had never known before. . . . She could feel the weight of an Indian baby hanging to her back as she climbed.

This potent sense of connection that Cather describes is the power of old places. It is what I feel when I think of that Kansas dugout where my ancestors made their home—the same thrill as visiting President Lincoln's cottage and grasping the same banister our former president held. It is how Stonehenge or the Great Bend of the Gila connects us to life thousands of years prior or how an old haunt connects us to the people and memories of our own past—including even ourselves.

In 1943, the psychologist Abraham Maslow came up with a theory of human motivation called the hierarchy of needs, which is now usually portrayed in the shape of a pyramid. The most fundamental needs of men and women form the base and more prosaic concerns lie at the top. After physiological needs like air, food, water, and personal safety, Maslow argued, the most powerful need felt by us is belonging.

Old places, Tom Mayes argues here, speak to that need for belonging in a way that little else can. They give us the chance to feel a connection to the broad community of human experience, a community that exists across time. And they help us understand that the lives we lead are not insignificant, that what we do will have an impact on the future.

That is why our work saving America's historic places is so important, not just for understanding our own history but for our sense of ourselves. Historic places connect us to the striving and struggles of earlier generations and of generations to come. They tell us who we are. And they help us understand that, though we ourselves may be mortal, our actions will echo on after we are gone, just as those of previous generations inform our world today.

All the more reason why we must continue working to save the places that matter to us and to make sure they are playing an active role in the daily lives of our communities so that future generations can experience them, be enthralled by them, and feel that same powerful sense of connection to the great American past and to we who inhabited it.

Stephanie Meeks is the president and CEO of the National Trust for Historic Preservation.

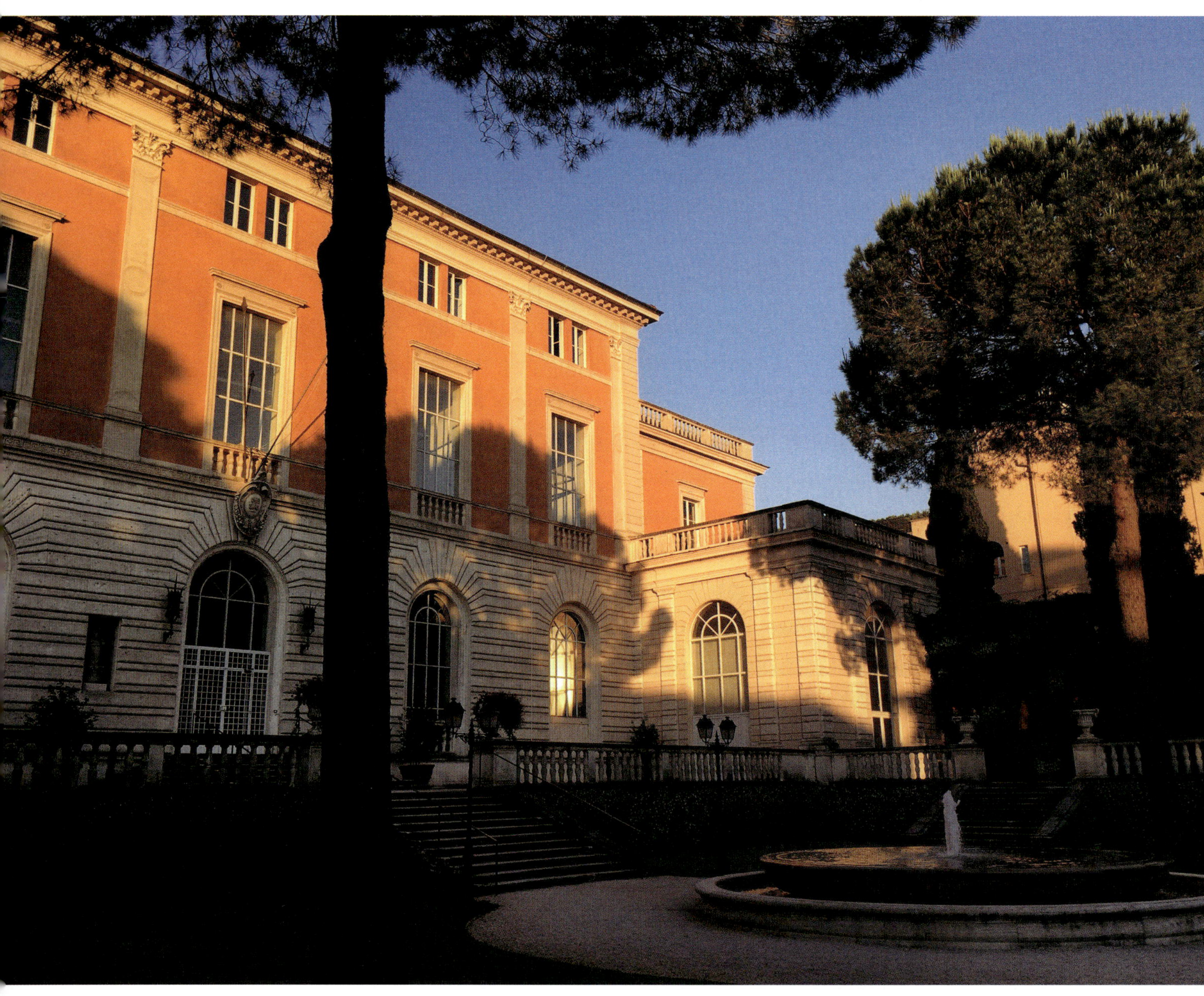

The American Academy in Rome, by McKim, Mead, and White, built in 1913. Charles Follen McKim was a founder and early supporter of the academy.

PAUL EDMONDSON/NATIONAL TRUST FOR HISTORIC PRESERVATION

Prologue

In 2013, I embarked on a journey both literal and figural. Thanks to support from the American Academy in Rome and the National Trust for Historic Preservation, I moved to Rome for six months so that I could investigate a question I had hoped to study for more than a decade: why do old places matter? What difference does it make to people if we save, reuse, or simply continue to use old places—or don't? Do old places enhance and improve people's lives and, if so, how? While exploring Rome and the many layers of history embedded in that astonishing palimpsest of an old city, I finally had the great gift of time to try to understand this central facet of both our work and our human experience.

Why did I embark on this journey? Aren't the reasons obvious? As someone posted on Facebook in response to one of my essays, "kinda crazy that the question even has to be asked." I was motivated to explore this topic because I had a sense that people who care about old places—many of whom may not even be conscious that they care until something is threatened or lost—didn't have ready words to express why old places make such a difference to them and to their communities, even though many of us feel the importance intuitively and often very deeply. Though explanations existed in textbooks, statutes, books, and articles, the reasons, to my knowledge, had never been gathered and stated together concisely in one publication.

After decades as a preservation professional for the National Trust for Historic Preservation—a lawyer, teacher, trainer, practitioner—I thought collecting these reasons would be a relatively simple task. I quickly realized that this project was going to be more daunting than I had imagined. Yet what I also discovered, to my delight, was a much larger world of people thinking and writing about place from multiple perspectives related to historic preservation but not in the preservation field, including environmental psychology, place attachment, place identity, cultural geography, phenomenology, aesthetic theory, sustainability, biophilia, geopsychology, health, and neuroscience, as well as the stalwarts of the field—architecture, planning, history, critical heritage studies, historic preservation, architectural history, and urbanism. I don't pretend to be an expert in all or even most of these fields, but I've sought to understand the work of scholars looking at place from these individual disciplines and to discern the key points that might be meaningful for people of all backgrounds who care about older places.

What I found is that, yes, old places do indeed matter—and for more reasons than I thought. From memory and identity, to architecture and history, to beauty and sacredness, to economics and sustainability, old places matter for reasons so numerous, all encompassing, and essential to who we are as individuals and as a society that their place in our lives is difficult to fully recognize. The kaleidoscopic list of reasons in this book suggests just how important older places are. Yet even these essays, which treat the topics singly, can only hint at the totality—the all-encompassing *world* of meaning that old places have for us. The old places of our lives are like the air we breathe: surrounding us, sustaining us, influencing us, and even a part of us.

Ultimately, I wrote about the fourteen ideas I heard most frequently when I talked with people about why old places mattered to them. These words capture many of the main concepts, but I continue to hear more. Among the other words I heard were *comfort*, *reconciliation*, *craftsmanship*, *knowledge*, *grounding*, *and belonging*, all worthy of further exploration. Our living relationship with old places is supple, subtle, and changeable. Any one place may reflect many of these reasons. Different ideas will resonate with different people at the same place. Some people will respond to one place but not another. And our relationships with places may change over a lifetime.

Although many people study place, only a handful choose to focus their work on older and existing places. Almost all the attention is on *new* places—on place*making* rather than place *sustaining*. For example, in the world of environmental sustainability, much attention is given to green products and to building new green buildings, but little attention is given to the importance of continuing to use the resources we already have. Similarly, in the world of planning, particularly new urbanism, much attention is given to building new communities that are walkable and dense in a way that fosters people's capacity to form community, but very little attention is given to sustaining existing communities, which have already become *community* through the intertwining of people and place over time. It's almost as if these existing older places are so much a part of our lives that they are invisible. One of my goals here is to make older places more visible.

By the very nature of the individual disciplines that study place, almost none of them strives to see the whole—the overarching totality of the role old places play in our lives. That's a key reason why I believe this series of essays is necessary—to try to get a greater glimpse of the meaning of old places by gathering the individual reasons together. Altogether, the old places of our lives give us, to borrow a phrase from a program at the University of North Carolina Greensboro, an internal compass that orients us in our lives and helps us know who, what, where, and sometimes even why we are.

The essays that follow were issued serially through the National Trust's *Preservation Forum* blog from November 2013 through April 2015 and were followed by an issue of the *Forum Journal* dedicated to the topic with articles by other writers. My ideas developed as I explored the individual topics. Had I known at the beginning what I knew at the end, I obviously might have changed the order or emphasis.

That learning process has not ended with the publication of these essays. I've since been inspired by the comments and reactions that these essays have sparked, particularly from people who are working to save places that they care about. Here are a few of my favorites:

> Old buildings are more than stones and creaky floors; they hold deep human memory, both painful and exultant.—Sr. Maureen

> I'm so happy to read and share with others how important connectivity with our past is to living in the present day. I've been discouraged many days but today my spirit is renewed.—Evelyn Terry

> Old places matter, as they are places of the heart.—Mechelle Lawrence Adams

It is my hope that this book encourages more people to think about why old places matter to them. I hope that it gives people phrases and words to help them articulate and express their deeply held feelings about the old places of their lives and that it helps to build a stronger ethic of appreciating, saving, and continuing to use old places.

This ethic is necessary to build both the political support for laws and policies—and the simple goodwill—that helps people and communities retain the places that matter. We need to be able to express the reasons—and share the evidence that supports them—with mayors, elected officials, planners, developers, and each other and to continue to build the case for retaining and nurturing the existing places where we live, work, and play. But more importantly, if we broaden our understanding of the old places in our communities and our own lives, we may help people lead more fulfilling and richer lives. These places spur our memory, delight us with beauty, help us understand others, give us a deep sense of belonging, and, perhaps most fundamentally, remind us who we are.

Introduction

People like old places. They like to live in places like Ghent in Norfolk, Virginia, and Logan Circle in Washington, D.C. They like to live in old houses—in white farmhouses in Vermont, brick mansions in Virginia, and in arts-and-crafts bungalows in Los Angeles. People like to visit old cities on vacation. They like Santa Fe, Provincetown, Mendocino, and Saugatuck. They like Rome, New York, Paris, and Kyoto. They like Brooklyn and Charleston and thousands of towns and cities and countrysides across America and throughout the world. They like ancient troglodytic hotels (Matera, Italy), and Greek Revival houses (Athens, Georgia). They like adobe houses in New Mexico, farmhouses in Ohio, and townhouses in Philadelphia.

Why? Why do people like old places? And why do old places matter to people? Do old places make people's lives better and, if so, how?

This series of essays explores the reasons that old places are good for people. It begins with what I consider the main reason—that old places are important for people to define who they are through memory, continuity, and identity—that "sense of orientation"

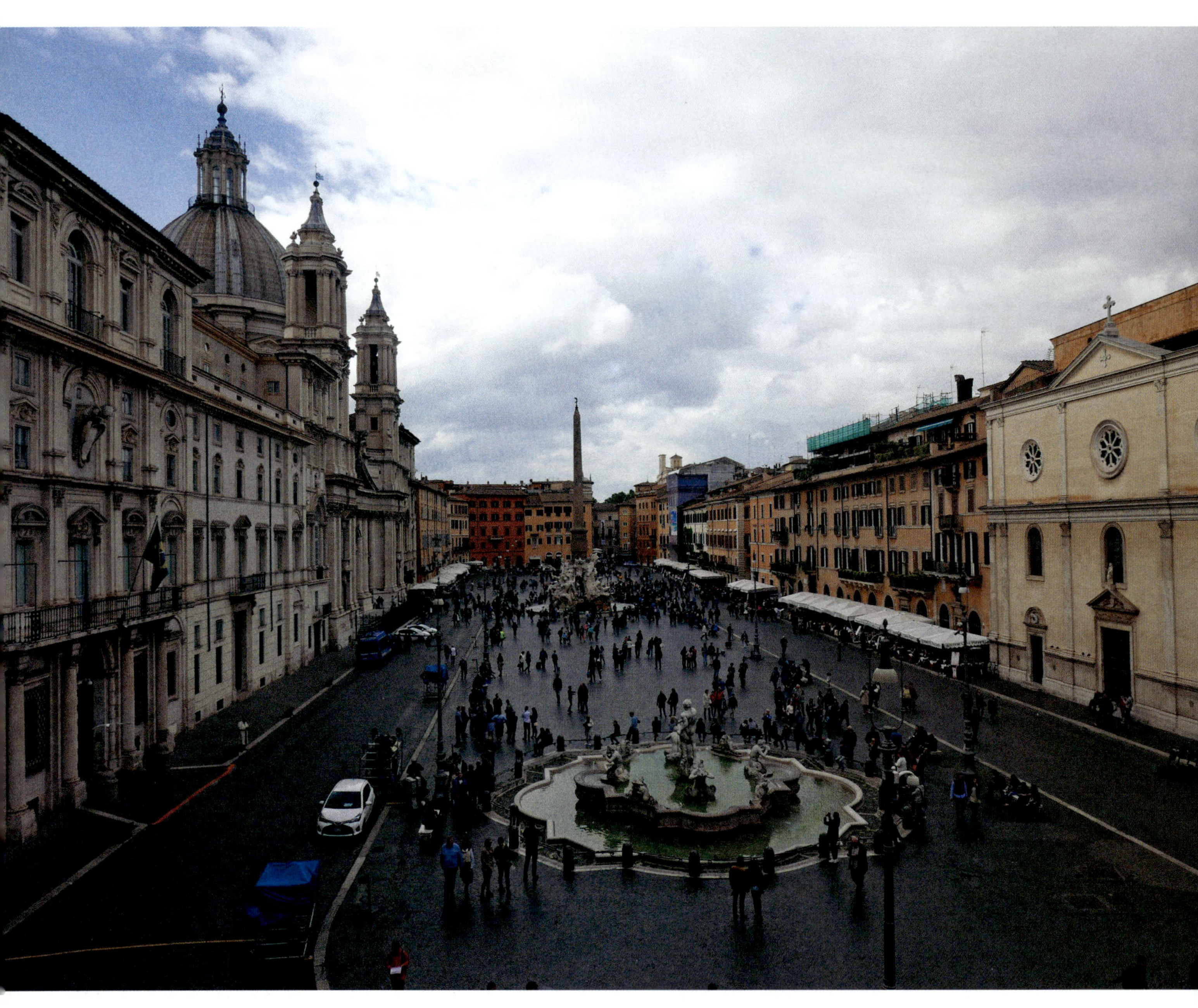

Piazza Navona in Rome, Italy, occupies the site of a Roman circus and is one of the most popular tourist destinations in the world
PAUL EDMONDSON/NATIONAL TRUST FOR HISTORIC PRESERVATION

referred to in the 1966 book *With Heritage So Rich*, which led to the enactment of the National Historic Preservation Act. These fundamental reasons inform all of the other reasons that follow: commemoration, beauty, civic identity, and the reasons that are more pragmatic—preservation as a tool for community revitalization, the stabilization of property values, economic development, and sustainability.

The notion that old places matter is not primarily about the past. It is about why old places matter to people *today* and for the future. It is about why old places are critical

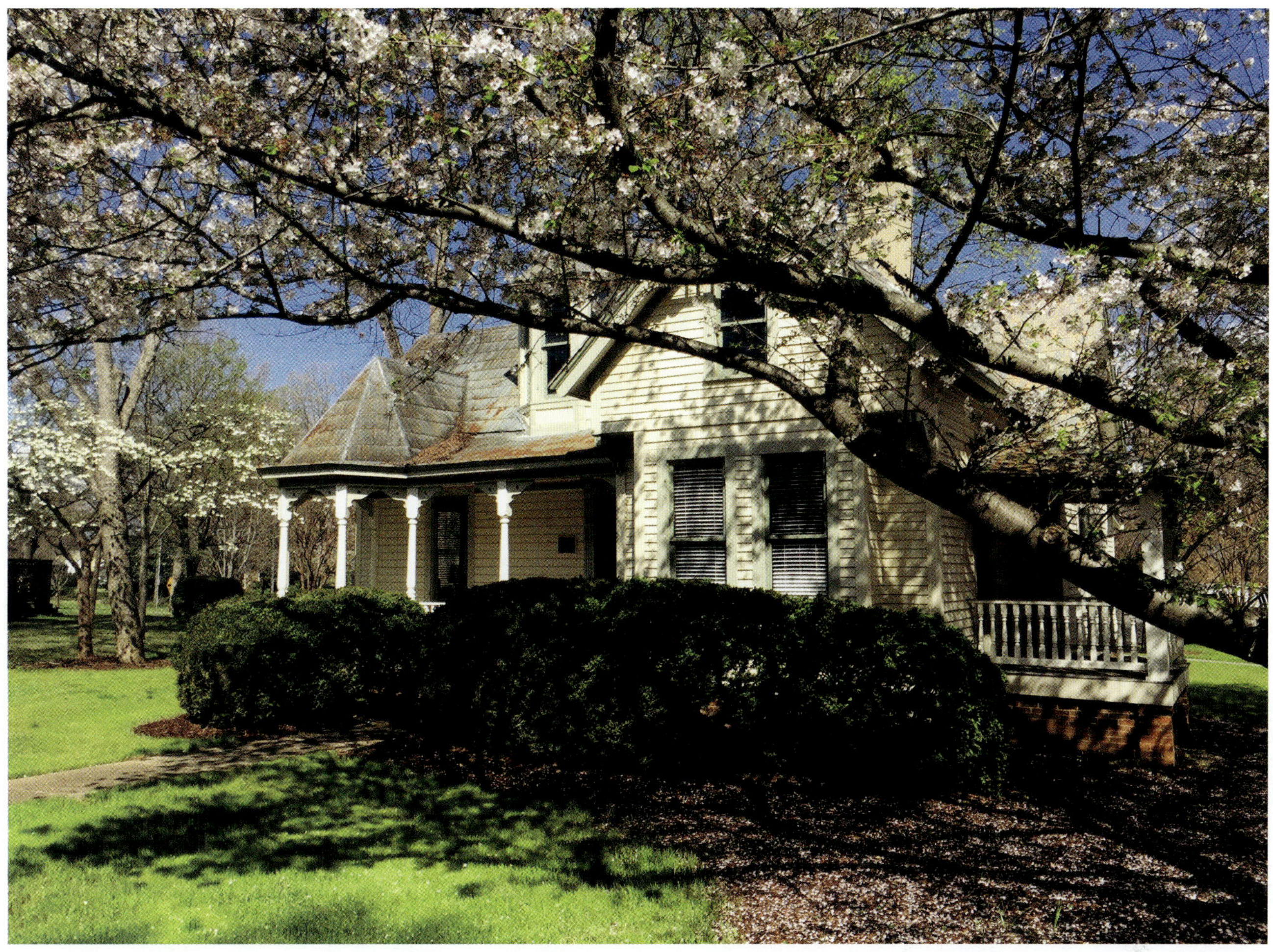

The Sloan House in Davidson, North Carolina, contributes to the beauty and charm of the town
TOM MAYES/NATIONAL TRUST FOR HISTORIC PRESERVATION

to people's sense of who they are, to their capacity to find meaning in their lives, and to see a future.

I am an unabashed advocate for keeping, saving, and continuing to use old places. Immense and overwhelming economic and political forces cause the destruction of old places at an astonishing pace every minute of every day. We see it in the loss of treasured places both large and small. From the removal of a single, gnarled pear tree that has delighted us with its bloom in the spring and its fruit in the fall, to the inexcusable demolition of public buildings such as schools and churches that give our communities their identity, we are steadily losing our old places. The loss is a soul-destroying severing of people from place, identity, and memory.

There are many critics of the idea of saving old places. Some say that saving old places stifles economic growth and that historic preservation has become too strong a force. They say that preservation is out of balance with the need for change. I see no

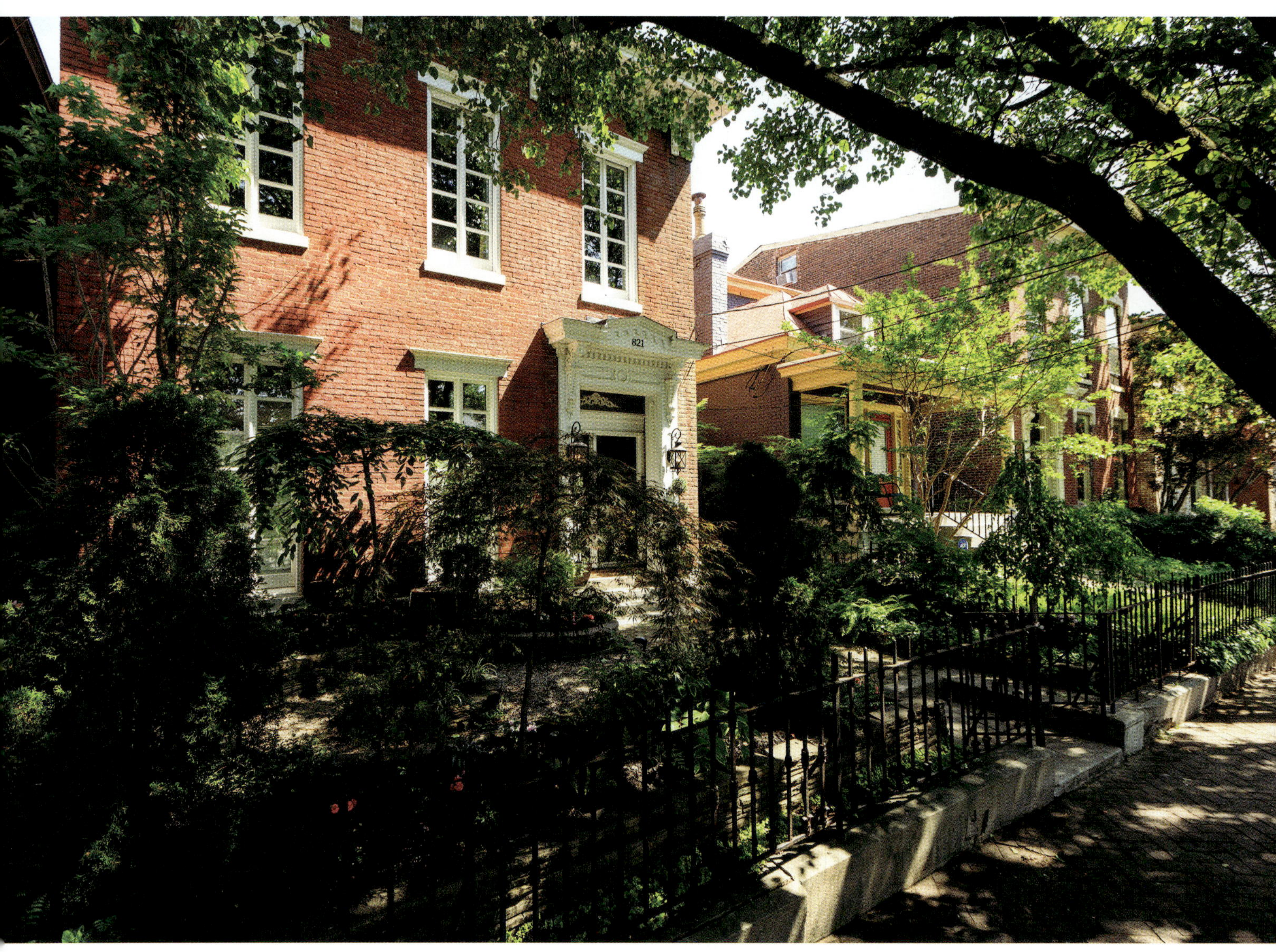

A streetscape in the Butchertown neighborhood in Louisville, Kentucky
ANDY SNOW

evidence whatsoever that the forces of preservation in the United States pose a threat to the capacity of the United States to have a vibrant and strong economy. Quite the contrary, old places actually seem to increase creativity and economic growth.

Are there things we should do better? Yes. Are there disagreements among the people who work to save old places? Yes. Are there arguments about what we retain and how we retain it? Yes. There should be. But the fundamental point remains: the history, memory, and continuity provided through old places are necessary for our self-worth—and are good for people.[1]

NOTE

1. A note about terminology: I use the term "old places" throughout these brief essays because the term includes not only places that are officially determined to be historic through the National Register of Historic Places or state or local designations, but also the majority of old places in America, most of which are not officially designated. The term also includes places that are not buildings—it captures streets, landscapes, gardens, farms, archaeological sites, cemeteries, and the many other old places that people value. I have also consciously avoided using terms that create an emotional distance between people and place, such as the term "historic resource."

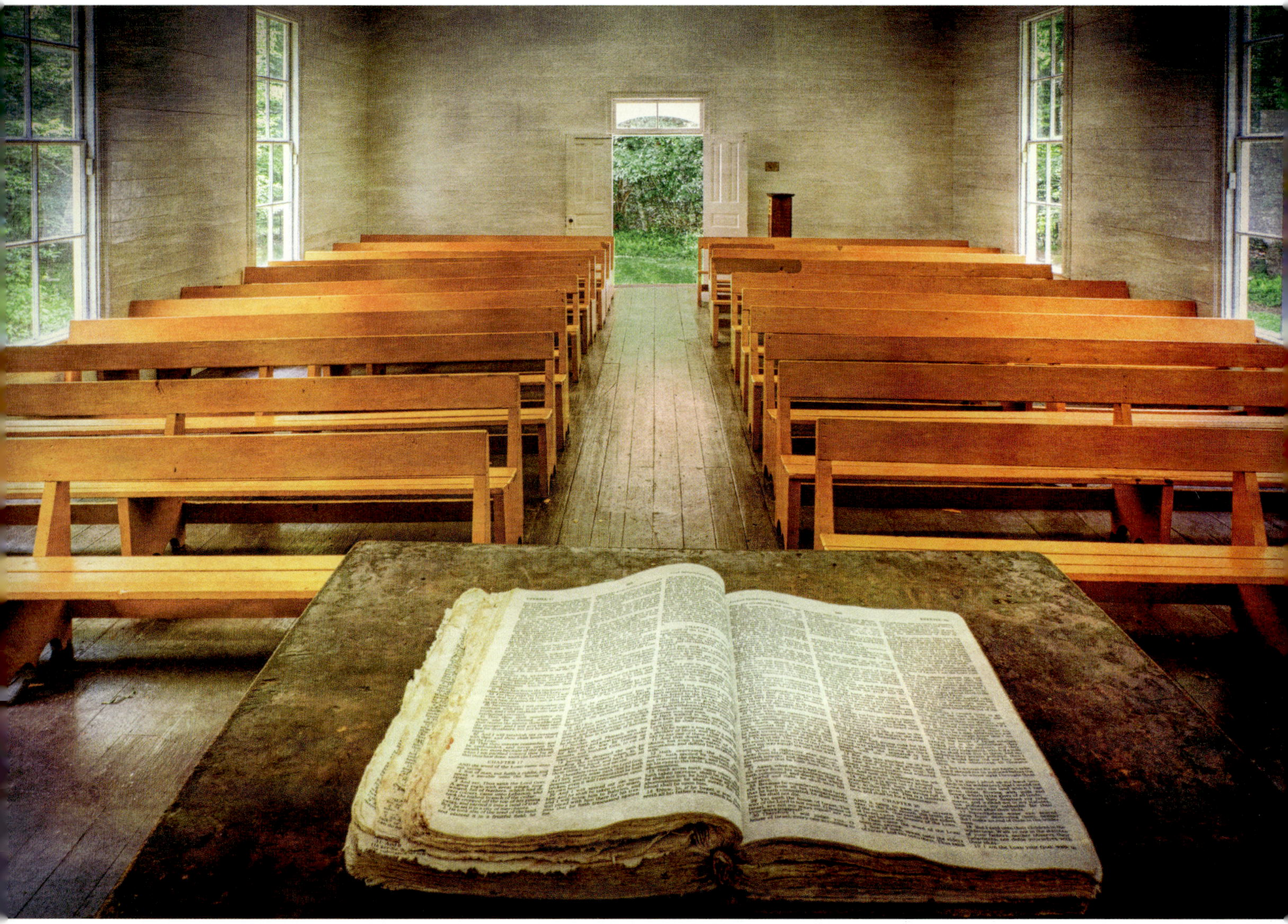

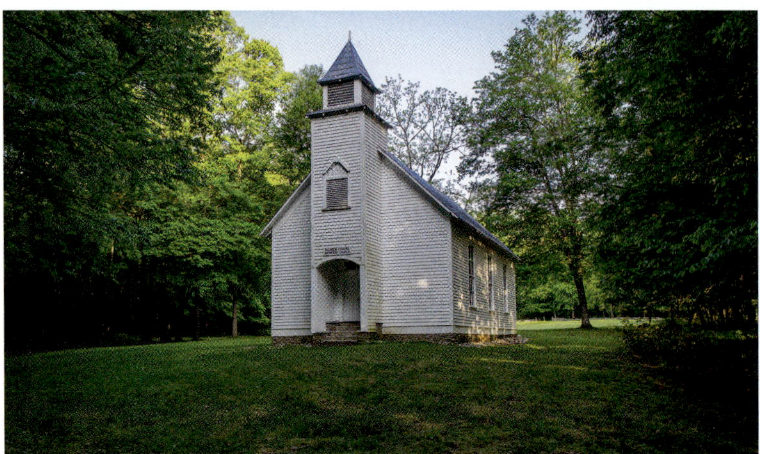

The interior of Palmer Chapel
JEFFREY STONER PHOTOGRAPHY

Palmer Chapel, in the Great Smoky Mountains National Park, where generations of former residents return for an annual reunion, providing descendants with a sense of continuity between the past and the present
JEFF CLARK/INTERNET BROTHERS

Continuity

***OLD PLACES** create a sense of continuity that helps people feel more balanced, stable, and healthy.*

When I ask people why old places are important, a frequent answer is that old places provide people with a sense of continuity. But this idea of a sense of continuity, which so many people obviously feel, is not often explained. What does this sense of continuity mean, how does it tie to old places, and why is it good for people?

Based on my conversations and the research I've done at the American Academy in Rome, the idea of continuity is that, in a world that is constantly changing, old places provide people with a sense of being part of a continuum, which is necessary for them to be psychologically and emotionally healthy. This is an idea that people have long recognized as an underlying value of historic preservation, though it is not often explained. In the influential 1966 book *With Heritage So Rich*, the idea of continuity is captured in the phrase "sense of orientation," the idea that preservation gives "a sense of orientation to our society, using structures and objects of the past to establish values of time and place."[1] Juhani Pallasmaa, the internationally known architect and architectural theorist, was a resident at the American Academy during my time there, and I've been privileged

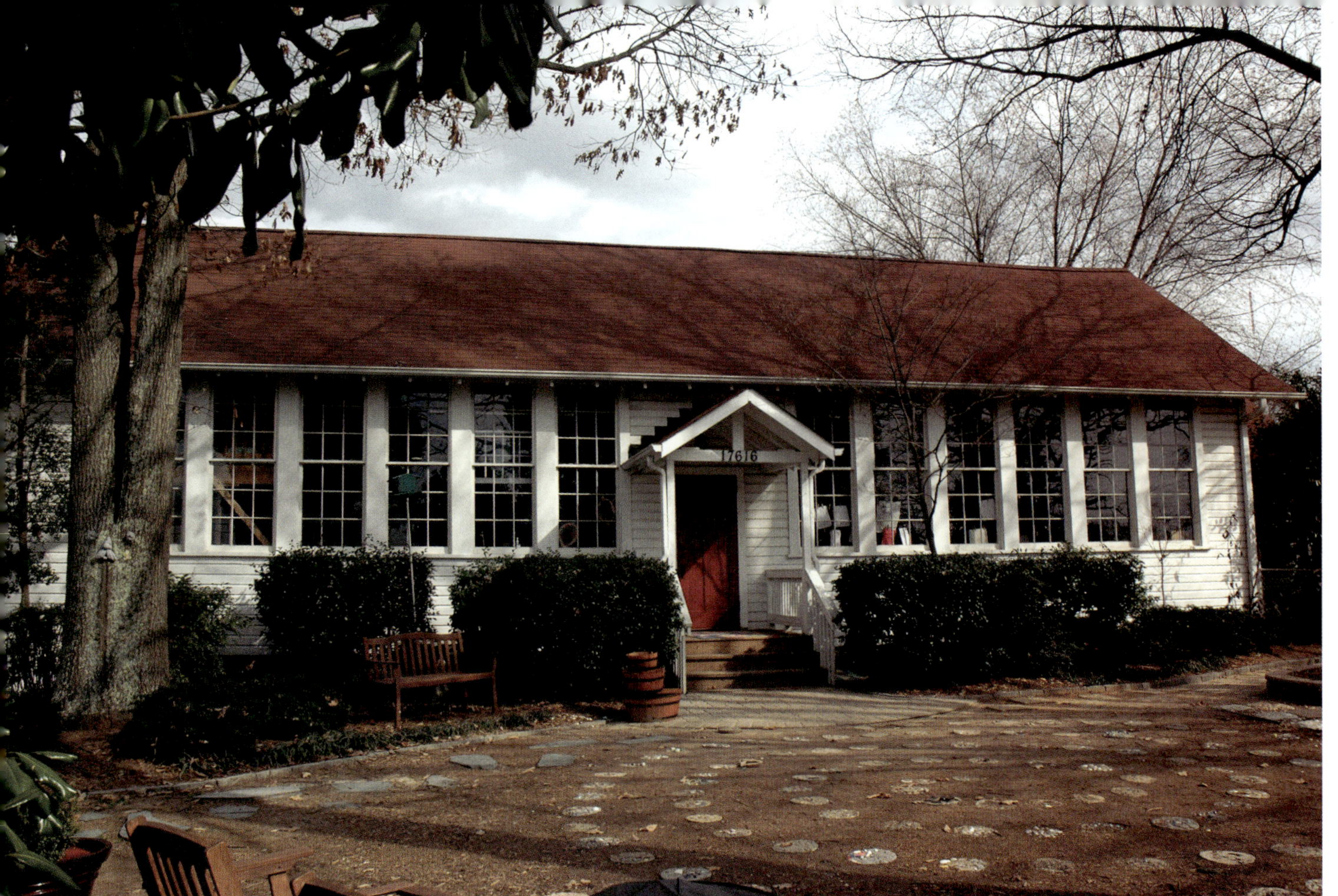

Caldwell Station School, in Huntersville, North Carolina, where earlier generations of my family attended school
STEWART GRAY

to talk with him about old places. Juhani puts it this way in an essay he wrote: "we have a mental need to experience that we are rooted in the continuity of time. We do not only inhabit space, we also dwell in time." He continues: "Buildings and cities are museums of time. They emancipate us from the hurried time of the present and help us to experience the slow, healing time of the past. Architecture enables us to see and understand the slow processes of history and to participate in time cycles that surpass the scope of an individual life."[2]

We see and hear this idea in the way people talk about the places they care about—in blogs, public hearings, newspaper articles, and anywhere people talk about threats to places they love. Discussing the potential loss of his one-hundred-year-old elementary school, for example, a resident says, "It's been a part of my life as long as I can remember. . . . My great-grandmother graduated in 1917. . . . It's the heart of the community."

People share stories of the experiences that they, their parents, and other people have had at theaters, restaurants, parks, and houses—as well as events that happened long before their parents were alive. They not only feel the need to be part of a time line of history, both personal and beyond themselves, but their connection to these old places makes them aware that they are part of the continuum, connected to people of the past, the present, and, hopefully, the future.

Environmental psychologists have explored many aspects of peoples' attachment to place, including the idea of continuity. Maria Lewicka, in her review of studies on "place attachment," says, "the majority of authors agree that development of emotional bonds with places is a prerequisite of psychological balance and good adjustment and that it helps to overcome identity crises and gives people the sense of stability they need in the everchanging world."

Although studies relating specifically to old places are limited, Lewicka summarizes the studies this way: "Research in environmental aesthetics shows that people generally prefer historical places to modern architecture. Historical sites create a sense of continuity with the past, embody the group traditions, and facilitate place attachment."

Lewicka's summary of one study captures a key idea: "The important part . . . is the emphasis placed on the link between sense of place, developed through rootedness in place, and individual self-continuity. Rootedness, that is, the person-place bond, is considered a prerequisite of an ability to integrate various life experiences into a coherent life story, and thus it enables smooth transition from one identity stage to another in the life course."[3]

Life story. This phrase captures the way people create a narrative out of their lives and make their lives meaningful and coherent. Old places help people to create meaningful life stories. This may sound a bit touchy-feely for our American sense of practicality and hard-nosed realism. But the point is that people need this sense of continuity, this capacity to develop coherent life stories, in order to be psychologically healthy.

We can see the importance of continuity in the places where continuity has been intentionally or unintentionally broken. People who have been forcibly removed from their homes, such as those who lived on the land that became Great Smoky Mountains National Park and were removed in the 1930s, described themselves as heartbroken by the forced removal. These former residents continue to visit the sites of their former homes—the remains of an old chimney, the foundation of an apple cellar, and the family graveyard—and to participate in homecomings, such as at the one at an old church named Palmer Chapel. Although they had been forcibly removed, the attachment to the place continued and has continued through later generations who never lived on the land but feel a sense of connection to the place.[4]

On a trip to Puglia, the fellows of the American Academy visited a World Heritage site, Matera, where the residents had been removed from their community during the mid-twentieth century. Our guide at one of the churches, a descendant of one of the

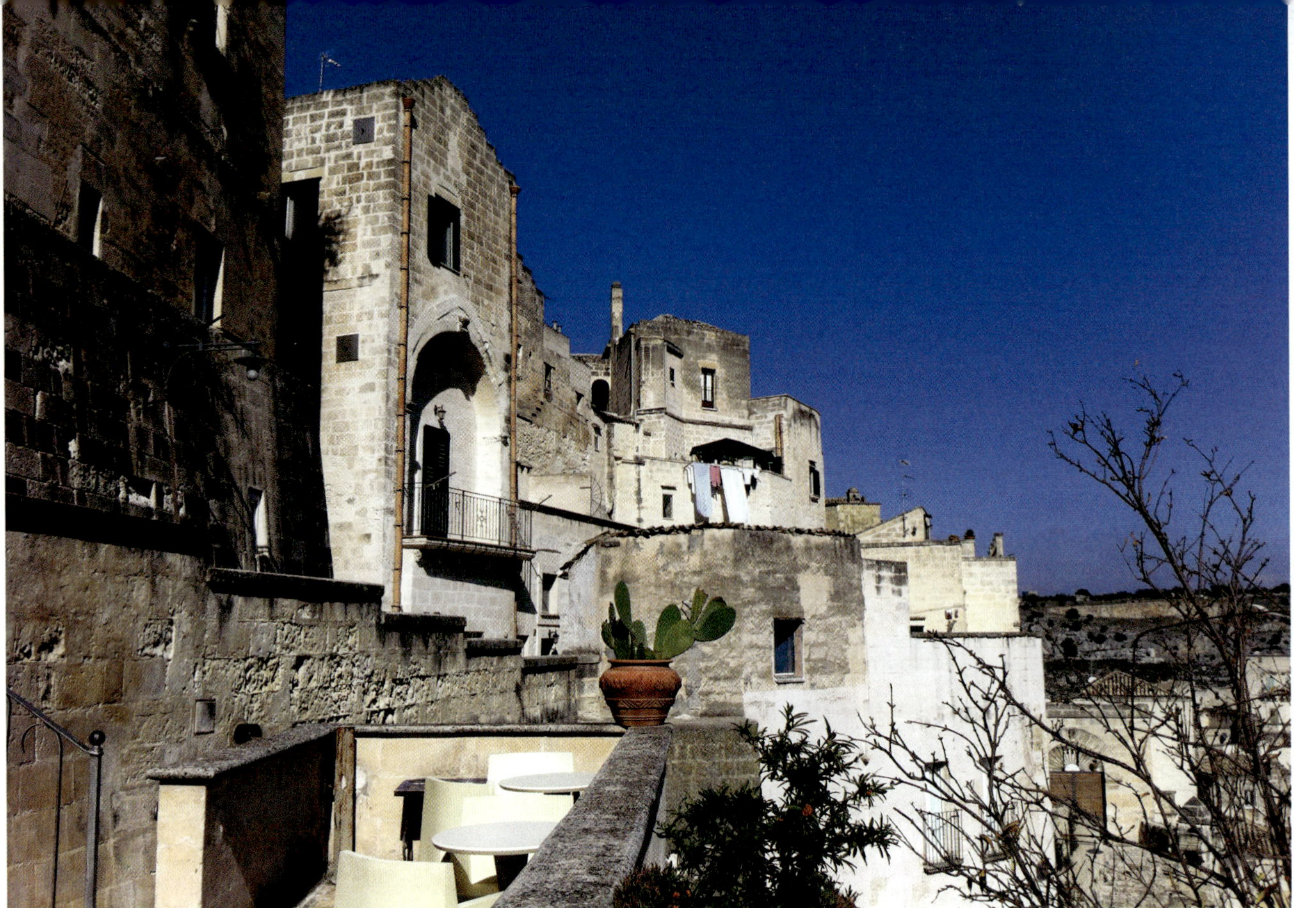

Residents of Matera, Italy, were displaced for supposedly better housing but many say their community was never the same
TOM MAYES/NATIONAL TRUST FOR HISTORIC PRESERVATION

families removed from the site, said that her grandmother hated moving and felt that the community never recovered from the forced removal. Studies have shown that the loss of the sense of continuity from uncontrollable change in the physical environment may even cause a grief reaction.[5] Put simply, people need the continuity of old places.

Continuity is not, however, only about the past, but also about the present and the future. That's what continuity means—bringing the relevance of the past to give meaning to the present and the future. Paul Goldberger, the architectural critic, says about preservation,

> Perhaps the most important thing to say about preservation when it is really working as it should is that it uses the past not to make us nostalgic, but to make us feel that we live in a better present, a present that has a broad reach and a great, sweeping arc, and that is not narrowly defined, but broadly defined by its connections to other eras, and its ability to embrace them in a larger, cumulative whole. Successful preservation makes time a continuum, not a series of disjointed, disconnected eras.[6]

Old places help people place themselves in that "great, sweeping arc" of time. The continued presence of old places—of the schools and playgrounds, parks and public

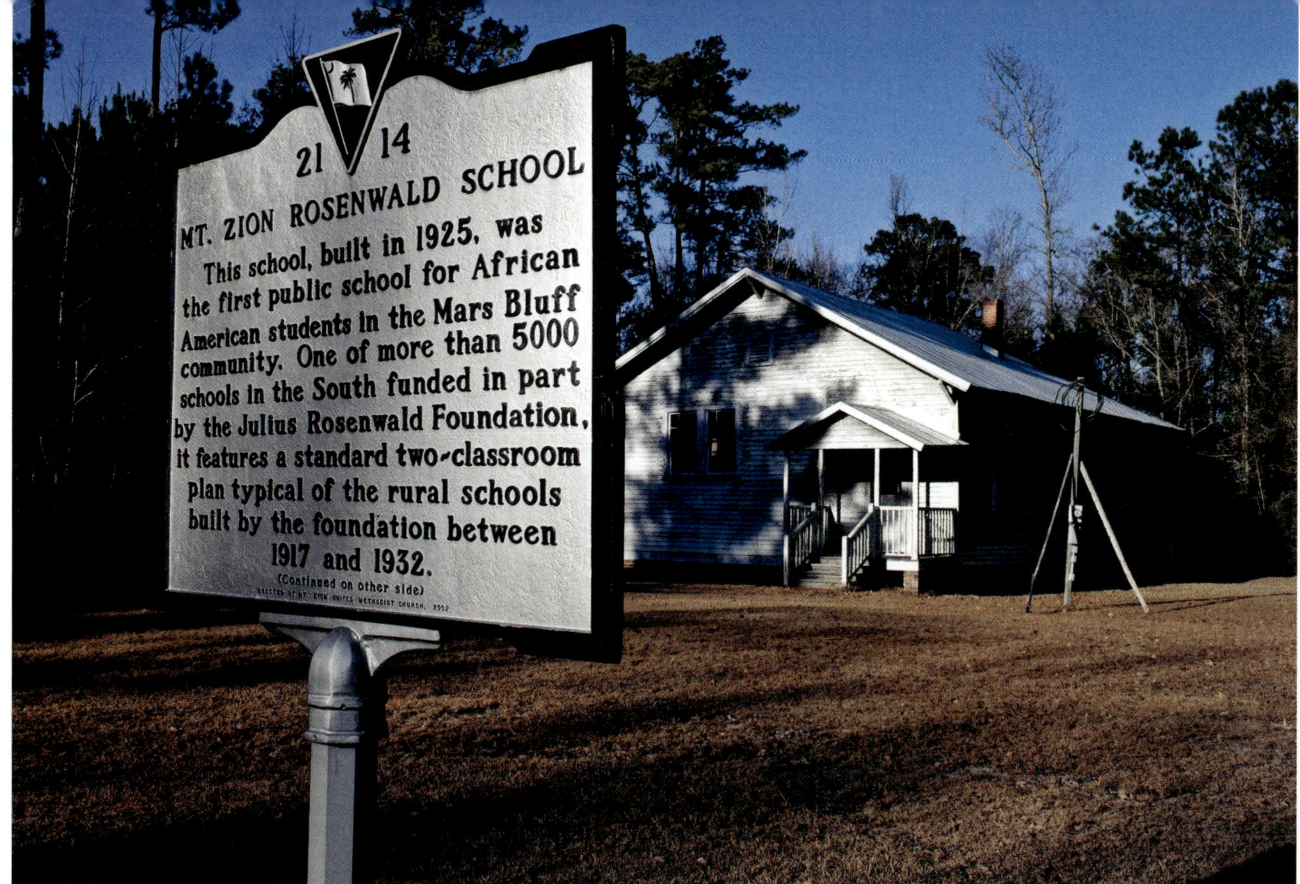

Schools, such as Mt. Zion Rosenwald School in Mars Bluff, South Carolina, provide continuity between generations
JASON CLEMENT/NATIONAL TRUST FOR HISTORIC PRESERVATION

squares, churches and houses and farms and fields that people value—contributes to people's sense of being on a continuum with the past. That awareness gives meaning to the present and enhances the human capacity to envision the future. All of this contributes to people's sense of well-being—to their psychological health.

NOTES

1. Special Committee on Historic Preservation United States Conference of Mayors, *With Heritage So Rich* (Washington, DC: Preservation Books, 1999).
2. Juhani Pallasmaa, *Encounters 1: Architectural Essays*, ed. Peter MacKeith (Helsinki, Finland: Rakennustieto Oy Publishing, 2012), 309, 312.
3. Maria Lewicka, "Place Attachment: How Far Have We Come in the Last 40 Years?" *Journal of Environmental Psychology* 31 (2011): 211, 225 and "Place Attachment, Place Identity, and Place Memory: Restoring the Forgotten City Past," *Journal of Environmental Psychology* 28 (2008): 211.
4. Michael Ann Williams, "Vernacular Architecture and the Park Removals: Traditionalization As Justification and Resistance," *TDSR* 13, no. 1 (2001): 38.
5. Clare L. Twigger-Ross and David L. Uzzell, "Place and Identity Processes," *Journal of Environmental Psychology* 16 (1996): 205–20.
6. Paul Goldberger, "Preservation Is Not Just about the Past," speech, Salt Lake City, April 26, 2007.

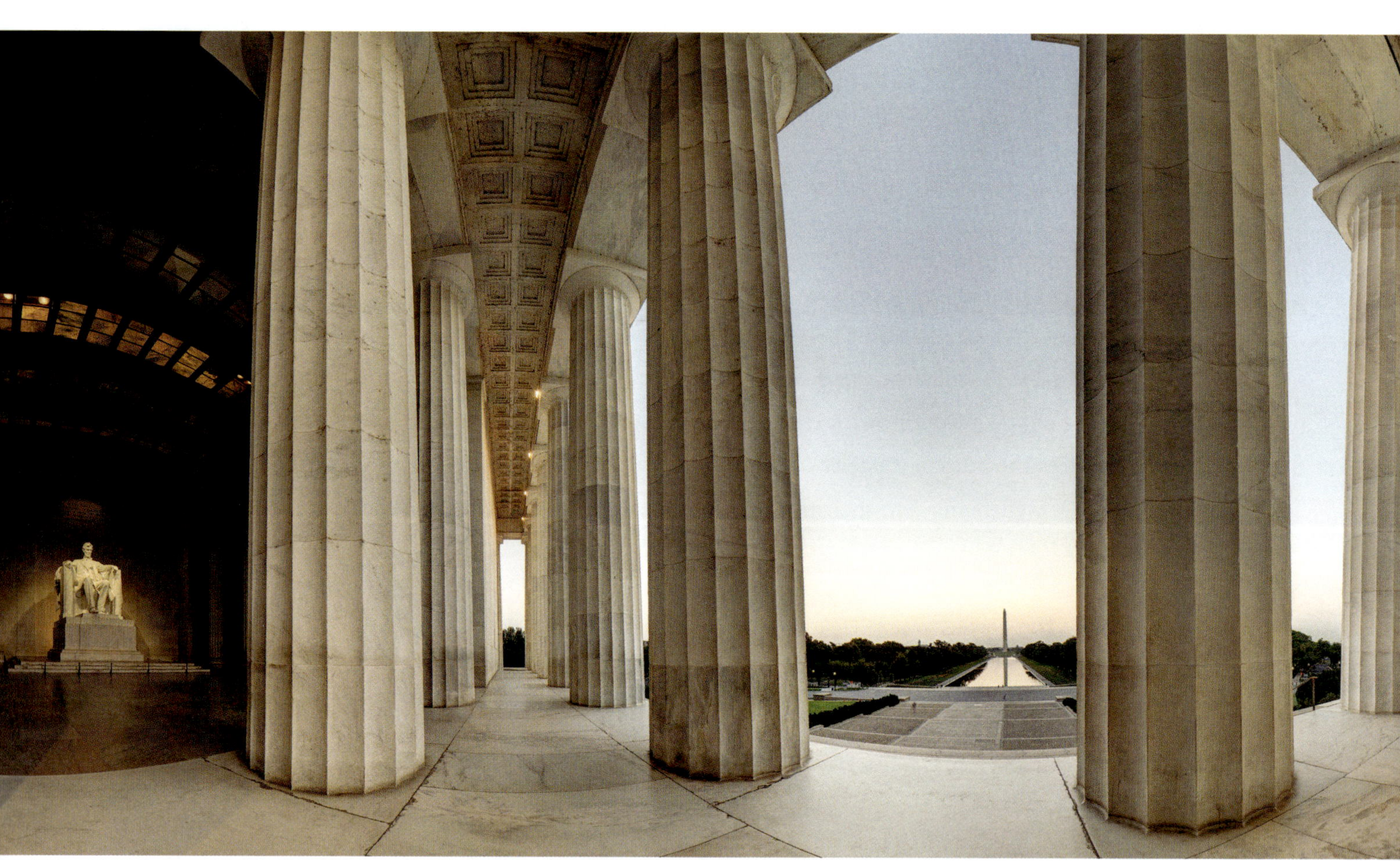

The Lincoln Memorial and the Reflecting Pool remind people of shared memories of national events
SAM KITTNER

Memory

OLD PLACES help us to remember.

Like many people, my earliest memories are of places—a pasture on our old farm where I napped in the warm sun until a cow licked me and the dining room of my grandfather's house where we watched President Kennedy's funeral cortege. Simply seeing a place again may bring back a flood of memories—whether it's Caffe Reggio in Greenwich Village, which I frequented in my twenties or the Davidson College Library where I pored over architectural history books as a teenager. "Old buildings are like memories you can touch," the architect Mary DeNadai tells her granddaughter. It's a succinct explanation of how old places—our homes, libraries, schools, barns, and parks—seem to hold and embody our memories.

Most people experience this connection between memory and place. The connection was acknowledged by John Ruskin, who wrote in "The Lamp of Memory" about architecture, "We may live without her, and worship without her, but we cannot remember without her."[1] But how important are places to memory? Does preserving old places—

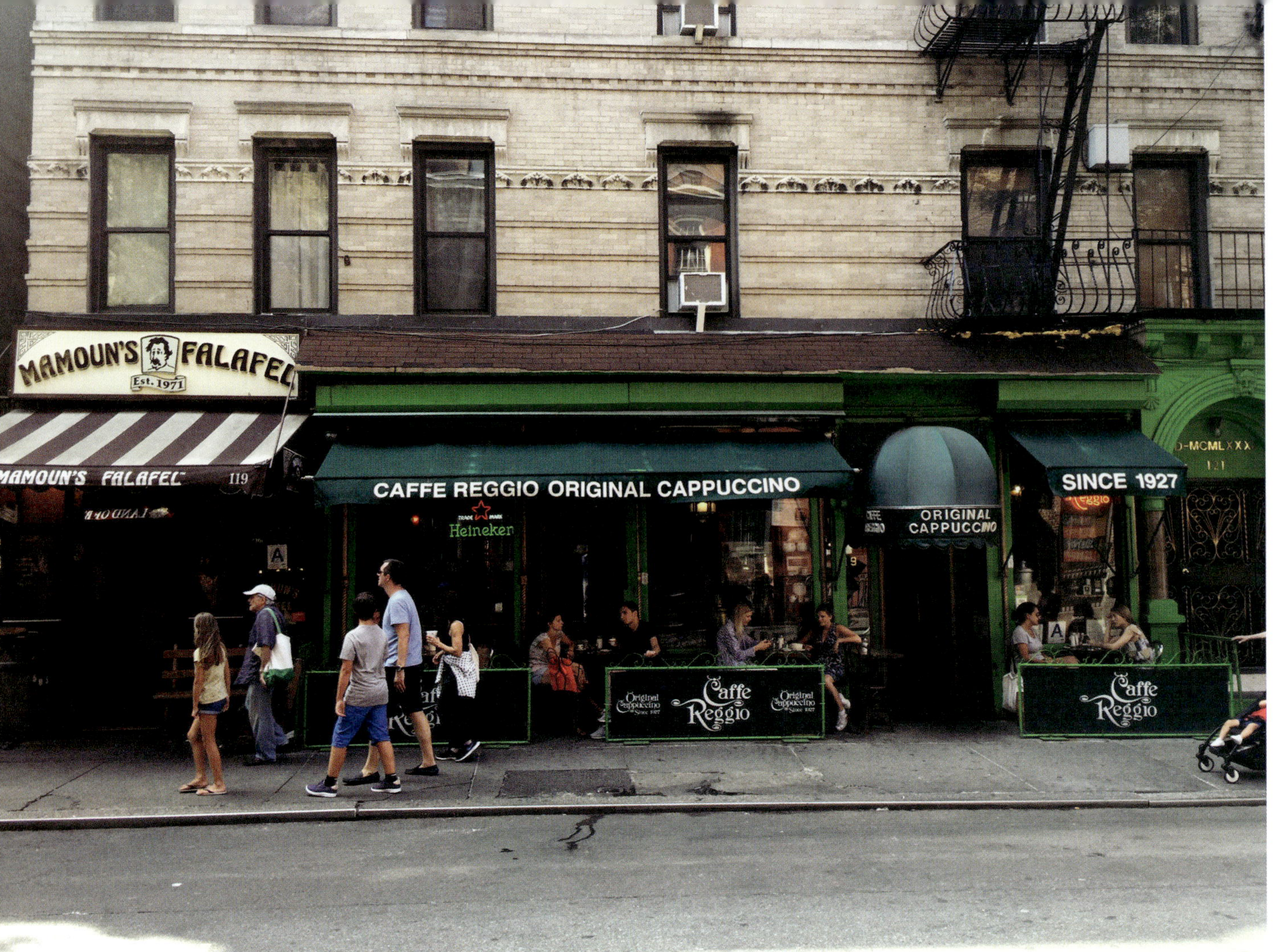

Caffe Reggio in Greenwich Village, New York
TOM MAYES/NATIONAL TRUST FOR HISTORIC PRESERVATION

and the memories they represent—matter? Do the individual and collective memories embodied in old places help people have better lives?

"Memory is an essential part of consciousness," says Randall Mason, chair of the graduate program in historic preservation at the University of Pennsylvania, talking to me about the large and ever-growing topic of memory studies. Philosophers, psychologists, writers, geographers, sociologists, and historians have written, studied, and theorized about memory, from Proust (yes, that famous madeleine that triggered memories of—what else?—a place) to Freud to French historian Pierre Nora, who coined the term *Lieux de Memoire*—"sites of memory."[2] Among the thousands of books, studies, and essays on memory and place, many, including Nora, analyze or critique the way memories are shaped or manipulated, including how historic preservationists and others choose what places to preserve and why. Yet even taking into account the criticism of what we preserve and why, most of these writers seem to support what geographers Steven Hoelsher and Derek Alderman refer to as the "inextricable link between memory and place." Places embody our memories, even when those memories are contested or controversial. As Hoelsher and Alderman put it, "What . . . groups share in their efforts to utilize the past is the near universal activity of anchoring their divergent memories in place."[3]

Places are key triggers for both *individual memory*, such as those very personal memories I recalled above, and *collective memory*, the memory shared by the larger society. Diane Barthel, in *Historic Preservation: Collective Memory and Historic Identity*, captures the relationship between individual memory and collective memory in a discussion of religious buildings: "Religious structures play a specially significant part in the collective memory as places where moments in personal history become part of the flow of collective history. This collective history transcends individual experiences and lifetimes."[4]

One need only think about important national sites to see the blending of the two types of memory and how they are tied to place. How many of us remember something both about ourselves and about us collectively when we see the Lincoln Memorial and its reflecting pool or images of the World Trade Center?

People writing about memory have described the mechanisms that drive the connection between place and memory. Places serve as mnemonic aids—they remind us of our memories, both individual (coffee at the Caffe Reggio) and collective (marches at the Lincoln Memorial)—but they also spur people to investigate broader societal memories they don't yet fully know. Pierre Nora writes, "Memory takes root in the concrete, in spaces, gestures, images, and objects."[5] Environmental psychologist Maria Lewicka refers to studies that discuss "historical traces" and "urban reminders." As she states, "urban reminders, the leftovers from previous inhabitants of a place, may influence memory of places either directly, by conveying historical information, or indirectly—by arousing curiosity and increasing motivation to discover the place's forgotten past."[6]

Old places seem to trigger memories people already have, give specificity to memories, and arouse curiosity about memories people don't yet know.

And why is "place memory" important? Earlier, I wrote about continuity—that old places contribute to a sense of continuity that is necessary for people. Memory contributes to the sense of continuity. Memory also gives people identity—both individual identity and a collective identity. As Hoelsher and Alderman put it,

> Whether one refers to "collective memory," "social memory," "public memory," "historical memory," "popular memory," or "cultural memory," most would agree with Edward Said [who stated] that many "people now look to this refashioned memory, especially in its collective forms,

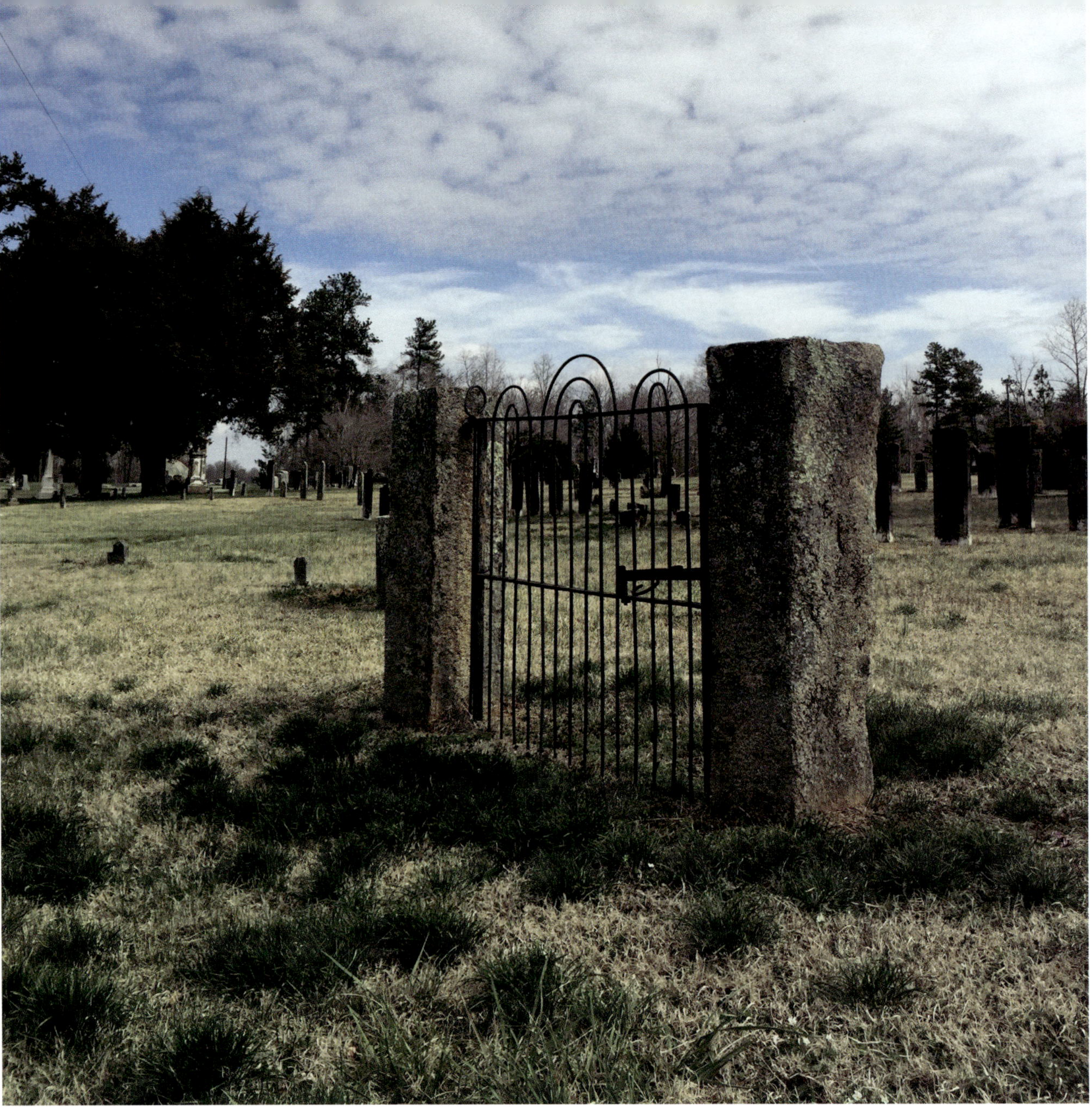

The gate at Ramah Presbyterian Church, in Huntersville, North Carolina, retains the memory of the wall that once surrounded the cemetery
TOM MAYES/NATIONAL TRUST FOR HISTORIC PRESERVATION

to give themselves a coherent identity, a national narrative, a place in the world."[7]

This sense of identity provided by memory is largely what defines us as individuals and as a society.

Memories and identities are often contested. We see people argue over the meaning of old places—a restored southern plantation house, which may or may not acknowledge the painful memory of slavery, a battlefield that may or may not present the memory of both the victor and the vanquished. People have different approaches about how places should be remembered. They argue over memorials, from the Vietnam Veterans Memorial to the World Trade Center. The history of an old place may be viewed differ-

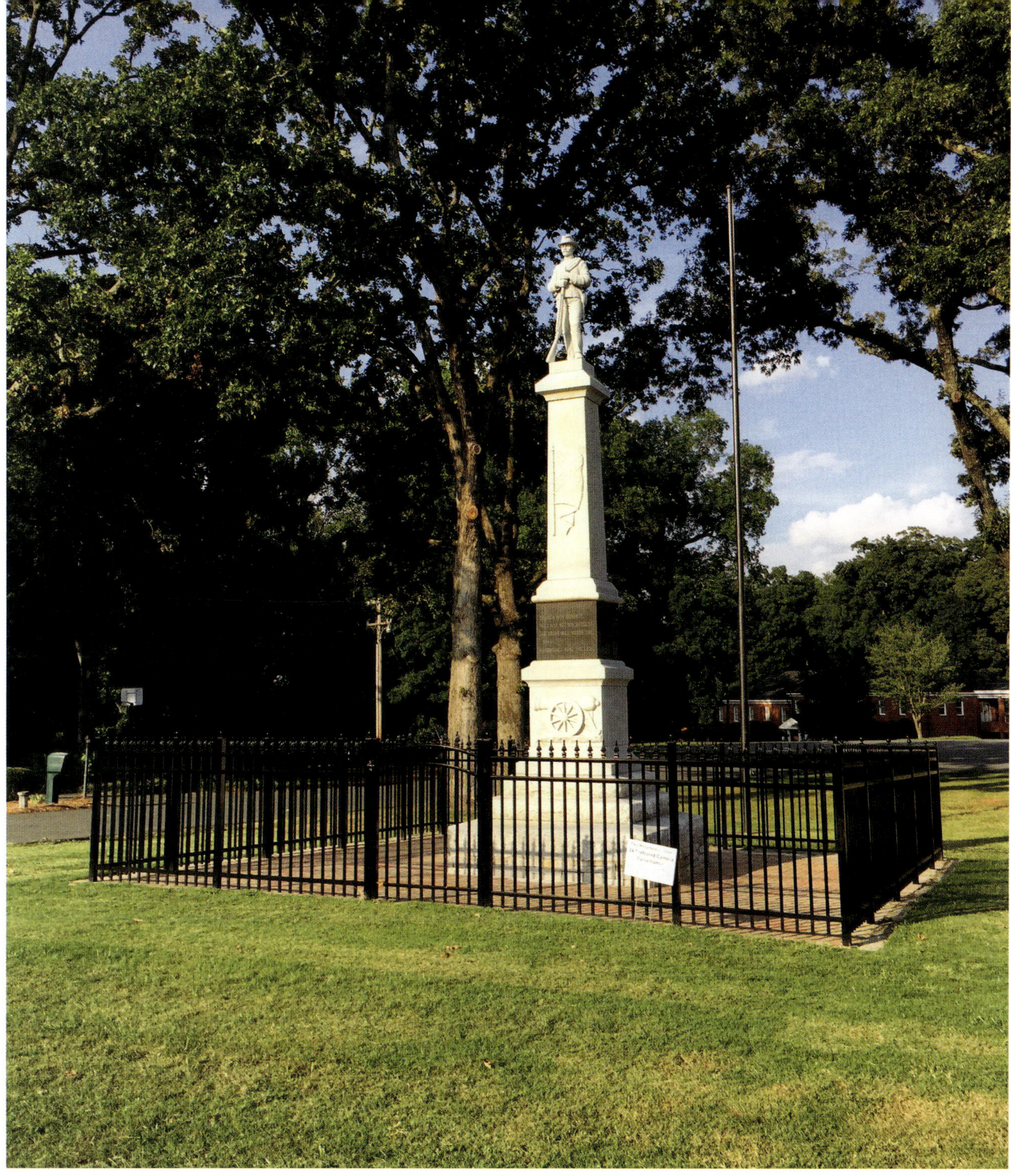

The Confederate memorial in Cornelius, North Carolina, was spray-painted and then cleaned. Old places serve as flash points for our changing national identity.
TOM MAYES/NATIONAL TRUST FOR HISTORIC PRESERVATION

ently over time—and interpreted and reinterpreted as our conception of who we are as a people changes.[8]

But here's the key point. The fact that these arguments occur highlights the importance of the *place*. Regardless of conflicting points of view, the place itself transcends a specific interpretation. The place is the vortex, the common ground, the center point, and the focus where divergent views about memory can be felt and expressed. The continued existence of the place permits the revision, reevaluation, and reinterpretation of memories over time. As Paul Goldberger, the architecture writer and critic, said to me in an interview in July, the continued existence of the place "allows new memories to be created."[9] Preservationists often think of historic sites from the viewpoint of significance for architecture or design. Yet architecture critic for the *New York Times*, Herbert Muschamp, wrote, "The essential feature of a landmark is not its design, but the place it holds in a city's memory. Compared to the place it occupies in social history, a landmark's artistic qualities are incidental."[10]

People ask, "but won't the memories survive even if the place is gone?" Yes, memory sometimes outlasts the place. I remember still the smell of the kettle of hot tea on the stove of my grandmother's house in North Carolina on Christmas Eve, though the house has been gone for many years. Memories can survive if places disappear. But memory—collective or individual—will not prove as durable—nor as flexible—when that vortex of memory, that mnemonic aid, that urban reminder, that historical trace—*the old place*—is gone.

NOTES

1. John Ruskin, "The Lamp of Memory," in *The Seven Lamps of Architecture* (New York: Dover Publications, 1989), 178.
2. Nora, "Between Memory and History: Les Lieux de Mémoire." *Representations* 26 (Spring 1989): 7.
3. Steven Hoelsher and Derek Alderman, "Memory and Place: Geographies of a Critical Relationship," *Social & Cultural Geography* 5 (2004): 348.
4. Diane Barthel, *Historic Preservation: Collective Memory and Historic Identity* (New Brunswick, NJ: Rutgers University Press, 1996), Kindle Locations 1199–1200.
5. Nora, "Between Memory and History," 9.
6. Maria Lewicka, "Place Attachment, Place Identity, and Place Memory: Restoring the Forgotten City Past," *Journal of Environmental Psychology* 28 (2008): 211, 214.
7. Hoelsher and Alderman, "Memory and Place," 348–49.
8. Since this essay was written, the debates over identity in the United States have intensified and the flashpoints for those debates have often been memorials, especially memorials to Confederate leaders or soldiers. These debates have also extended to other memorials, including Christopher Columbus, Theodore Roosevelt, Junipero Serra, and Juan de Oñate. The National Trust issued guidance about the treatment of Confederate memorials, which read in part: "These Confederate monuments are historically significant and essential to understanding a critical period of our nation's history. Just as many of them do not reflect, and are in fact abhorrent to, our values as a diverse and inclusive nation. We cannot and should not erase our history. But we also want our public monuments, on public land and supported by public funding, to uphold our public values." See Stephanie Meeks, "Statement on Confederate Memorials: Confronting Difficult History," National Trust for Historic Preservation, June 19, 2017, accessed February 19, 2018. https://savingplaces.org/press-center/media-resources/national-trust-statement-on-confederate-memorials#.WpLb8Ely74h. The statement was updated

after the violent protests in Charlottesville, Virginia, in August 2017. See Stephanie Meeks, "After Charlottesville: How to Approach Confederate Memorials in Your Community," National Trust for Historic Preservation, August 21, 2017, accessed February 19, 2018. https://savingplaces.org/stories/after-charlottesville-confederate-memorials#.WpLbjkly74g. These debates suggest just how important historic places and memorials are to people and the way that they can become venues for discussions of our changing identity. Many statues are being moved, recontextualized, or destroyed. From my perspective, these monuments should become the venue and opportunity for discussions that lead to acknowledgment, recognition, and, hopefully, reconciliation.

9. Paul Goldberger, interview with the author, July 18, 2013.
10. Herbert Muschamp, "The Secret History of 2 Columbus Circle," *The New York Times*, January 8, 2006.

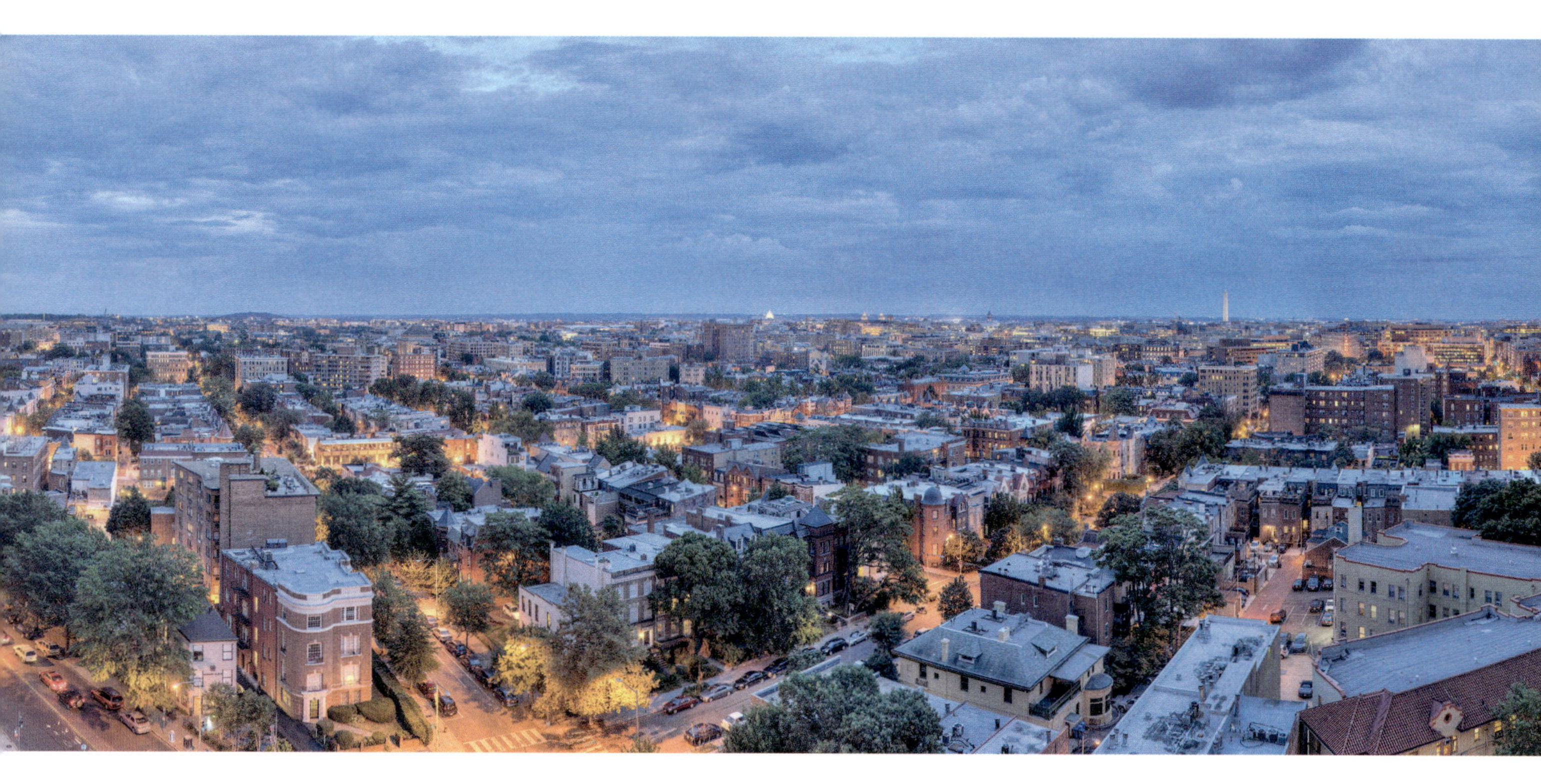

Dupont Circle, in Washington, D.C., where the author lives. Our sense of identity changes over our lifetime, and we may identify with places we come to know.
SAM KITTNER

Individual Identity

OLD PLACES embody our identity

"Old places are who we are." "They give us a sense of self." "They tell us who we are as a people." People frequently use these phrases when talking to me about why old places matter. Sofia Bosco, the Rome director of Fondo Ambiente Italiano, an Italian preservation organization, told me, "These places are testimonials of who we are. They represent the identity of every one of us."[1] Old places—our homes and churches, our neighborhoods, schools, main streets, and courthouse squares—are all part of our identity and of who *we* are.

People have long recognized the crucial connection between identity and old places. In the ancient world, Cicero chronicled the "indescribable feeling insensibly pervading my soul and sense" on returning to the place where he was born and where his father and grandfather lived.[2] More recently, architect and preservationist James Marston Fitch wrote that preservation "affords the opportunity for the citizens to regain a sense of identity with their own origins of which they have often been robbed by the sheer process of urbanization."[3]

Each of us can probably think of a place, like Cicero's childhood home, that seems to embody our identity, but how do old places "tell us who we are"? What exactly is this relationship between old places and identity? Earlier, I described how old places are critical for people to maintain a sense of continuity and memory. Identity is closely related to both continuity and memory—they are part of the same package. I'll look first at individual identity and address national or civic identity in the next essay.

For more than thirty years, psychologists, sociologists, philosophers, and architectural theorists from all over the world have actively studied the relationship between place and identity and have developed a variety of definitions and processes for looking at "place attachment" and "place identity"—how a person's identity is tied to place. Although there is no consensus about the definitions or processes, most studies accept the notion that "the use of the physical environment as a strategy for the maintenance of self" is a pervasive aspect of identity and that "place is inextricably linked with the development and maintenance of continuity of self."[4]

The way places inform our identity and the way we create identity out of place is complex and multilayered, and there is no agreement about how it works. The Turkish architect Humeyra Birol Akkurt offers a useful summary of a number of other scholars' definitions of how our identity ties to place:

> a set of links that allows and guarantees the distinctiveness and continuity of place in time, . . . the bond between people and their environment, based on emotion and cognition, . . . symbolic forms that link people and land: links through history or family lineage, links due to loss or destruction of land, economic links such as ownership, inheritance or politics, universal links through religion, myth and spirituality, links through religion and festive cultural events, and finally narrative links through storytelling or place naming.

Other writers have noted a sense of pride by association and a sense of self-esteem tied to place. Akkurt notes that one scholar theorizes that for any particular place there are as many different place identities as there are people using that place.[5]

The Norwegian architect Ashild Lappegard Hauge summarizes a key finding as "aspects of identity derived from places we belong to arise because places have symbols that have meaning and significance to us. Places represent personal memories, and . . .

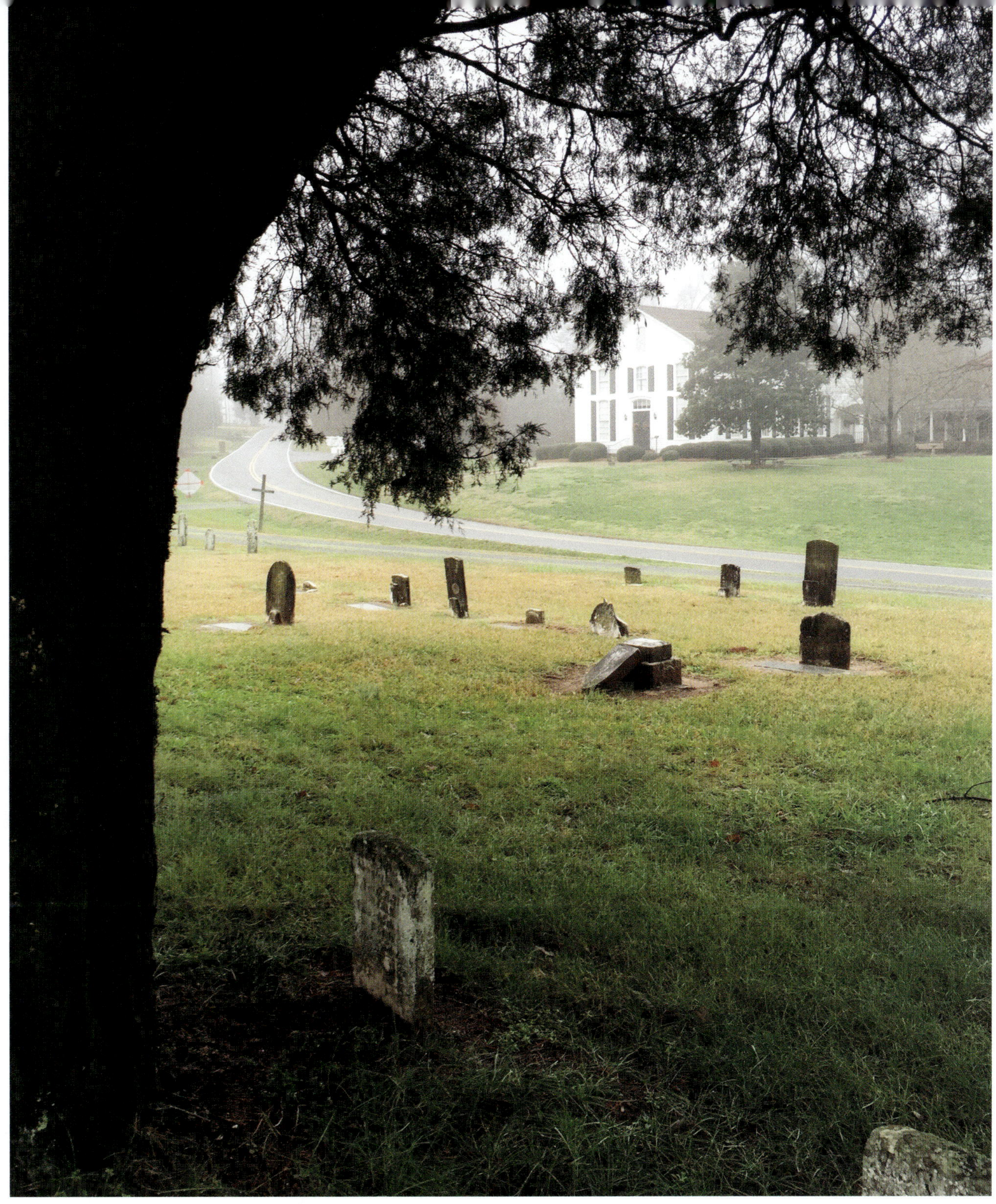

social memories (shared histories)." Hauge concludes that "places are not only contexts or backdrops, but also an integral part of identity."[6]

Old churches, such as Ramah Presbyterian Church, are often associated with identity
TOM MAYES/NATIONAL TRUST FOR HISTORIC PRESERVATION

People seem to recognize intuitively the way older places symbolize meaning, significance, and memories. Yi-Fu Tuan, the influential geographer who pioneered the study of people's relationship to place, wrote, "What can the past mean to us? People look back for various reasons, but shared by all is the need to acquire a sense of self and

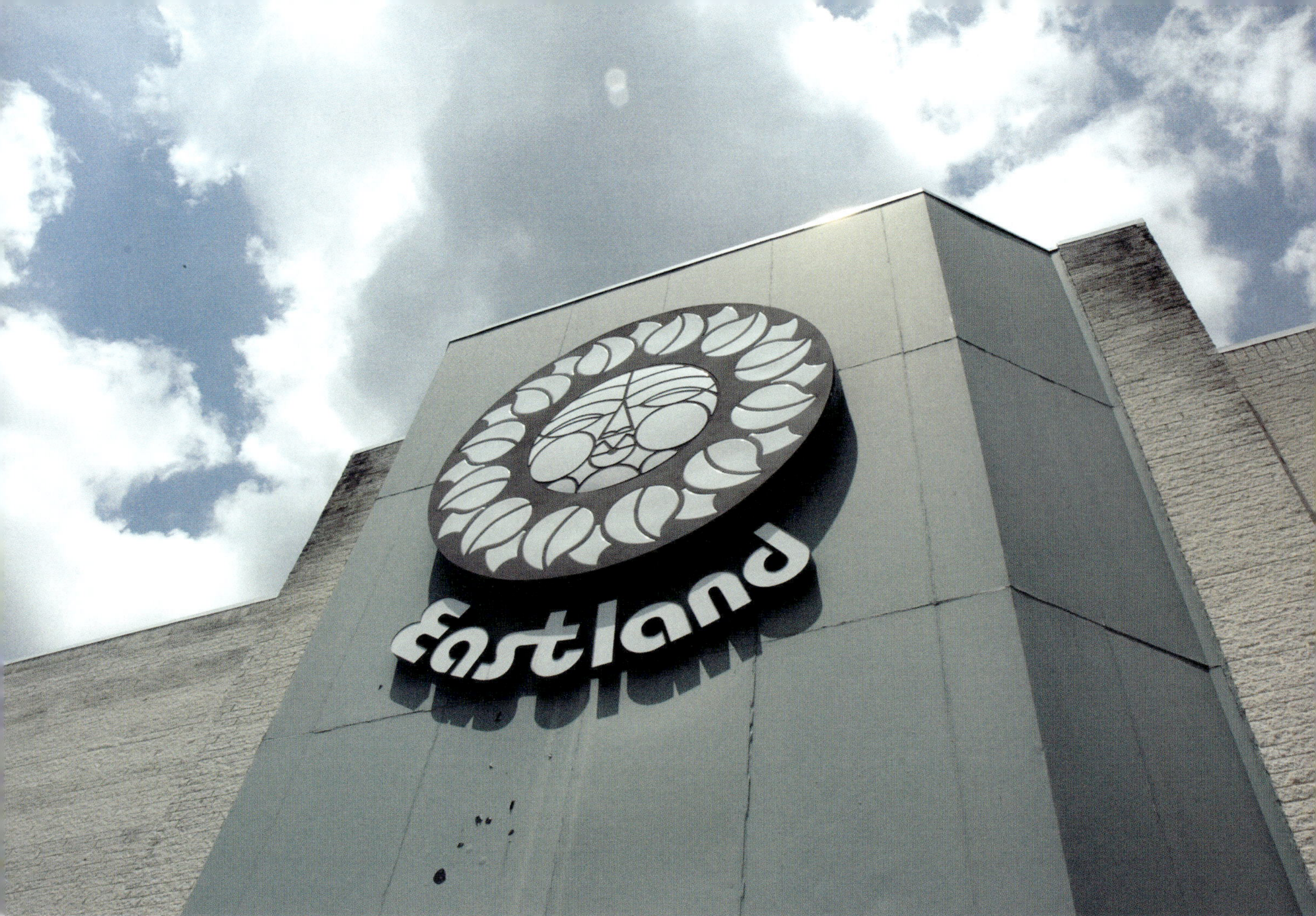

The sign for Eastland Mall in Charlotte, North Carolina, which the preservation organization E.A.S.T. successfully saved as part of the identity of the community
STEWART GRAY

of identity. . . . The passion for preservation arises out of the need for tangible objects that can support a sense of identity."[7] Tuan was not uncritical of what and how people choose to preserve and the identities that are reinforced. Yet the fact remains that old places provide tangible support for our sense of identity.

But there also seems to be something bigger at work. It's not as if we simply decide what our identity with place is. In fact, some theorists say the relationship between place and identity is inseparable. One writer, summarizing the findings of Edward Relph, another geographer who pioneered theories about place, stated, "the essence of place lies in its largely unselfconscious intentionality, which defines places as profound centres of human existence."[8] Or as David Seamon summarized Relph's idea, place is "not a bit of space, nor another word for landscape or environment, it is not a figment of individual experience, nor a social construct. . . . It is, instead, the foundation of being both human and nonhuman; experience, actions, and life itself begin and end with place."[9]

Our place identity is not static, however. It is dynamic. It changes over time. As noted previously, I grew up on a farm in North Carolina. Without any question, my identity is tied to that place—to the frame farmhouse where I was raised, to the cedar trees that line the fences (I can smell the cedar as I write this), to the very quality of the light on the green grass of the cow pastures. I am nurtured when I return to that place. But my identity is not tied only to that place. I also have an identity connected to places where I have lived, worked, or visited—from the leafy green campus at Chapel Hill, to the brick sidewalks and apartment buildings of Dupont Circle, to 1785 Massachusetts Avenue, the former National Trust headquarters, to a 1950s cement block riverside fishing cabin in West Virginia. And I look forward to having my identity further defined, enhanced, expanded, or clarified by Rome and by other places I will know in the future.

Although our identity with place changes over time (and can be re-created in different places), the places that form our identity act as tangible objects that support our identity. Our old places—if they continue to exist—serve as reference points for measuring, refreshing, and recalibrating our identity over time. They are literally the landmarks of our identity.

A place that supports our identity may not be particularly old, although many of them are (or have become so over the course of our lives). Eastland Mall, which opened in 1975 in east Charlotte and was part of my adolescence, was demolished in 2013. Its "rising sun" logo signs are being preserved as public art through the efforts of the grassroots E.A.S.T. community group, the Charlotte-Mecklenburg Historic Preservation Foundation, and the City of Charlotte to continue the community memory of a place that was once considered to have "embodied the spirit of the city."[10] The demolition company tearing the building down established a contest for people to share their memories (the head of the company met his wife ice skating at the mall). A man has even had the rising sun logo tattooed on his arm.

I'm glad E.A.S.T. saved the signs, but I wish that more of the place remained. Documented by the Charlotte-Mecklenburg Historic Preservation Foundation before its demolition, the vacant building had an evocative beauty that makes me think that the city might have been a richer place in the future if we had figured out how to reinvent the old mall in a way that saved this "tangible object" of my teenage memories and identity. Perhaps our society would be a bit more stable and humane—and sustainable—if we didn't build and replace our buildings every thirty-five years, with the resulting erasure of recent memories and identity embodied in them and the inexcusable waste of demolition.

When the places that are part of our identity are threatened, lost, or destroyed, our identity may be damaged. As indicated previously in the discussion on continuity,

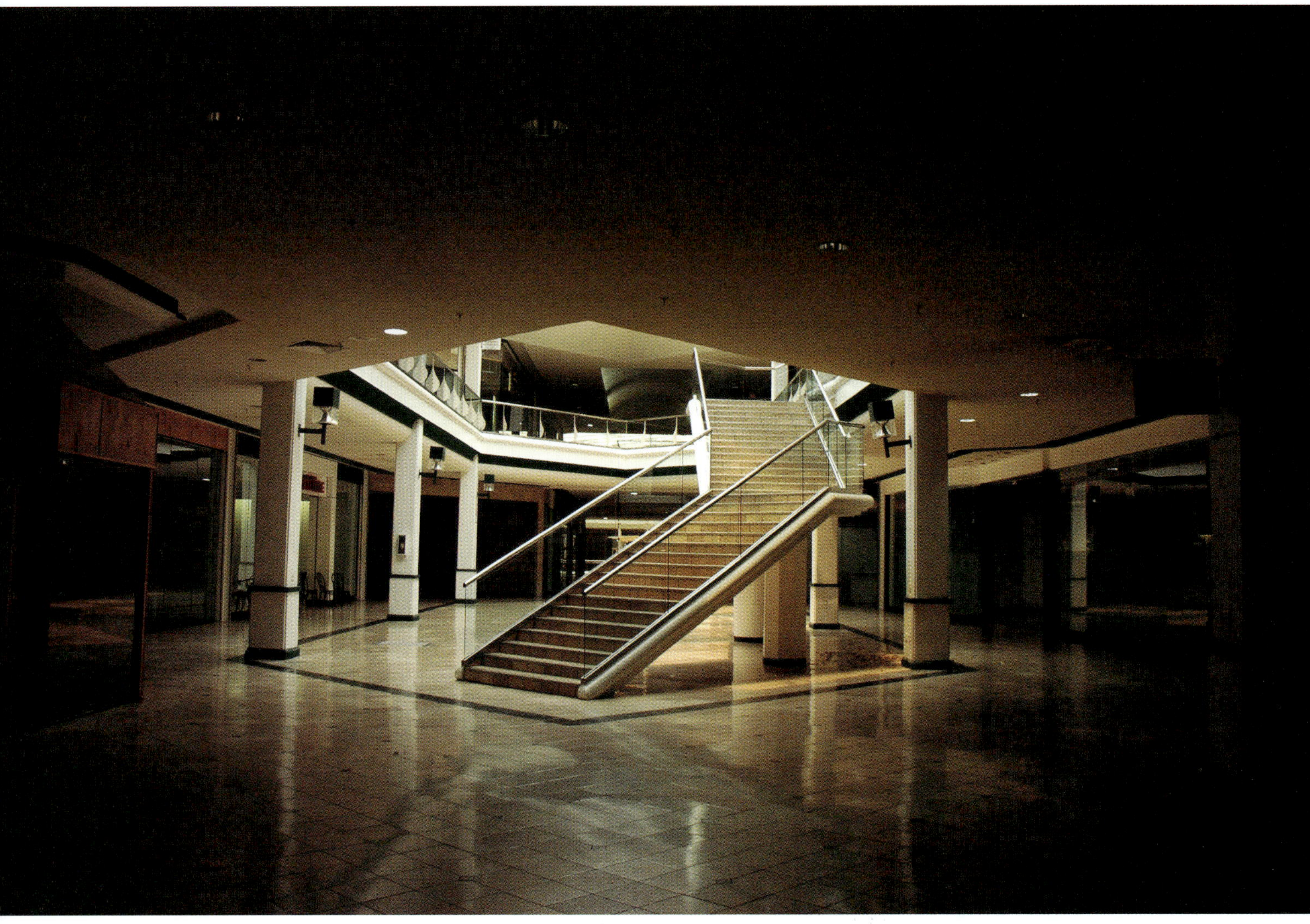

The interior of Eastland Mall, photographed before its destruction in 2013
STEWART GRAY

when the place is lost, there can be devastating effects on people—a reaction comparable to grief. I grieve for many lost places. I'm sometimes *mad* about the unnecessary loss—from New York's Penn Station (which I never even knew), to Chicago's Prentice Hospital, to my great-grandfather's gentle white clapboard house.

People survive the loss of places that support their identity. And many times these places survive in memory. But the continued presence of old places helps us know who we are and who we may become in the future.

NOTES

1. Sofia Bosco, interview with author, November 25, 2013.
2. Cicero, *The Treatises of M. T. Cicero*, ed. C. Yonge (London: H. G. Bohn, 1853), 428.

3. James Marston Fitch, *Historic Preservation: Curatorial Management of the Built World* (New York: McGraw-Hill, 1982), 404.
4. Clare L. Twigger-Ross and David L. Uzzell, "Place and Identity Processes," *Journal of Environmental Psychology* 16 (1996): 206, 208.
5. Humeyra Birol Akkurt, "Reconstitution of the Place Identity within the Intervention Efforts in the Historic Built Environment," in *The Role of Place Identity in the Perception, Understanding, and Design of Built Environments*, ed. Hernan Casakin and Fátima Bernardo (Bentham E-books), 64–65. https://ebooks.benthamscience.com/book/9781608054138.
6. Ashild Lappegard Hauge, "Identity and Place: A Critical Comparison of Three Identity Theories," *Architectural Science Review* (March 1, 2007): 6, 10. www.highbeam.com/docID=1G1:160922464.
7. Yi-Fu Tuan, *Space and Place: The Perspective of Experience* (Minneapolis: University of Minnesota Press, 1977), e-book locations 2826, 2990.
8. Akkurt, "Reconstruction of the Place Identity," 64.
9. David Seamon, "Place, Place Identity, and Phenomenology: A Triadic Interpretation Based on J. G. Bennett's Systematics." In *The Role of Place Identity in the Perception, Understanding, and Design of Built Environments*, ed. Hernan Casakin and Fátima Bernardo (Bentham E-books), 5. https://ebooks.benthamscience.com/book/9781608054138.
10. Stewart Gray, Survey and Research Report on the Eastland Mall Signs, Charlotte-Mecklenburg Historic Preservation Foundation, May 30, 2013. www.cmhpf.org/Survey%20Commttee%20Agendas/Eastland%20Mall%20SR.pdf.

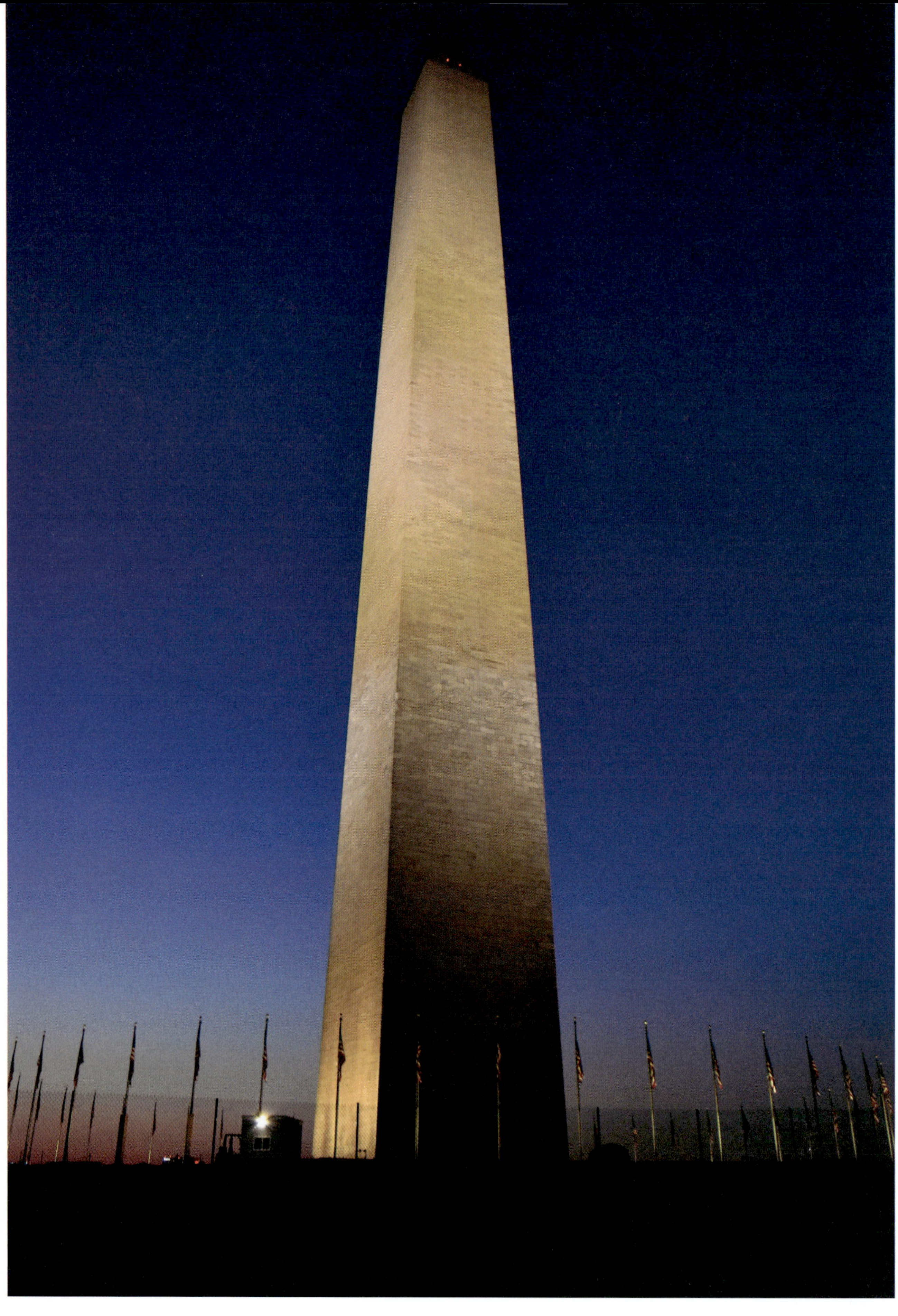

The Washington Monument reflects the national identity of the United States
MICHAEL POLLOCK

Civic, State, National, and Universal Identity

OLD PLACES embody our civic, state, national, and universal identity.

Jamestown. Mount Vernon. Independence Hall. Old South Meetinghouse. Valley Forge. The Missions of California. Fort McHenry. The Alamo. Sutter's Mill. Harpers Ferry. Fort Sumter. Gettysburg. Appomattox. Little Bighorn. Pearl Harbor. Dexter Avenue Baptist Church. The very recitation of these names conjures the long time line of American history. These places—and countless others—embody the history and principles of the United States. For generations, these places have inspired Americans to learn our uniquely American story.

Just as these places embody an American identity, old places throughout the world embody civic, state, national, and universal identity. Stone cottages with thatched roofs embody Irishness. English country houses and cozy pubs stand as symbols of something particularly English. Temples and Zen gardens symbolize Japan. The pyramids of Egypt and the Parthenon in Greece are valued throughout the world as symbols of our common humanity. Old places help form, maintain, and transform civic identity—whether it's a city, county, state, region, country, or even the world.

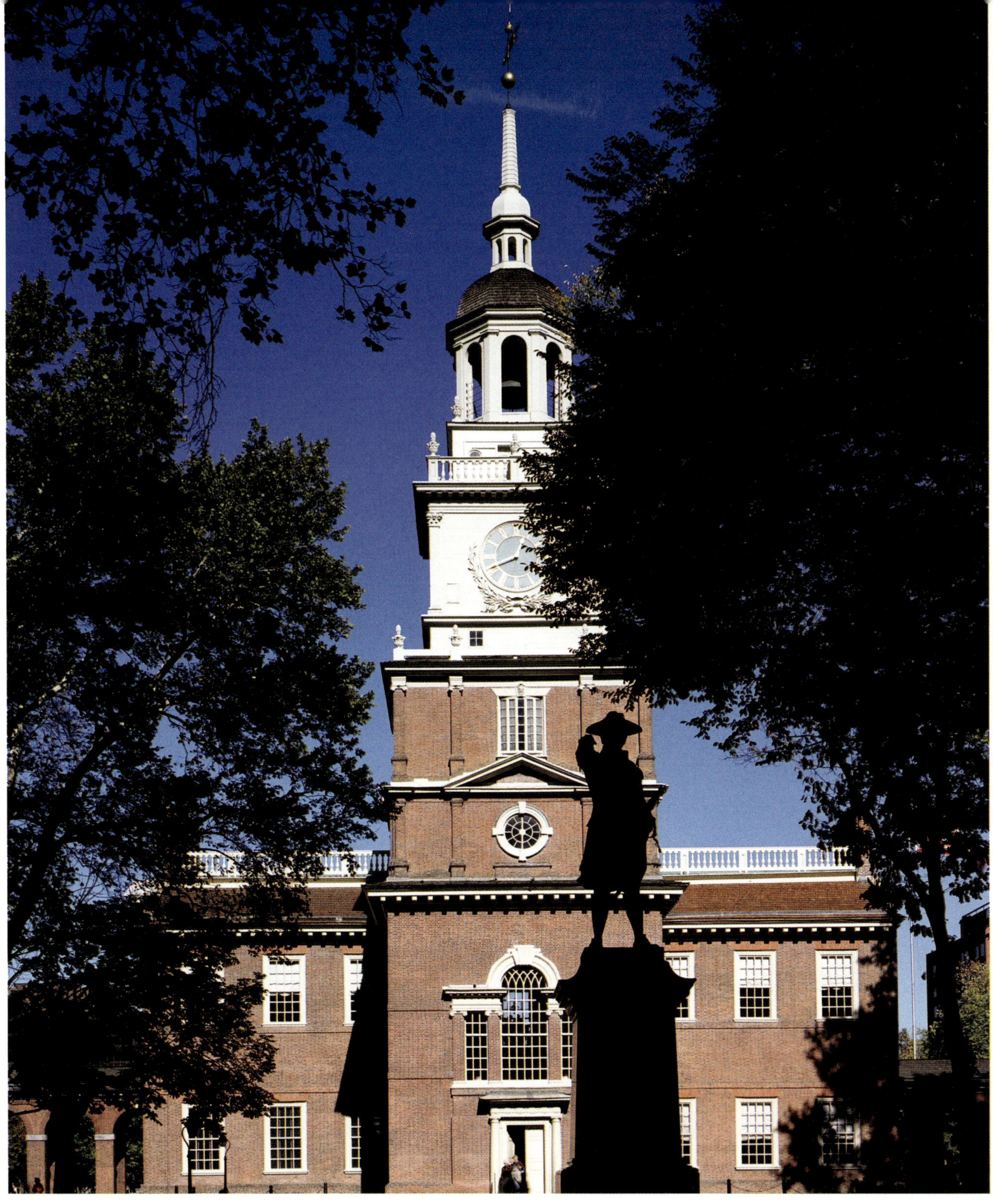

Independence Hall in Philadelphia, Pennsylvania, epitomizes the history and identity of the United States for generations of Americans
ISTOCK

Americans—and people everywhere—care deeply about the old places that embody their shared identity, whether national, civic, or more broadly cultural. They speak forcefully and eloquently about these places when they are threatened. From the Tomb of the Unknown Soldier to the Virginia countryside where the Battle of the Wilderness took place, people strive to save these places because they matter to our collective sense of who we are. As the Civil War Trust notes on its website:

> Can you imagine a fast-food restaurant in the middle of Arlington Cemetery? Can you imagine paving over the Vietnam Veterans Memorial? Can you imagine destroying the remaining original copies of the Declaration of Independence or the Constitution? Of course not. But with each square foot of battlefield land that is consumed, whole chapters of America's history are being ripped out of the book of our national memory, and an irreplaceable piece of our important heritage is lost forever."[1]

In America, we've had policies to preserve places of national identity for more than seventy-five years, and patriotism and national identity have been key drivers of movements to save old places.[2] But we aren't as single-minded or as uncritical about our civic or national identity as we may have once been. As I listened to people talk about the reasons that old places matter, I noticed that although many people mentioned national identity and patriotism, others were reticent to refer to national identity—or patriotism—as a reason for saving old places. This reticence seems to reflect what American academic and literary critic Edward Said described as the "vexed issue of nationalism and national identity, of how memories of the past are shaped in accordance with a certain notion of what 'we' or, for that matter, 'they' really are."[3]

What is this "vexed" issue of national identity, and how do we responsibly talk about places that reflect our national or other identities? Many of the places we first deemed worthy of preservation were saved to celebrate and promote an idea of a shared American heritage—essentially an American identity. The Daughters of the American Revolution, the National Society of the Colonial Dames of America, and many other state or local organizations saved old places to promote American ideals. These places inspired people about American history and American institutions, while also acting to form an American identity. The places we sought to preserve represented what we valued from the past. At the same time, they also represented what those who saved these places aspired for America to be.

Countless writers and scholars have criticized the selective choice of what was preserved as part of our national identity, by whom, and for what purpose.[4] As someone who has cared about old places for most of my life, I am painfully aware of the exclusive character of many early preservation efforts and the conscious attempts to use old places to tell only a selective view of American history—essentially to define American identity in a way that left out some people or issues. Slavery and enslaved people were

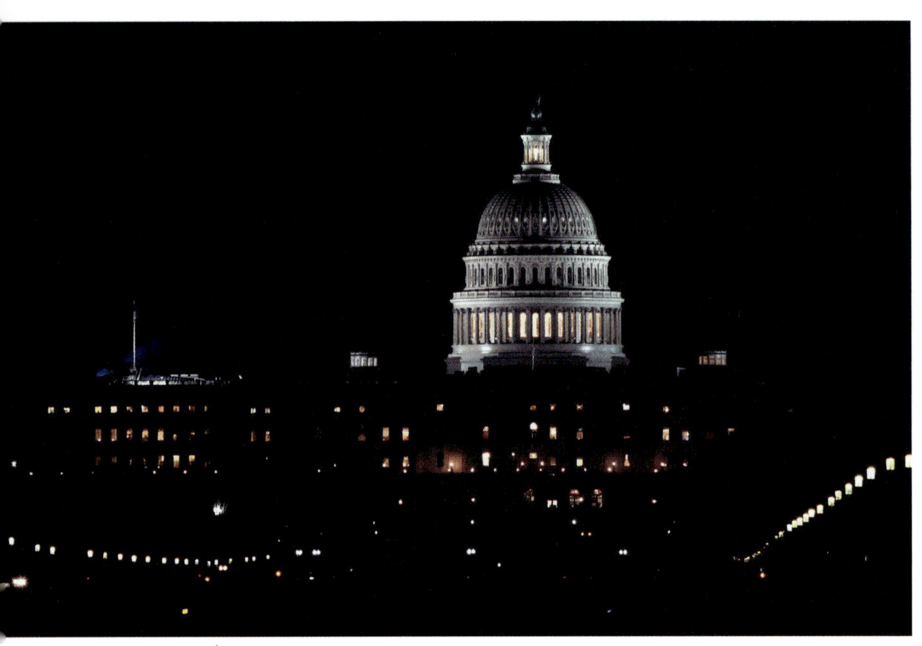

Capitol of the United States at night
MICHAEL POLLOCK

not acknowledged at plantation houses. Native Americans were treated as an inhuman enemy at frontier sites. The presence of Irish, German, and Eastern European people was not recognized at a host of places that they built or where they lived and worked. For many years, mill workers, farmers, mechanics, and shopkeepers were not visible in the old places that were preserved as sites of our national identity.

The process of redefining who "we" are is continuous, and today our old places increasingly reflect a more diverse history. Lowell, a textile mill town in Massachusetts, has been a national park since 1978. Steel mills are preserved in Pittsburgh. The reality of slavery is acknowledged at plantations. In my view, it is critically important for people who care about old places to acknowledge the sometimes exclusive history of the preservation movement and to continue to push to have all the stories included in the places that define who we are as Americans. Americans argue vociferously about what our country is, who it is for, and what it means. These debates help reshape and reform and—hopefully—deepen our understanding of history and identity. The old places that embody our identity are the perfect venues for those discussions and debates.

Edward Relph, a geographer who pioneered theories about place, noted when he reflected back on his early work,

> I realize that place and sense of place, which I then represented as mostly positive, have some very ugly aspects. They can, for instance, be the basis for exclusionary practices, for parochialism, and for xenophobia. There is ample evidence of this in such things as NIMBY attitudes, gated communities, and, more dramatically, the political fragmentation and ethnic cleansing that beset parts of Europe and Africa and that are sometimes justified by appeals to place identity.[5]

Bitter disputes over old places are a testament to how much these places matter. They matter. Sometimes they matter so much that their meaning may lead to war and to the destruction, as in times of conflict, of sites that symbolize a specific identity. A famous example is the destruction of Old Town Warsaw during World War II or, more recently, sites during the Bosnian War, in which "factions attacked the cultural heritage of other groups, acts that both violated the laws and customs of war and served to destroy these groups' collective memory, both internally and to the outside world."[6]

Nationalism and national identity have a dark history. One of the surprises of Rome for me is the prominent presence of buildings from the Fascist era. Mussolini made dramatic changes to the city plan and built hundreds of buildings, many of which consciously sought to tie the Fascist regime with the image of imperial Rome. The buildings are often monumental, stripped-down versions of classical buildings—a distinctive style developed to create a new national identity, just as Americans built Greek and Roman style buildings to tie our nation to the republican and democratic ideals of the classical world. The Fascist identity Mussolini sought to create was utterly discredited with the defeat of the Axis in World War II. But the buildings remain and are actively used today. People differ about whether and how the meaning and history of these buildings should be acknowledged and recognized.

Reynold Reynolds, a filmmaker and a fellow during my tenure at the American Academy, shared with me a film he made about the demolition of the Palace of the Republic in Berlin, the former home of the People's Assembly of East Germany. The palace was originally built in 1973 to 1974 on the site of the Berliner Schloss (which was heavily damaged by bombs in World War II and destroyed by the German Democratic Republic (GDR) in 1950), perhaps the most symbolically powerful site in Berlin. As a representation of the ideals of the GDR, the palace was without question a symbol of a national identity. But it was a national identity that was no longer valued when Germany was reunited in 1990. Despite the fact that the building represented a discredited regime, Reynolds's project shows that many Berliners viewed the demolition as the erasure of their history and the loss of the opportunity for that history to be acknowledged and transformed. As Reynolds said, "thousands of citizens demonstrated against the planned demolition and hoped the building would be protected against historical censorship, but alas, one day twenty years after the fall of the Berlin Wall, the palace completely disappeared."[7]

The continued presence of old places permits the acknowledgment of history—and former identities—and the transformation of identity over time—the necessary and continuous critical revision of identity informed by the past. Monticello now doesn't

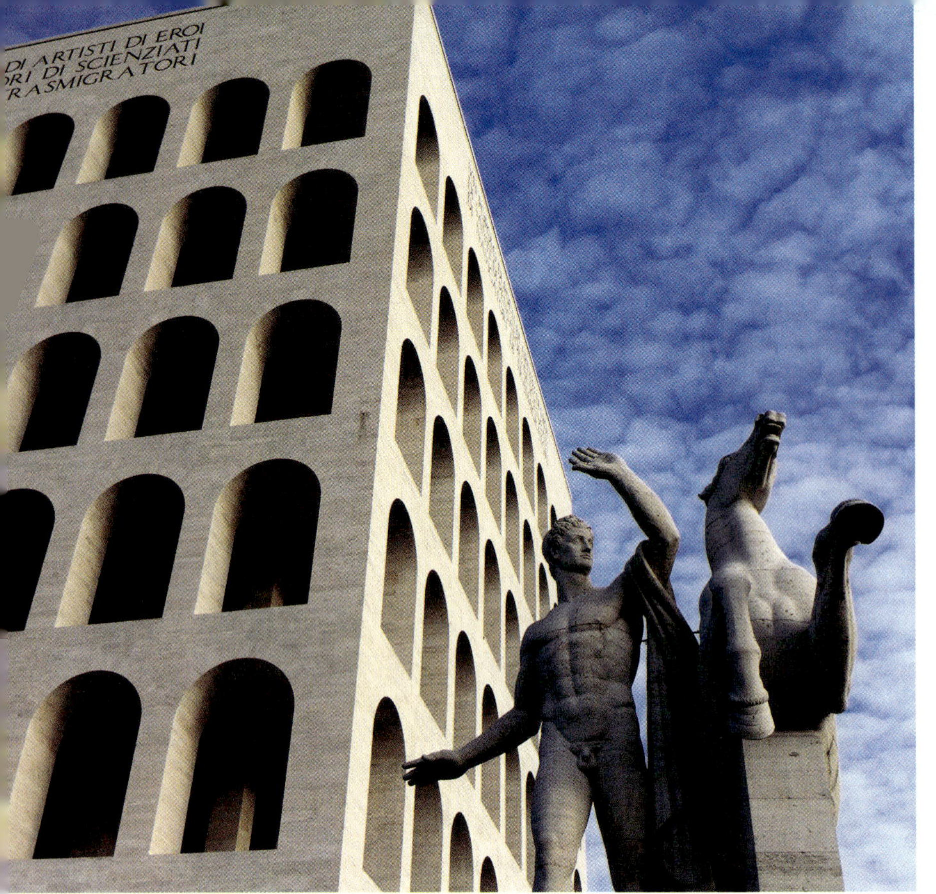

The "Square Coliseum" tied Mussolini's fascist regime to the history of the Roman empire
TOM MAYES/NATIONAL TRUST FOR HISTORIC PRESERVATION

hide the reality of Jefferson's life with the enslaved people he owned, although that was not always the case. The enslaved people and their descendants—both literal and metaphorical—are now visible and present at the site. Monticello is the venue for understanding this history, which leads to a deeper understanding of our national identity.

I have heard people say that identity is different in America than in European countries, which have a more homogenous culture. As French historian Pierre Nora stated, "In the United States, for example, a country of plural memories and diverse traditions, historiography is more pragmatic. Different interpretations of the Revolution and the Civil War do not threaten the American tradition because, in some sense, no such thing exists."[8]

Although I don't necessarily agree with Nora's statement, as I think about old places that represent an American national identity, it seems to me to be very American to voice critiques about that identity and to express diverse viewpoints about what the place means. Our old places of national identity can be the forum for this very American expression of views. What could be more patriotic than that?

When I was in Rome, I interviewed Jukka Jokilehto, who has been developing ideas about universal cultural value for the International Centre for the Study of the Preservation and Restoration of Cultural Property, about the fraught nature of identity. Jokilehto shared a critically important idea during our conversation. Places that reflect universal human values also reflect the diversity of cultural identities. In other words, places that are important to all of us arise from places that are important to some of us. When I spoke with Sofia Bosco, the Rome director of Fondo Ambiente Italiano (FAI), an Italian preservation organization, about old places in Italy, she clearly didn't think about old places in Italy as only Italian. The FAI website features people all over the world talking about why places in Italy are important to them. As she told me: "Italy is a public museum of the history of everyone. . . . The physical identity of a country is more than a library or a warehouse. It's there for you, for everyone."

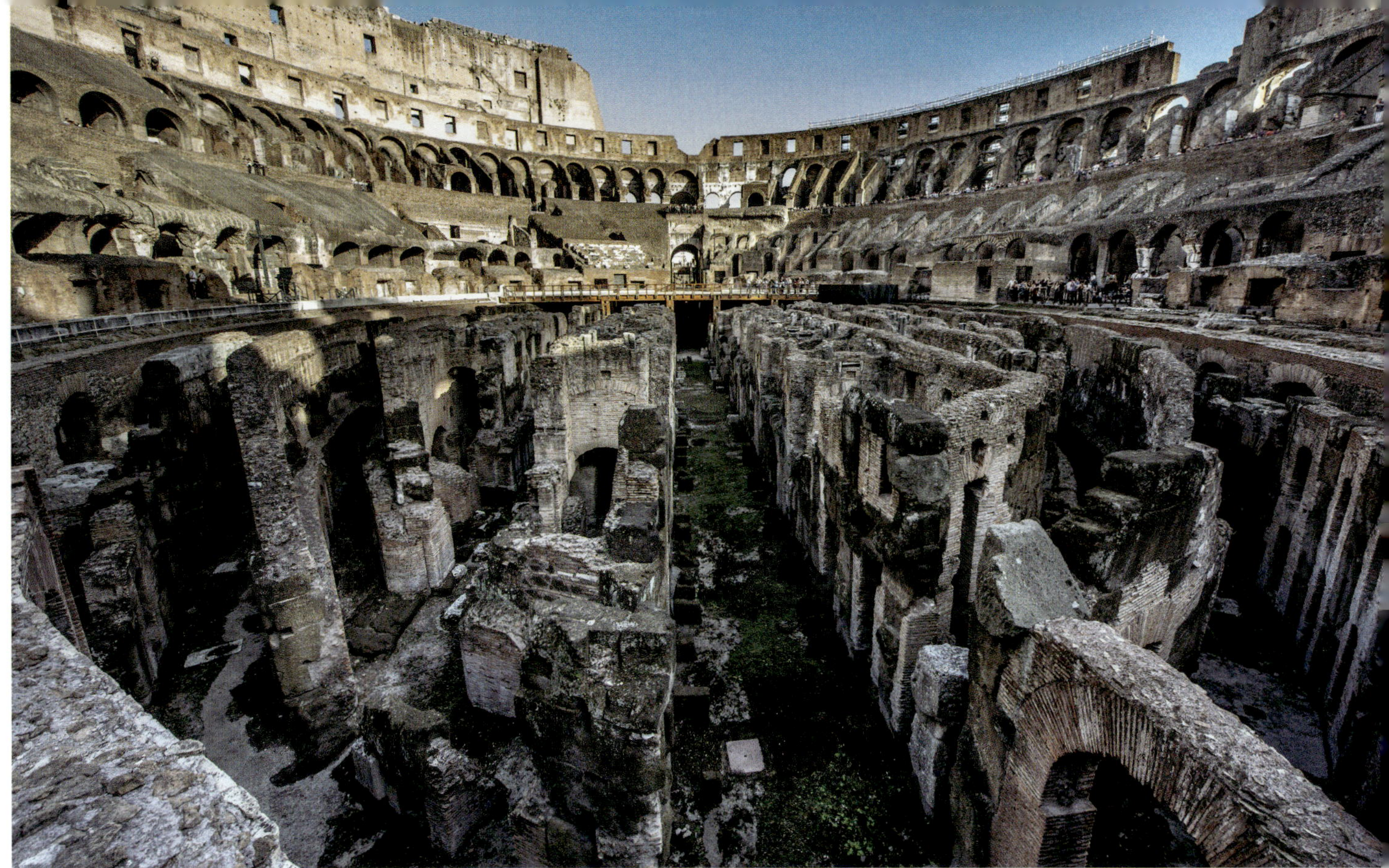

The Coliseum in Rome, a place that gives visitors a palpable sense of time
PETER KROGH

Old places embody our ever-changing shared identities and serve as tangible sites for transforming identity. Although we should guard against the dangers of nationalism, these old places, through the diversity of identities, reflect our universal humanity.

NOTES

1. "FAQs: Battlefield Preservation," Civil War Trust, accessed February 7, 2018, www.civilwar.org/about/faqs-battlefield-preservation.
2. The Historic Sites, Buildings, and Antiquities Act, codified at U.S. Code 16 (2018), section 461. The Historic Sites Act of 1935 expressly declared a national policy "to preserve for public use historic sites, buildings, and objects of national significance for the inspiration and benefit of the people of the United States."
3. Edward W. Said, "Invention, Memory, and Place," *Critical Inquiry* 26, no. 2 (2000): 177.
4. See, e.g., Diane Barthel, *Historic Preservation Collective Memory and Historical Identity* (New Brunswick, NJ: Rutgers University Press, 1996); Max Page and Randall Mason, eds., *Giving Preservation a History: Histories of Historic Preservation in the United States* (New York: Routledge, 2004).
5. Edward C. Relph, "Reflections on Place and Placelessness," *Environment & Architectural Phenomenology Newsletter* 7, no. 3 (Fall 1996), accessed February 23, 2018, www.arch.ksu.edu/seamon/Relph96.htm.
6. Shannon Supple, "Memory Slain: Recovering Cultural Heritage in Post-War Bosnia," *InterActions: UCLA Journal of Education and Information Studies* 1, no. 2 (2005), https://cloudfront.escholarship.org/dist/prd/content/qt28c783b6/qt28c783b6.pdf?t=kro8fd&v=lg., 2.
7. Gerhard Falkner and Reynold Reynolds, *The Last Day of the Republic* (Nurnberg: Starfruit Publications, 2011), http://artstudio reynolds.com/artworks/city-films. See also Brian Ladd, *The Ghosts of Berlin: Confronting German History in the Urban Landscape* (Chicago: University of Chicago Press, 1997).
8. Pierre Nora, "Between Memory and History: Les Lieux de Memoire," *Representations* 26 (1989): 10.

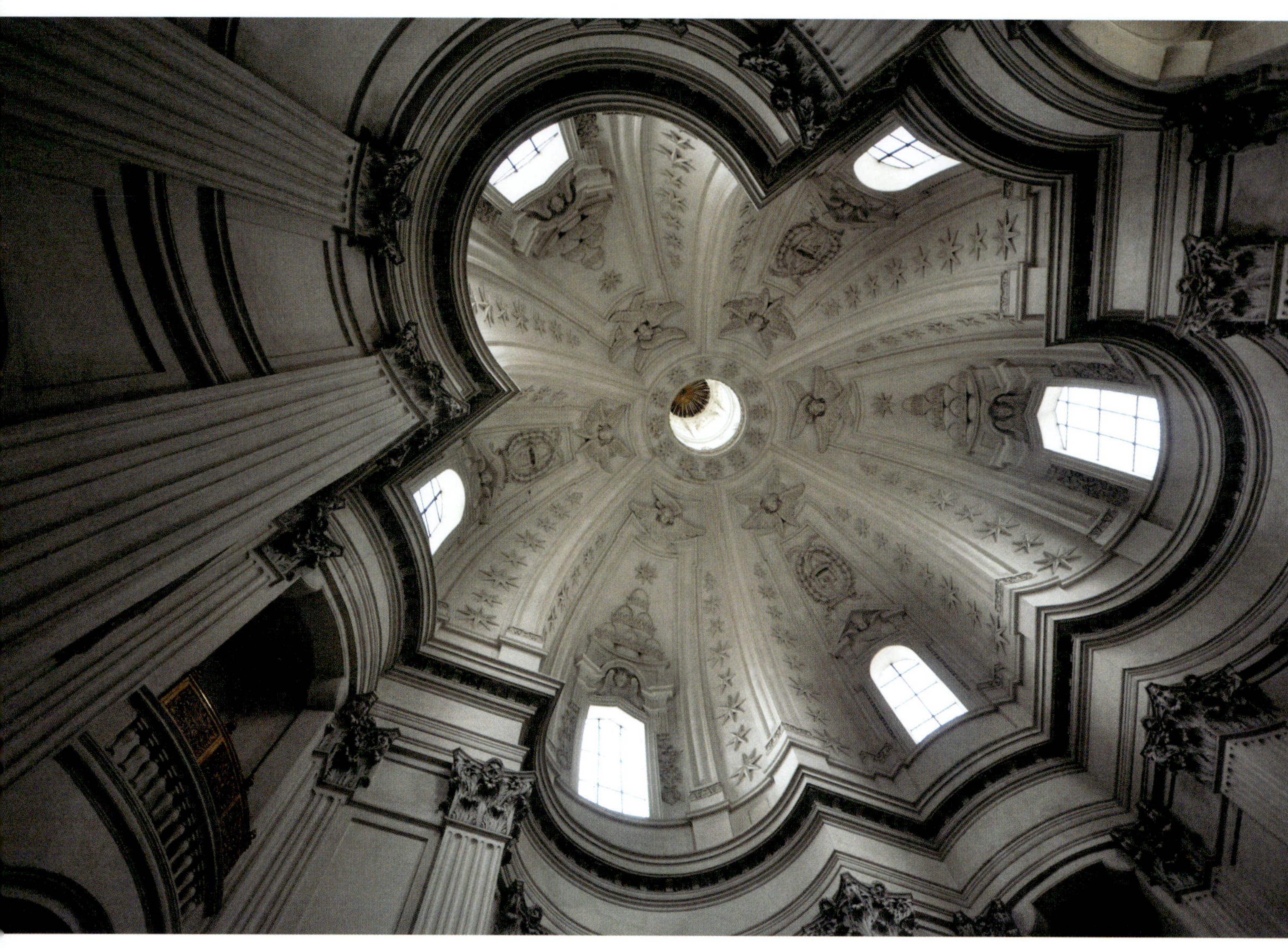

The church of Sant'Ivo alla Sapienza in Rome, Italy, considered a masterpiece of the baroque architect Francesco Borromini and widely regarded as beautiful
CATIE NEWELL

Beauty

OLD PLACES are beautiful.

When asked once why old places matter, Mark McDonald, president of the Georgia Trust, exclaimed without hesitation, "Because they are beautiful!" Google the phrase "beautiful places," and the results typically show old cities, old towns, and old buildings, along with natural places and a smattering of newer places. From the Zen gardens of Kyoto, to Bernini's colonnade at St. Peter's Square, to the Ruins of Windsor in Port Gibson, Mississippi—beautiful old places are treasured throughout the world as places where people experience the power of *beauty*.

Beauty—and the threat to beautiful places—was the driving force for many early preservation efforts. In Charleston, South Carolina, the people who formed the art movement known as the Charleston Renaissance sought to keep the beautiful and picturesque. As the Morris Museum of Art website states,

> Alice R. H. Smith, Elizabeth O'Neill Verner, and other Charleston artists helped inspire the historic preservation movement, awakening

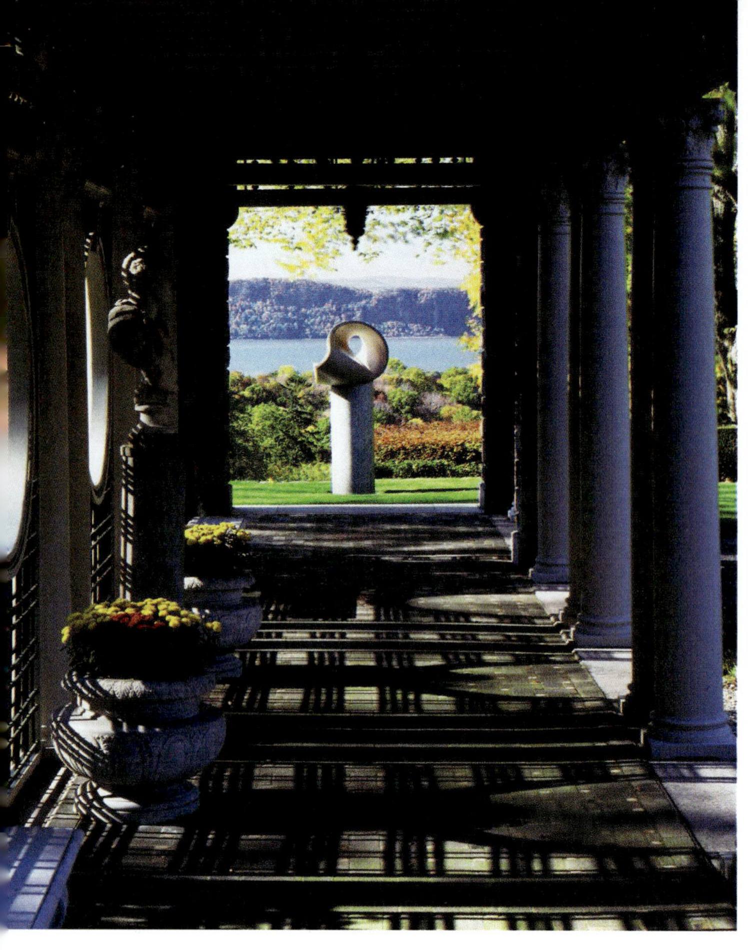

A sculpture placed against the landscape at Kykuit, a National Trust Historic site operated by the Rockefeller Brothers Fund
RON BLUNT

their neighbors to the charm and significance of the city's architectural heritage, through their images. As a result, the city's architectural and cultural heritage became the focus of pioneering efforts in historic preservation.[1]

Similarly, in Texas, the San Antonio Conservation Society was created by artists who were concerned about the loss of beautiful places in their city. In places throughout the world, artists who care about beauty were—and are—often at the forefront of saving threatened places. Today Charleston and San Antonio now reap a rich harvest of benefits—including economic benefits—because they kept their beautiful old places.

Beauty remains at the heart of why people care about old places. As Marta de la Torre and Randall Mason put it in their study of the values of cultural heritage, "The many interpretations of beauty, of the sublime, of ruins, and of the quality of formal relationships considered more broadly have long been among the most important criteria for labeling things and places as heritage."[2] Or as Dan Hurlin, one of the visual artists at the American Academy, said to me, "The primary reason to save old places is because they are beautiful, whether it's Penn Station or Fallingwater."[3]

Beauty, however, as Dan hints in using two very different places as examples, is not a simple topic. Philosophers, artists, architects, planners, and poets have explored the idea of what beauty means for more than two millennia. From Plato and Aristotle, to Vitruvius, to Burke, to Keats, to Kant, to Dave Hickey,[4] people have debated, defined, redefined, dismissed, and rediscovered the meaning of beauty. Is beauty balance and harmony? Is it proportion? Is beauty about truth? Moral goodness? Awe or transcendence? Is beauty inherent or subjective? Is beauty what only one person perceives or is it universal? The idea of beauty raises seemingly endless philosophical questions. Reviewing the many attempts to define beauty over the course of human civilization is a fascinating journey through history and art.[5] Yet regardless of how beauty is defined, people perceive and desire beauty in their lives and in their communities. And they find beauty in old places.

As I read and talk to people about beauty, a few words and phrases capture the experiences I've had—and that I believe other people also have—at beautiful old places: *delight*, *exhilarating surprise*, *speechlessness*, *the language of timeless reality*, *echo of an ideal*, *sudden unexpected harmony of the body, mind, and world.*[6]

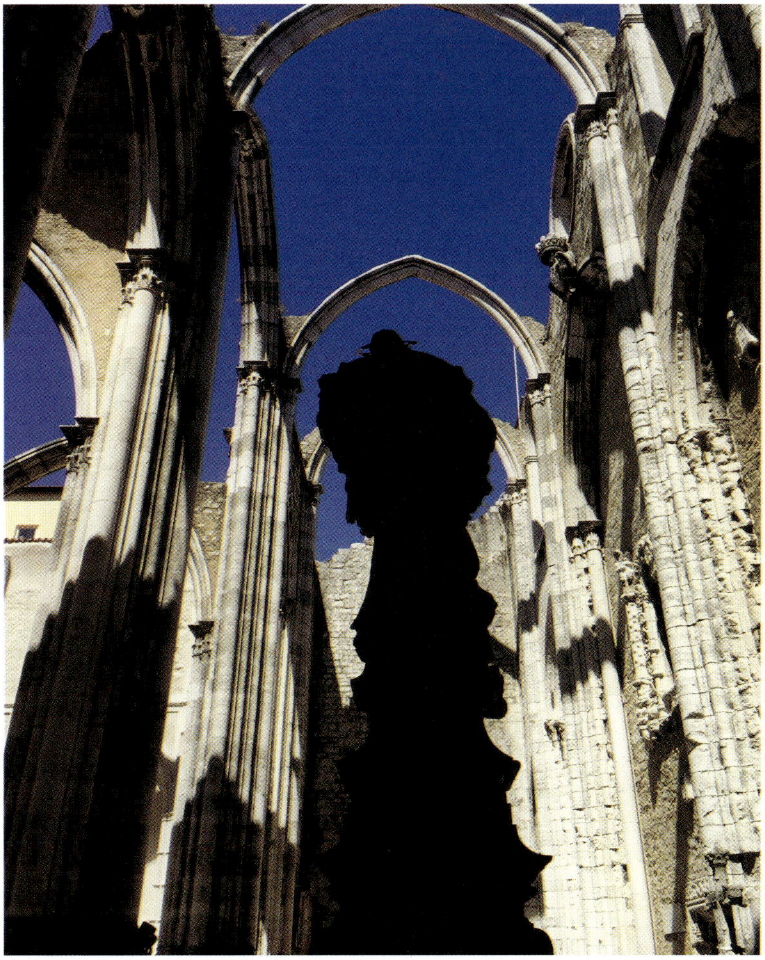

One of the many buildings in Rome that is open only for a few hours every week on Sunday morning is Sant'Ivo, a baroque church designed by Francesco Borromini. The interior is light filled and tall and plays with scale and perspective. The form of the space is a complex of triangles and curves, convex and concave. The pilasters are gray. The walls are plain. My eyes were drawn upward, and I felt amazement and awe, and somehow, in that moment, in that lofty space, the world was a great and wonderful place. Altogether, it's what the architect Catie Newell, another fellow at the academy, described to me as "that moment of *gasp*." A moment when we are stopped in our tracks and taken out of ourselves, when we feel that the universe is a big and amazing place and that we are part of it. That may be as close to my own subjective idea about a moment of beauty as I can get.[7]

Ruins have long been associated with the idea of the sublime and are often considered beautiful, such as Carmo Convent in Lisbon, Portugal

TOM MAYES/NATIONAL TRUST FOR HISTORIC PRESERVATION

Old places may be beautiful for their design, but sometimes they're beautiful because of their very age—because of the mark that time has left upon them. Ruins have been the exemplars of the concept of the sublime for hundreds of years, epitomized by the famous gothic ruins of Tintern Abbey on the River Wye in Wales.

The Ruins of Windsor—monumental Corinthian columns that are all that remain of a vanished plantation house—in Port Gibson, Mississippi, have been a southern pilgrimage site for generations because of the palpable sense of time and loss. The same holds true for the ruins of Barboursville in Virginia, where one can see the structure of a Jeffersonian building that burnt to the ground on Christmas Day 1884. Today, we have

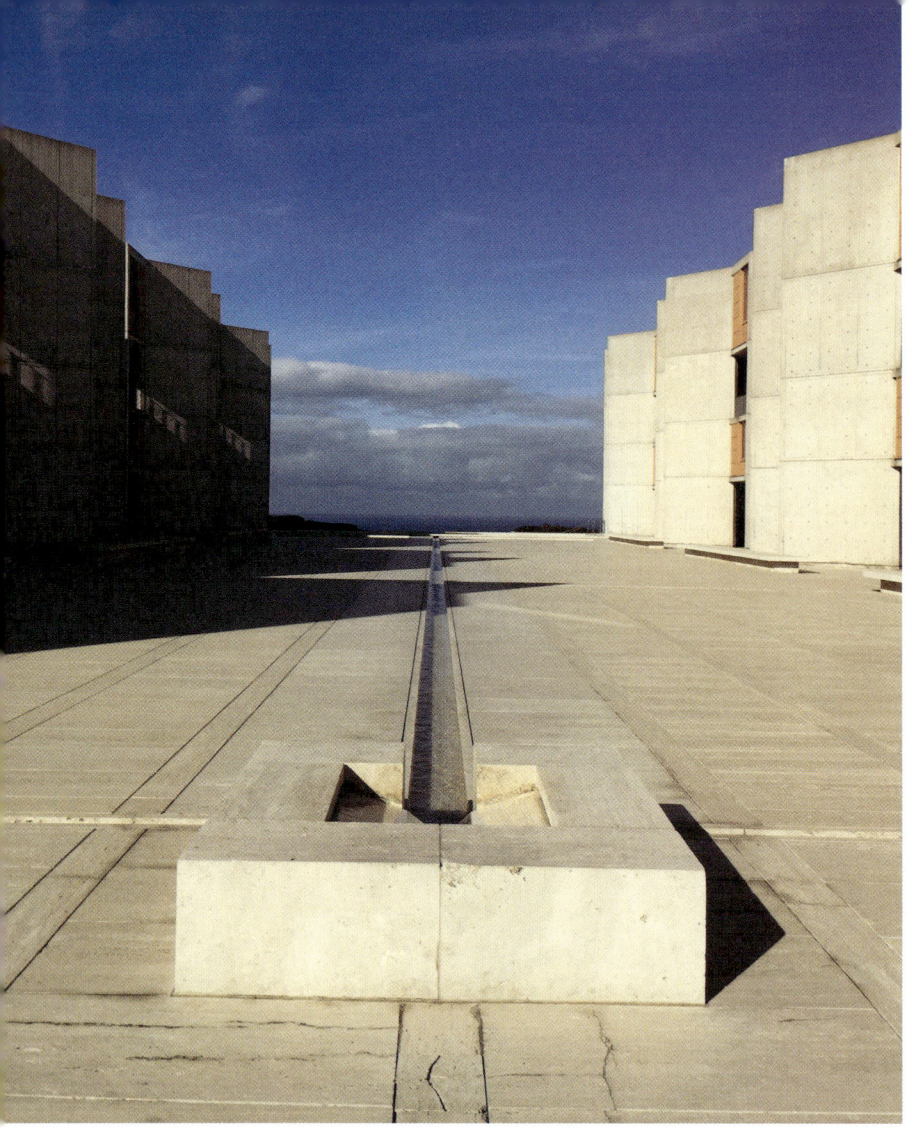

The Salk Institute, by Louis Kahn, is constructed of poured concrete and is widely considered beautiful
TOM MAYES/NATIONAL TRUST FOR HISTORIC PRESERVATION

the proliferation of "ruin porn" sites on Facebook, Pinterest, and Flickr devoted to the evocative, gritty, and sad abandoned buildings of Detroit and other cities. All of these are about beauty—the beauty to be found in old places.

As I talk to people about beauty and old places, I note that many architects and artists—*like many preservationists*—hesitate to talk about beauty. The hesitancy is for many reasons—the difficulty of defining what beauty is, the loaded cultural aspects of beauty, the subjective nature of people's experience of beauty, or even the simple fact that decision makers sometimes consider beauty frivolous or expendable.

As Dan suggested by mentioning Penn Station *and* Fallingwater, beauty is found in many different types of places, and people's experiences of beauty often differ. Feelings and opinions about beauty also change over time. The history of preservation demonstrates a remarkable march of the *ugly* transforming into the *beautiful*. Victorian buildings were condemned as the worst expressions of a degraded era; art deco was considered commercial and hideous; industrial buildings were treated as having no architectural value; midcentury modern was dated. All of these were once considered ugly and are now (generally) considered—or starting to be considered—beautiful. It's always easier to save a place that people consider beautiful than a place—no matter how historically significant—that people think is ugly.

The many heated (to say the least) discussions I have had about my view that beauty can be found in the poured concrete walls of Brutalist buildings highlight the fact that the field of preservation is one of the venues in which concepts of beauty and ugliness are publicly debated. Even I was surprised by the lyric beauty of a video of parkour athletes performing amid the brightly graffitied and spalling concrete of Miami Marine Stadium.[8] A building may be considered beautiful when built, then ugly for a generation when "dated," then beautiful again. The march goes on.

Beauty has financial as well as psychological and sociological benefits. The Federal Reserve Bank of Philadelphia published a report in 2008 that analyzed the financial benefits of beautiful places. The definition of "beautiful cities" used in the report expressly included a determination of places that were historic through listing in the National Register of Historic Places. The authors recognized that leisure visitors and permanent residents were attracted to places because of an area's "special traits, such as proximity to the ocean, scenic views, historic districts, architectural beauty, and cultural and recreational opportunities."[9] They concluded that "beautiful cities disproportionally attracted highly educated individuals and experienced faster housing price appreciation."[10]

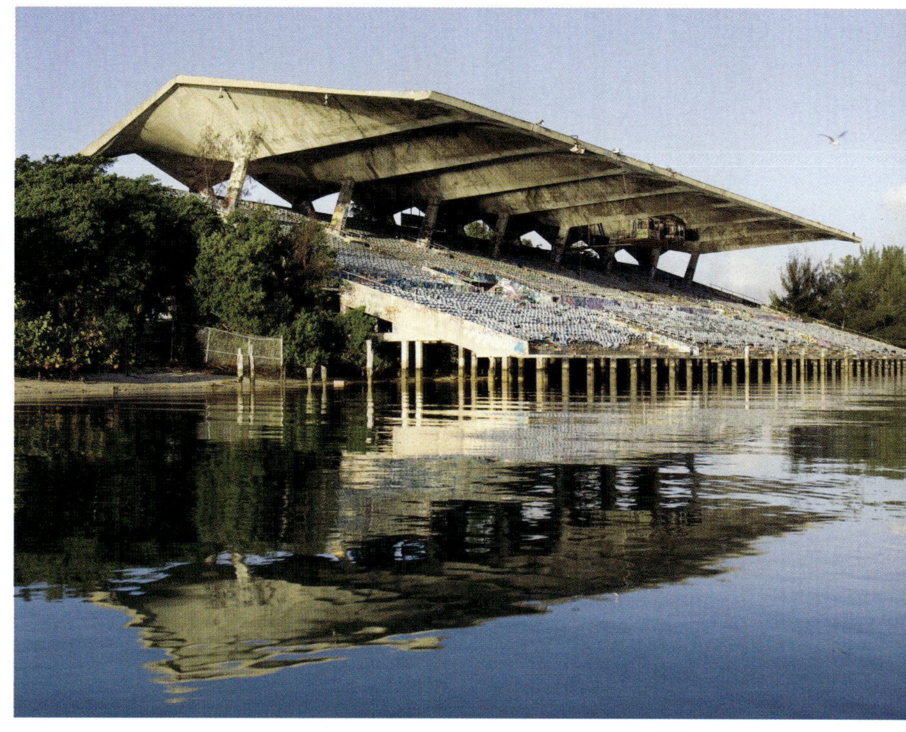

Miami Marine Stadium, a once-abandoned stadium for watching boat races, was named a National Treasure by the National Trust
KEN HAYDEN

When I mentioned Sant'Ivo earlier, I described a *moment* of beauty. These moments happen in unexpected places and at unexpected times. Yet I think it's important for people to live in beautiful communities every day, to be surrounded by beauty, and for it to be accessible to everyone, rich and poor. It's good for people, and we shouldn't be ashamed to talk about it and demand it, as many community leaders did during the City Beautiful movement more than a century ago.

In England, the Commission for Architecture and the Built Environment published a series of essays on beauty in 2010 to encourage people to engage in decisions about their built environment. As one essayist wrote,

> Whatever the reasons, as the 2010 Commission for Architecture and the Built Environment study *People and Places* suggests, beauty is fundamental to many people's lives. Where we find beauty varies, but we do agree that appreciating it is a deeply positive experience contributing to happiness and well-being. This fact alone is enough to justify taking

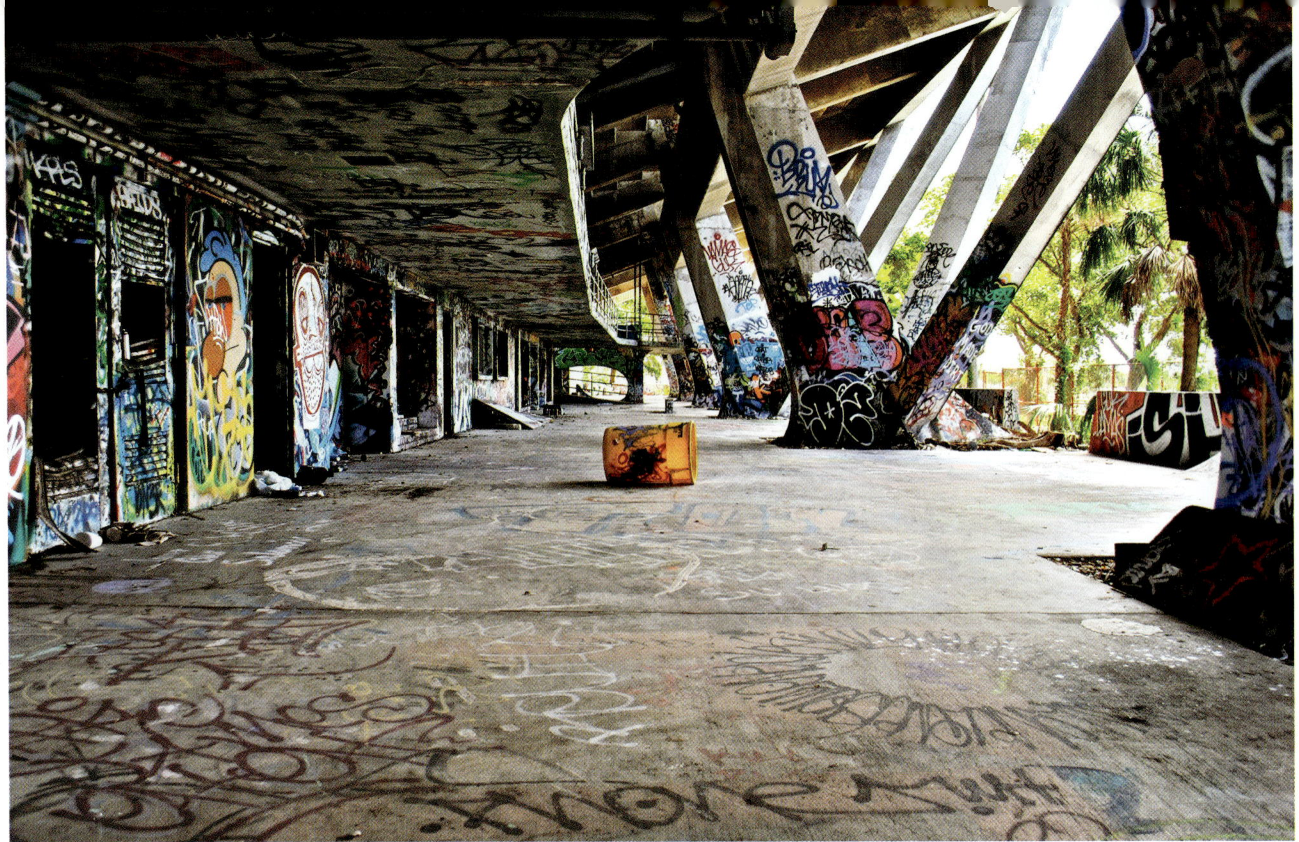

The heavily graffittied interior of Miami Marine Stadium
JASON CLEMENT/NATIONAL TRUST FOR HISTORIC PRESERVATION

beauty more seriously. And a proper understanding of what beauty is and the purposes it may serve will show why beauty should even be integral to planning and policy.[11]

Old places are a key aspect of what makes our communities beautiful. As Alan Powers said in *Beauty: A Short History*, preservation "was far more powerful as a means of restoring ideas of beauty in the public realm than architecture and planning of new buildings had ever been on their own. It was also a means of engaging a citizen population in debate and decision making about their environment."[12]

In an interview with Sofia Bosco from Fondo Ambiente Italiano, she told me that she thought Italians are incredibly talented and creative because they live in contact with beauty every day of their lives.[13] I'm an unabashed believer in the power of beauty. I think it's time not only to get comfortable with talking about beauty, but to *rise up and demand it* in our cities, towns, and countryside so that we can all have the experience of beauty.

President Kennedy said,

> I look forward to an America which will not be afraid of grace and beauty, which will protect the beauty of our natural environment, which will preserve the great old American houses and squares and parks of our national past, and which will build handsome and balanced cities for our future.[14]

I also want an America that is not afraid of grace and beauty—and that has daily access to the beauty of old places.

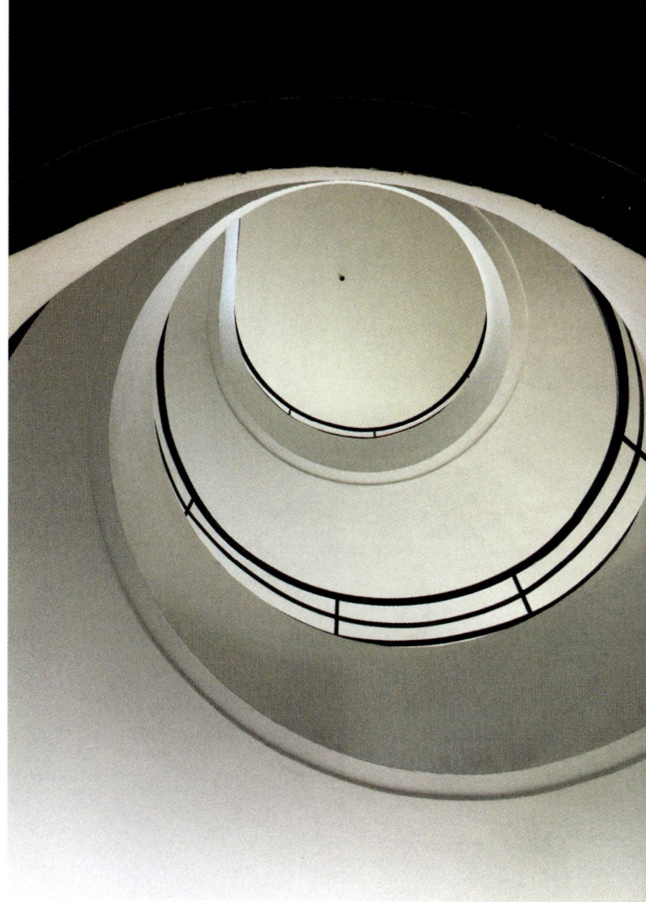

A stairway in the GIL building in Rome, by Luigi Moretti, who also designed the Watergate in Washington, D.C.

TOM MAYES/NATIONAL TRUST FOR HISTORIC PRESERVATION

NOTES

1. "The Charleston Renaissance," Morris Museum of Art, accessed February 7, 2018, http://tfaoi.org/newsm1/n1m526.htm.
2. Marta de la Torre and Randall Mason, *Assessing the Values of Cultural Heritage* (Los Angeles: Getty Conservation Institute, 2002). http://hdl.handle.net/10020/gci_pubs/values_cultural_heritage, 12.
3. Dan Hurlin, conversation with author, January 1, 2014.
4. Dave Hickey, *The Invisible Dragon: Four Essays on Beauty* (Los Angeles: Art Issues Press, 1993).
5. For further reading, see Umberto Eco, ed., *On Beauty* (London: Secker & Warburg, 2004); Alan Powers, *Beauty: A Short History* (London: Commission for Architecture and the Built Environment, 2010).
6. See Dave Hickey, *The Invisible Dragon*; Sarah Bainter Cunningham, "The Compass of Reason: Intellectual Interest in the Beautiful As a Mode of Orientation" (PhD diss., Vanderbilt University, 2004); Alain De Botton, *The Architecture of Happiness* (London: Penguin Books, 2006); Juhani Pallasmaa, *Encounters I: Architectural Essays*, ed. Peter MacKeith (Helsinki, Finland: Rakennustieto Oy Publishing, 2012).
7. Catie Newell, discussion with author, January 16, 2014. See also Hamlett Dobbins, *Sant'Ivo: June 29th, 2014* (Memphis, TN: H. Dobbins, 2015).
8. "Parkourplayhouse: Abandoned Stadium," YouTube video, June 27, 2012, accessed February 7, 2018. www.youtube.com/watch?v=mebaCC3MxcY.
9. Gerald A. Carlino and Albert Saiz, "Working Paper No. 08-22, City Beautiful" (Philadelphia: Federal Reserve Bank of Philadelphia, September 2008), 3.
10. Carlino and Saiz, *City Beautiful*, 33.
11. Matthew Kieran, "The X Factor: Beauty in Planning" (London: Commission for Architecture and the Built Environment, 2010), 5.
12. Powers, *Beauty*, 24.
13. Sofia Bosco, interview with author, November 25, 2013.
14. John F. Kennedy, "Remarks at Amherst College October 26, 1963," National Endowment for the Arts, accessed February 7, 2018. www.arts.gov/about/kennedy-transcript.

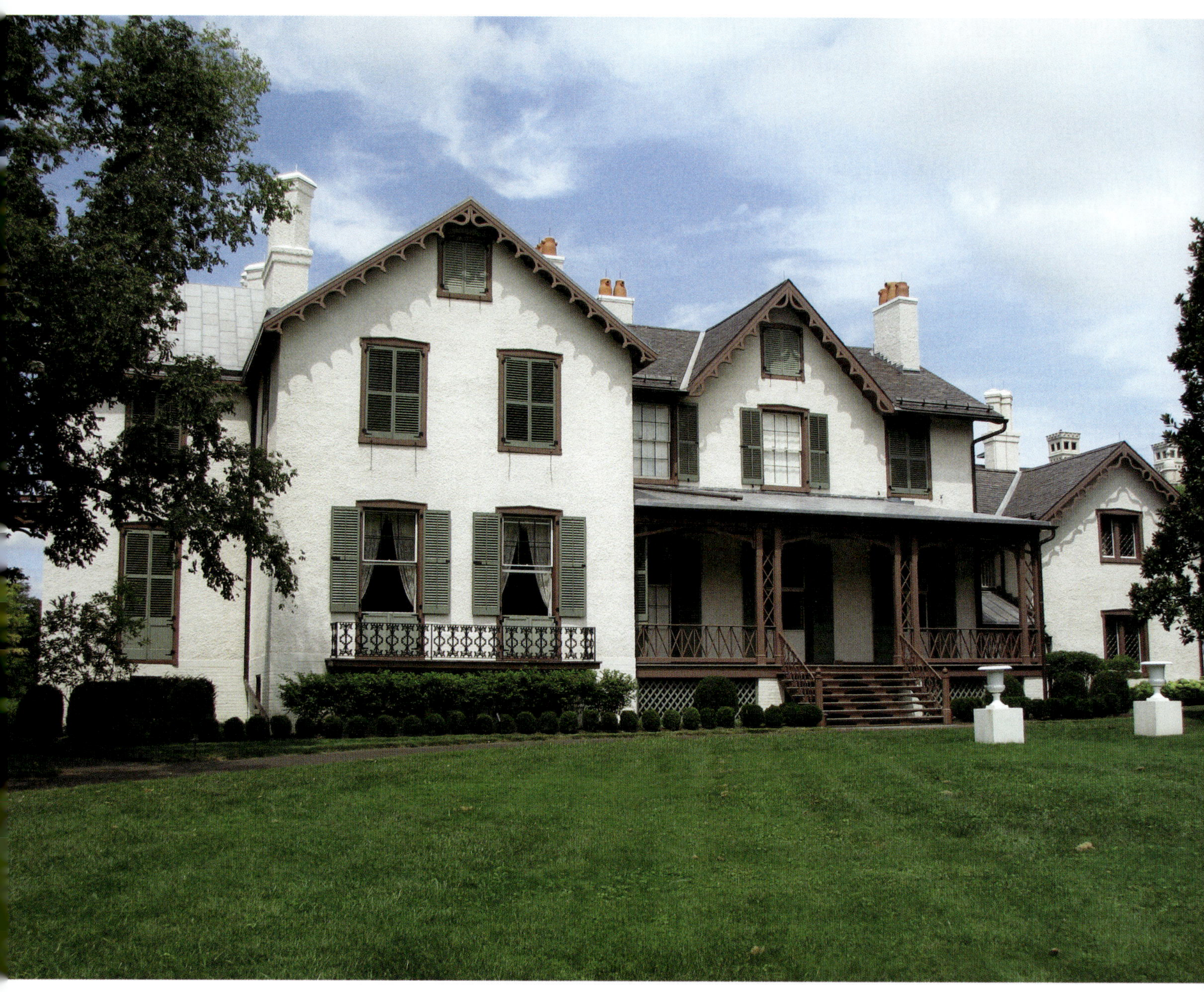

At President Lincoln's Cottage at the Armed Forces Retirement Home in Washington, D.C., visitors appreciate walking where Lincoln walked
NATIONAL TRUST FOR HISTORIC PRESERVATION

History

***OLD PLACES** give us an understanding of history that no other documents or evidence possibly can.*

As the National Park Service website for "Teaching with Historic Places" states, "Places make connections across time that give them a special ability to create an empathetic understanding of what happened and why."[1] Marta de la Torre and Randy Mason, in their report on heritage values, summarized the idea this way: "Historical values are at the root of the very notion of heritage. The capacity of a site to convey, embody, or stimulate a relation or reaction to the past is part of the fundamental nature and meaning of heritage objects.[2]

Simply put, old places tell us about the past. But what is it about old places that give them this unique capacity to "convey, embody, or stimulate a relation or reaction" to history? First, old places are tangible. Many people feel the excitement of experiencing the place where something actually happened, from the shimmering watery fortress of Fort Sumter, where the Civil War started, to the quiet rooms of Emily Dickinson's home in Amherst, Massachusetts.

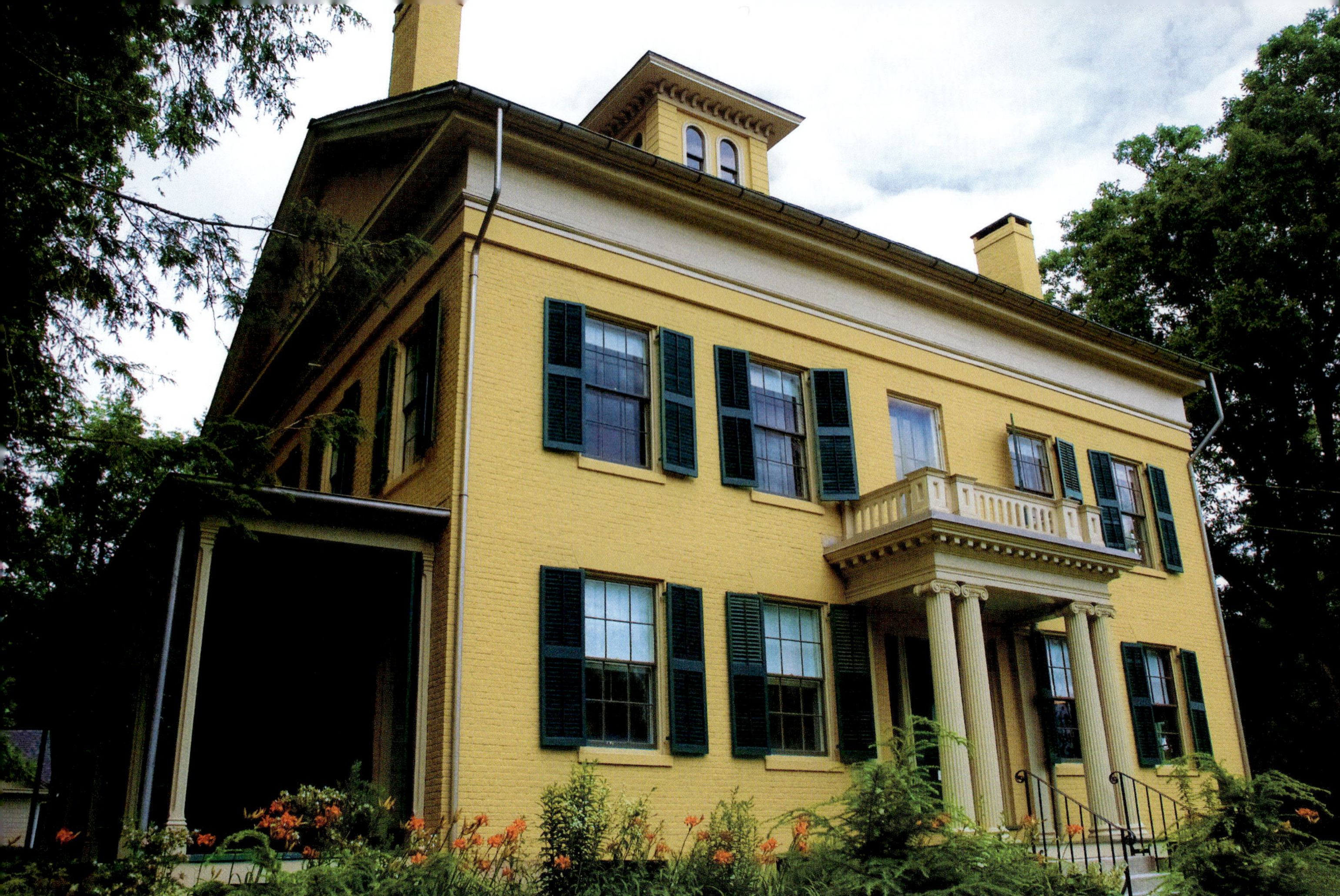

The home of Emily Dickinson in Amherst, Massachusetts, where visitors gain a greater context to understand Dickinson's poetry
DALLAS CLEMMONS

At President Lincoln's Cottage at the Soldiers' Home in Washington, D.C., visitors experience the place where President and Mrs. Lincoln sought refuge from the protocol, noise, and office seekers at the White House. Here, visitors pass through the same rooms the Lincolns used, they walk on the same ground that the Lincolns trod, they trail their hands along the same stair rail that Lincoln touched, they see the same distant view of the monuments of Washington, D.C. This capacity to engage all the senses in the experience of history is unique to old places—and it provides information that documentary history alone cannot provide.[3]

Other times the geography of the place tells the history. A stone wall, a sunken road, a long open field at a battlefield helps visitors understand troop movements and military tactics, as well as imagine the chaos, destruction, and loss of lives that occurred. Other places symbolize a decisive moment, such as the turn in the road at Wilderness Battlefield where Union troops cheered when they realized that the road chosen meant that General Grant was pursuing the Confederates rather than letting them retreat and regroup.

It is a common complaint that history education defaults to the tedious, dry, and rote memorization of dates and names. Knowing dates and names is necessary, but how do people really get excited about knowing history? It seems to me that history is most vividly learned and retained though experiencing the places where history happened. Joseph Farrell, professor of classical studies at the University of Pennsylvania wrote to me, "old places and old things stimulate my historical imagination in a personal way—that is, in a way that is different from reading about the past. . . . For many, places and things are a much more effective way of being in touch with the past than reading is."[4]

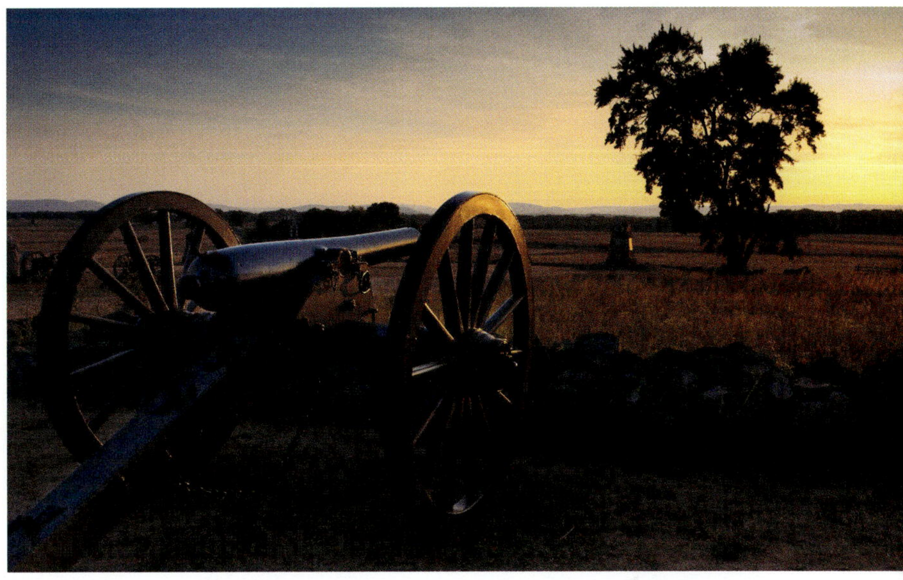

At places like Gettysburg Battlefield, visitors can understand how geography shaped history
ISTOCK

Why is it important for people to understand history?[5] A recent National Park Service report stated,

> "if we inventory the fundamental benefits that historical insight and historical thinking offer society, it is clear that they extend well beyond dates and facts to provide a well-spring of skills, and a dynamic array of tools and insights that people can use to approach both their own times and the welfare of society as a whole."[6]

The understanding of history provided by historic places, the report found, has the "promise of creating an inspired, informed and thinking citizenry."[7] Old places are perhaps the most evocative and powerful tools for us to tell and understand history.

Like civic identity and collective memory, history—the history we choose to tell—can be manipulated, and it is important to question who is telling the history and for what purpose. Mussolini, for example, consciously tried to tie the Fascist era to the history of imperial Rome. But people who are aware of history and capable of historical thinking—critical thinking based on evidence—are less likely to be duped by the manipulation of history by others. All of us can think of a time when our reaction to a political event has been: *Have we learned nothing? Don't they know we went through this in the 1920s, '30s, or '40s?* This type of historical thinking also acknowledges that the "historical understanding of any era, topic, or event in the past is a moving target,

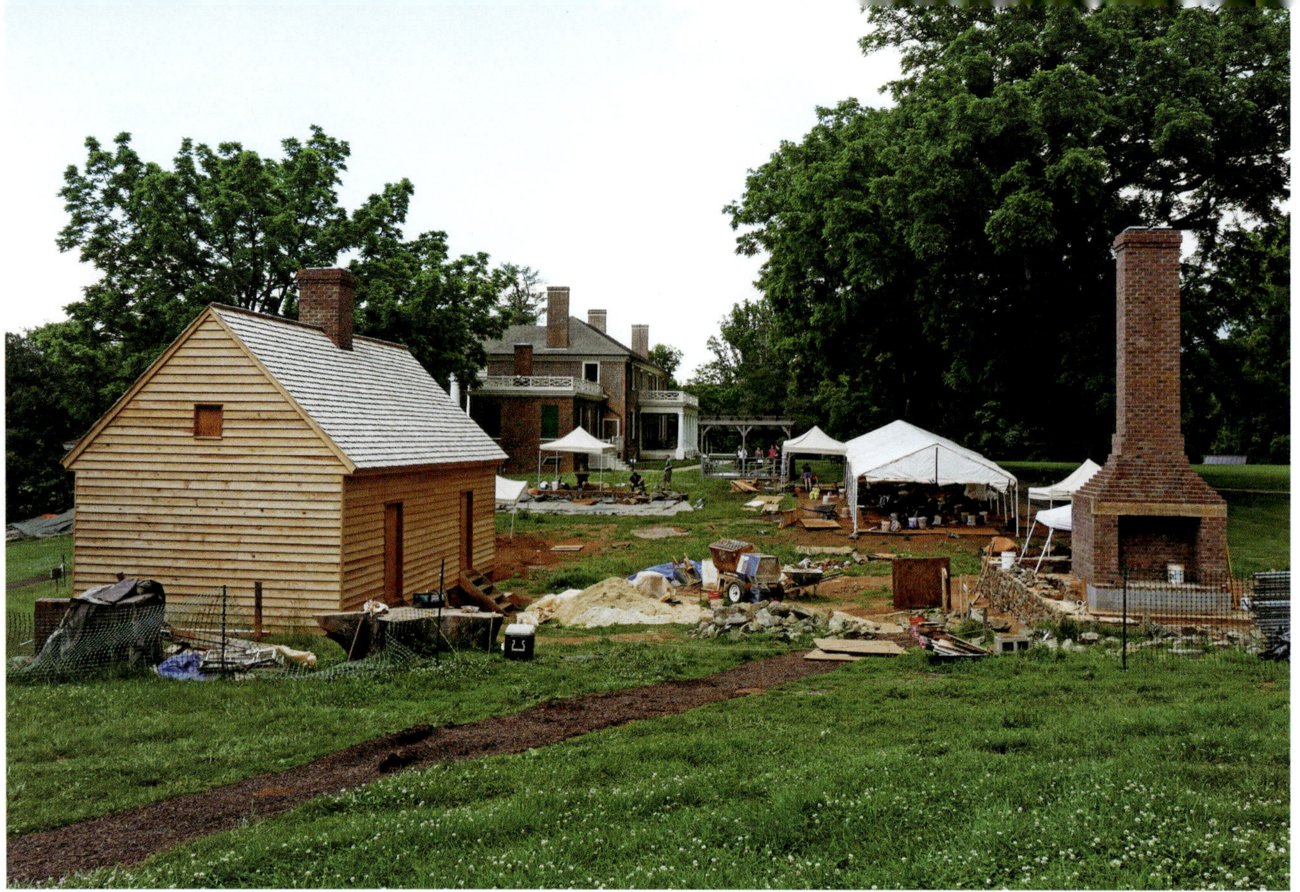

At Montpelier, a National Trust historic site, the Montpelier Foundation is researching and reconstructing the buildings where James Madison's slaves lived and worked
PAUL EDMONDSON/NATIONAL TRUST FOR HISTORIC PRESERVATION

a dynamic, ever-changing landscape of ideas, rather than a static narrative that once recovered need never be revisited."[8] Awareness of history is critical for an engaged and informed democratic society.

But something even deeper is also at work here. History is not simply a utilitarian tool to create an informed and thinking citizenry. History is central to the notion of our lives as humans. Joseph Farrell shared with me this idea about why old places matter:

> "My main point [is] about history and my belief that a conception of history is a distinctively human trait. I believe that not doing things that are characteristically or distinctively human means living a less fully human life. . . . To live in an eternal present is not to take advantage of all our human capacities."[9]

History is part of what makes us distinctly human, and it has the capacity to deepen and enrich our conceptions of ourselves and of our place in the world. We see this in people's desire to connect to history through many paths—visiting historic places, historical reenactments, collecting antiques, living in an old house, researching genealogy, and hearing the stories of our ancestors.

Old places have tremendous power to convey a sense of history. Sometimes, however, a visit to a historic site is not always interesting; in fact, it can be downright boring or even comical.[10] Although many historic sites are dynamic places to visit that engage all the senses, some are tedious, condescending, or even claustrophobic—and sometimes peddle bad history to boot. Catherine Wagner, an artist at the American Academy, told me that, from her perspective, "the moment someone tells you what the experience is supposed to be, they keep you from finding your own voice."[11] We see this in popular culture's view of historic sites—just take a look at the Alamo tour scene in the movie *Pee-Wee's Big Adventure*, which captures the sometimes condescending character of historic site tours with great humor.[12]

It's difficult to balance the amount of historical information provided with a more open-ended experience of place—and people absorb information in different ways. The National Trust for Historic Preservation, the American Association for State and Local History, the National Council on Public History and regional and state museum associations have been encouraging the field of public history toward more engaging interpretation and a more sophisticated view of history. Old places are uniquely capable of giving people a full-bodied experience of history. Let's take advantage of that natural strength.

The places I've mentioned so far are mostly historic sites open to the public with a stated purpose of education. But the scope of public history is much broader. It includes the many places where we might experience history—landscapes, gardens, and streets. The historian and poet Dolores Hayden writes about the need to acknowledge the histories of these places. "Creating public history within the urban landscape can use the forms of the cultural landscape itself, as well as words and images, to harness the power of places to connect the present and the past."[13] Hayden envisions the possibilities that this broad-based public history could unleash, "A socially inclusive urban landscape history can become the basis for new approaches to public history and urban preservation," she writes. And further, "Both citizens and planners may find that urban landscape history can help to reclaim the identities of deteriorating neighborhoods where generations of working people have spent their lives."[14]

I asked Max Page, professor of history and architecture at the University of Massachusetts, Amherst, and a fellow at the American Academy during my tenure there, what changes to historic preservation practice might be most beneficial to people and to the field. He suggested having the story of places on the National Register available at the places themselves so that people could become aware of and engaged with the history at the place. He also suggested that because public history uses oral history, architectural

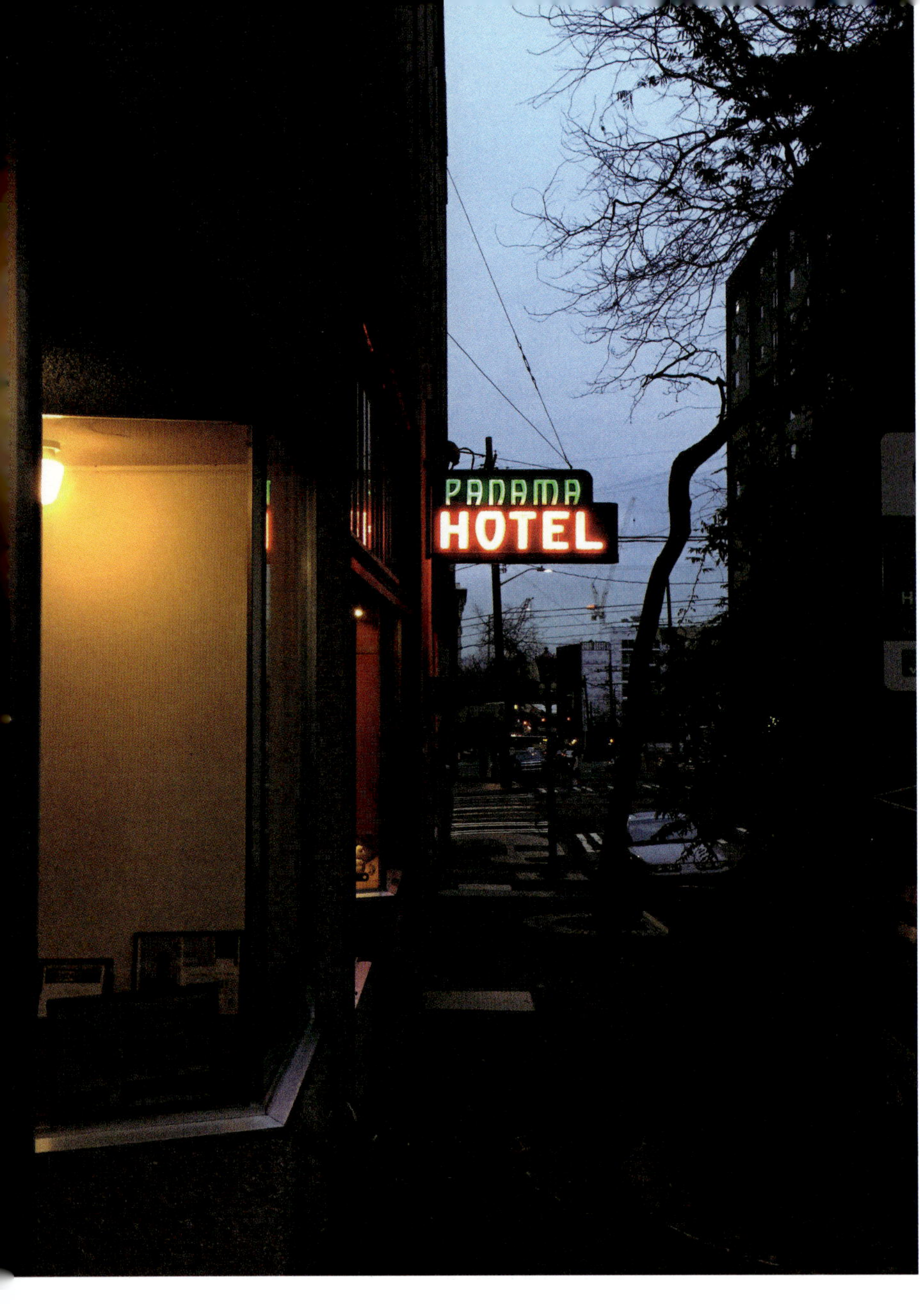

evidence, archaeology, and other sources, it has the capacity to give a fuller view of the historical record. In addition, because public history engages more people in the development of the history, it has the capacity to develop a broader and more inclusive view of and support for history.[15]

History is, and has been, a central rationale for laws and policies that protect old places. Virtually all systems that identify old places as worthy of preservation use history as a key criterion, from the National Register of Historic Places, which includes the phrase "associated with events that have made a significant contribution to the broad patterns of our history" in its criteria, to local historic preservation commissions, such as Seattle, which includes "location of, or is associated in a significant way with, a historic event with a significant effect upon the community, city, state, or nation."[16]

The Panama Hotel, in the International District of Seattle, Washington, evokes the lives of Japanese Americans before, during, and after the World War II internment period
TOM MAYES/NATIONAL TRUST FOR HISTORIC PRESERVATION

The National Park Service website says, "Historic places have powerful and provocative stories to tell. As witnesses to the past, they recall the events that shaped history and the people who faced those situations and issues."[17] I get excited about being at the place where history happened—even when it's in my own neighborhood. Thousands of others share this excitement, from visiting the battlefield of Gettysburg to the quiet home of Emily Dickinson.

NOTES

1. "Teaching with Historic Places," National Park Service, accessed February 7, 2018, www.nps.gov/subjects/teachingwithhistoricplaces/using-places.htm.
2. Marta de la Torre and Randall Mason, *Assessing the Values of Cultural Heritage* (Los Angeles: Getty Conservation Institute, 2002), 11.

3. The first chief historian for the Park Service, Verne E. Chatelain, is quoted saying "An historic site is source material for the study of history, just as truly as any written record." See "Imperiled Promise: The State of History in the National Park Service," prepared by the Organization of American Historians at the invitation of the National Park Service, 2011. Accessed February 9, 2018. www.oah.org/site/assets/documents/Imperiled_Promise.pdf., 21.
4. Joseph Farrell, e-mail to author, December 5, 2013.
5. See Peter N. Stearns, "Why Study History," American Historical Association, accessed February 9, 2018. www.historians.org/about-aha-and-membership/aha-history-and-archives/archives/why-study-history-(1998). See also information on the History Relevance campaign, which became a public campaign in 2013 and states, "We believe that history can have more impact when it connects the people, events, places, stories, and ideas of the past with people, events, places, stories, and ideas that are important and meaningful to communities, people, and audiences today." "The History Relevance Campaign," accessed February 28, 2018. www.historyrelevance.com.
6. "Imperiled Promise," 17.
7. "Imperiled Promise," 12.
8. "Imperiled Promise," 18.
9. Joseph Farrell, e-mail to author, December 5, 2013.
10. See, e.g., Sarah Vowell, *Assassination Vacation* (New York: Simon & Schuster, 2005).
11. Catherine Wagner, interview with author, January 20, 2014.
12. *Pee-Wee's Big Adventure*, Movie Clip: The Alamo Tour (2005), YouTube, January 2, 2015. Accessed February 7, 2018. www.youtube.com/watch?v=0PdeHy_87OM.
13. Dolores Hayden, *The Power of Place: Urban Landscapes As Public History* (Cambridge, MA: MIT Press, 1995), 246.
14. Hayden, *The Power of Place*, 12, 43.
15. Max Page, interview with author, February 9, 2014.
16. Seattle, Washington, municipal code, chapter 25, section 25.12.350. Accessed April 9, 2018. https://library.municode.com/wa/seattle/codes/municipal_code?nodeId=TIT25ENPRHIPR_CH25.12LAPR.
17. "Teaching with Historic Places," National Park Service, accessed February 7, 2018. www.nps.gov/nr/twhp/wwwlps.

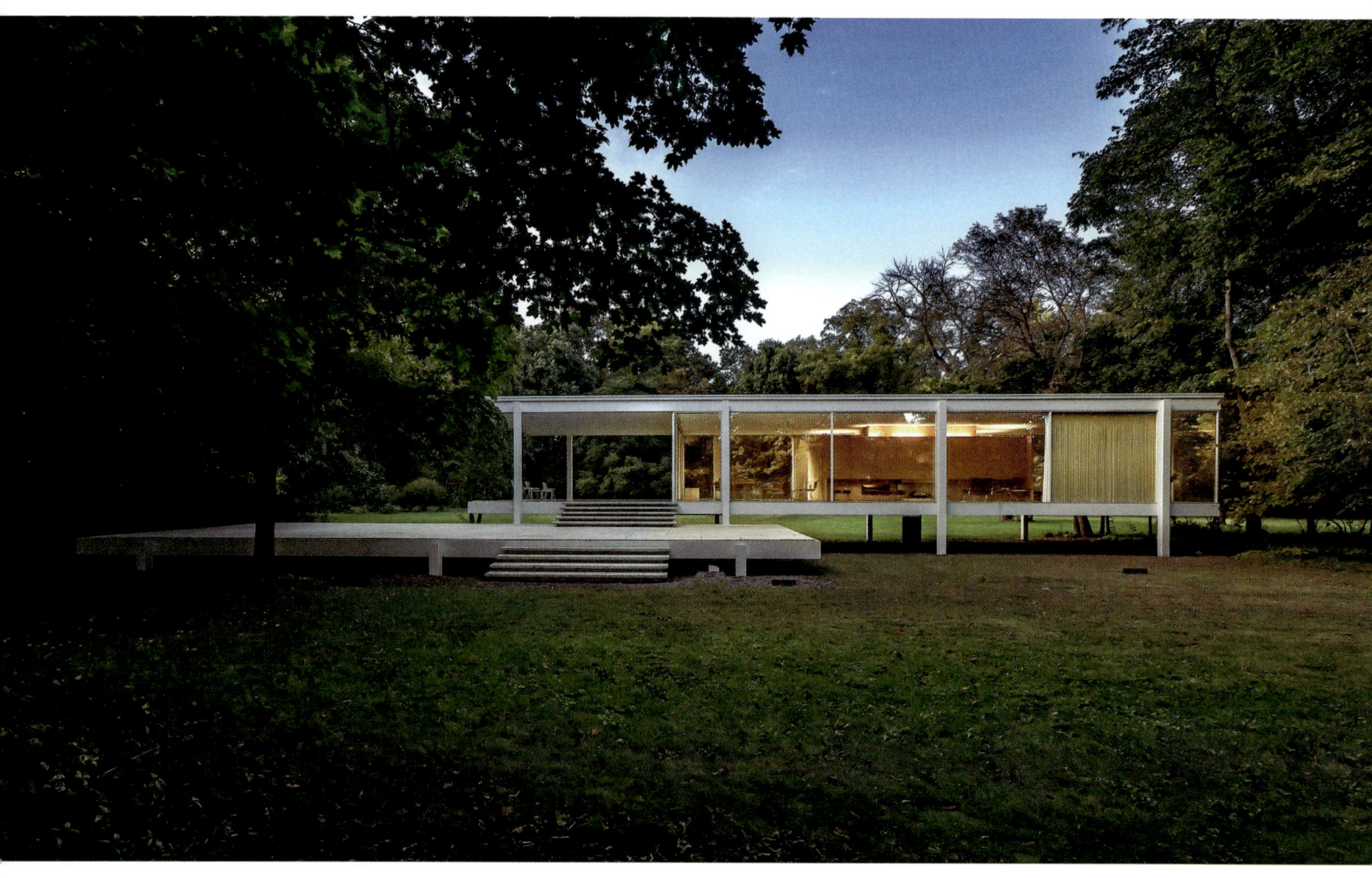

The Farnsworth House, in Plano, Illinois, by Mies van der Rohe, a National Trust historic site considered a masterpiece of international style architecture
MIKE CREWS

Architecture

People love and revere old buildings for their art and craftsmanship—and for the way they make us feel. As a boy, I was fascinated by an old house that my father's friend, Jim Withers, used as a barn. From the outside, it looked like a relatively modest, two-story house. It was dilapidated, to say the least—the glass was missing from almost all of the windows, and the shutters sagged from their hinges. But inside, there were all the marks of an architect or master builder. The high-ceilinged rooms had hand-carved woodwork, and the wide mantelpieces were supported by intricate molding. Decorative brackets unwound in a spiral on the edges of the steps of the curving stair. The woodwork, the relationship of the woodwork to the tall plaster walls, the size and height of the rooms, all felt like part of something whole. I didn't know then why the house made me feel the way it did, but I later learned that I was probably experiencing—despite the bales of hay stacked in the rooms—the concepts of proportion, balance, and harmony, as well as the marks of time.

I was experiencing Architecture—Architecture with a capital *A*.

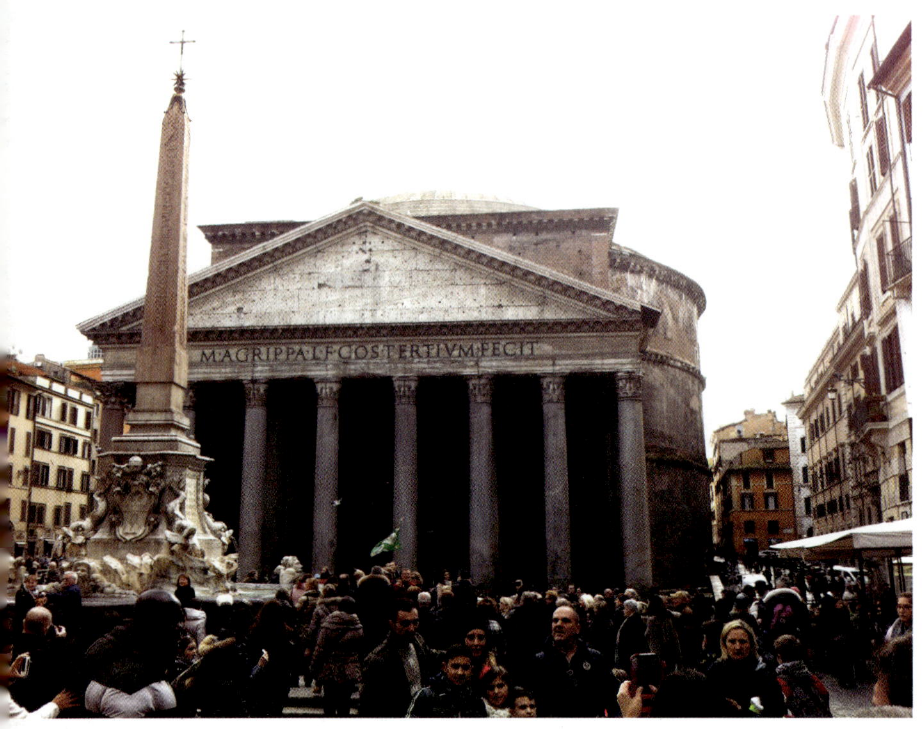

The Pantheon in Rome, one of the most intact monumental buildings of the ancient world, which has served as a model for generations of architects
TOM MAYES/NATIONAL TRUST FOR HISTORIC PRESERVATION

The feeling I felt in Jim Withers's old house is a feeling many of us experience when we're in the presence of certain buildings—that complex web of emotions ranging from wonder to comfort to nobility to delight. It's the reason that people fall silent under the oculus of the Pantheon in Rome or stare awestruck at the Farnsworth House. It's the reason people travel to see the Taj Mahal, the Empire State Building, or the relatively unknown residential masterpieces of Louis Kahn. It's the magic of architecture.[1]

This experience of architecture has been recognized and valued by people for thousands of years. From the Roman emperor Theodoric,[2] who commissioned architects to take care of ancient buildings, to Brunelleschi, who studied the Pantheon to determine its secrets of proportion and construction,[3] to Philip Johnson, who, despite being known for the brash modernism of his Glass House, channeled the entire history of world architecture in his experiments in design, people have looked to the buildings of the past for inspiration.

These special places, these works of architecture, are works of art. Like painting, music, or literature, these buildings help us understand our capacities as humans. No less than any other great art, architecture defines our civilization. The pyramids, the Parthenon, St. Paul's Cathedral, and Fallingwater, for example, are all icons of western civilization. Some of these icons represent watershed moments in the time line of human culture. I recently heard Ashley Wilson, Graham Gund Architect at the National Trust, explaining the importance of the Farnsworth House. She said,

> After the Farnsworth House, modern domestic architecture was forever altered. There are very few buildings that can be identified as the "first" of a movement. One that comes to mind is the early-fifteenth-century building that kickstarted the Renaissance, the Ospedale degli Innocenti in Florence. Nothing was the same after that building was built.[4]

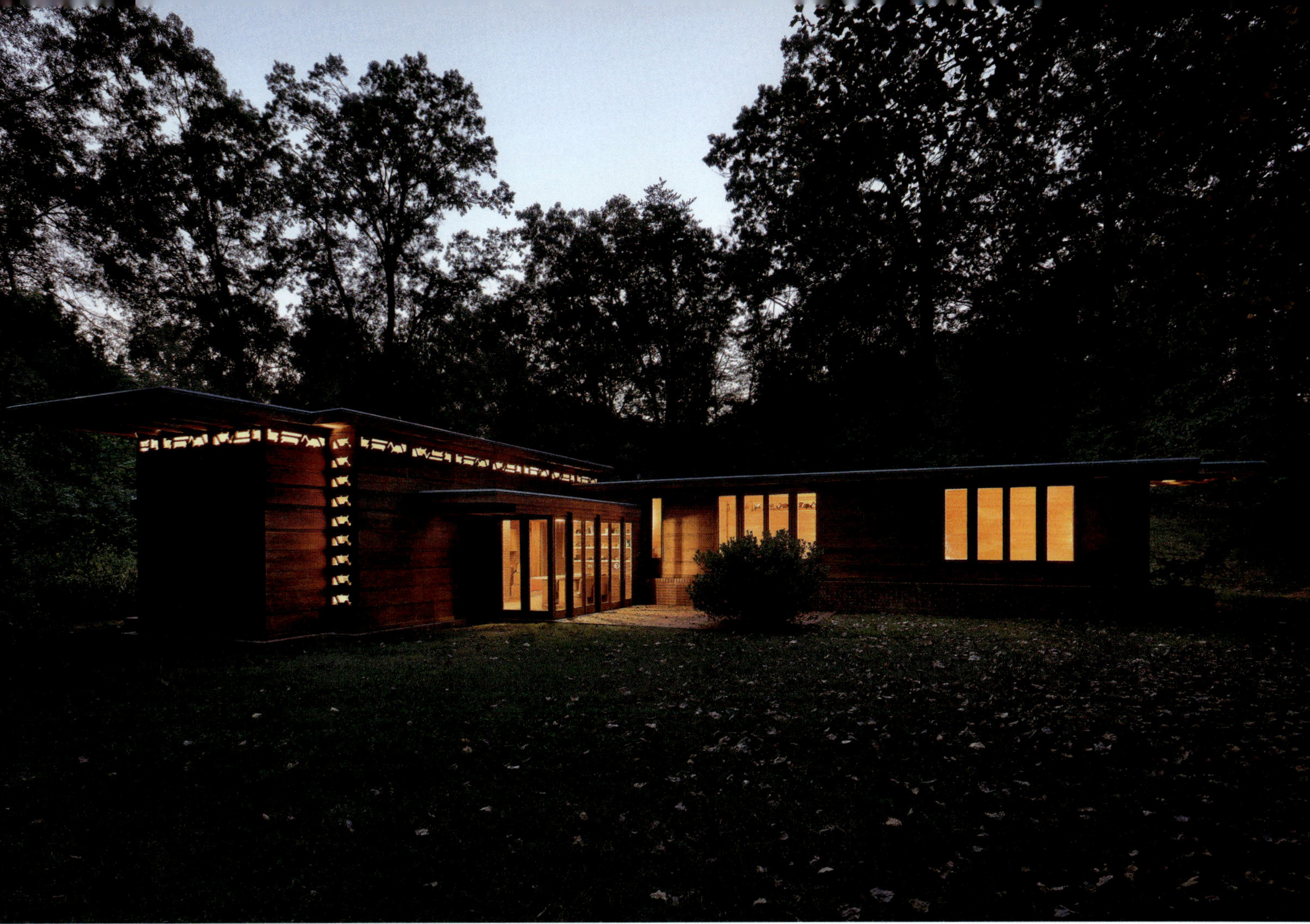

The Pope-Leighey House, in Mount Vernon, Virginia, a National Trust historic site that was designed by Frank Lloyd Wright as an affordable house
PAUL BURK

As Philip Kennicott wrote in *The Washington Post* in a discussion about the central library in downtown Washington designed by Mies van der Rohe, historic preservation experts, architecture critics, and other "cranks" (I love that) "ground their beliefs on the complicated and difficult to express fundamental value of retaining important cultural objects simply because they are beautiful or play an important role in the history of culture."[5] Old buildings are a critical part of our artistic and cultural heritage.

This phrase "cultural heritage" is one we use frequently in the preservation world. It's an abstract phrase, but it's useful shorthand to capture a cluster of concepts. When we refer to architecture—old buildings—as cultural heritage, it means we're not merely valuing these places as culture for culture's sake (though that's fine, too, and shouldn't be sneered at), but because these living symbols give meaning—identity, continuity, memory, and inspiration—to our lives today.

Old architecture contributes to our memory, our civilization, our history, and our understanding of ourselves. It's worth noting, however, that for architecture to be part of the continuity of civilization, the building doesn't necessarily have to be old. People throughout the world vociferously protested the impending loss of the former American

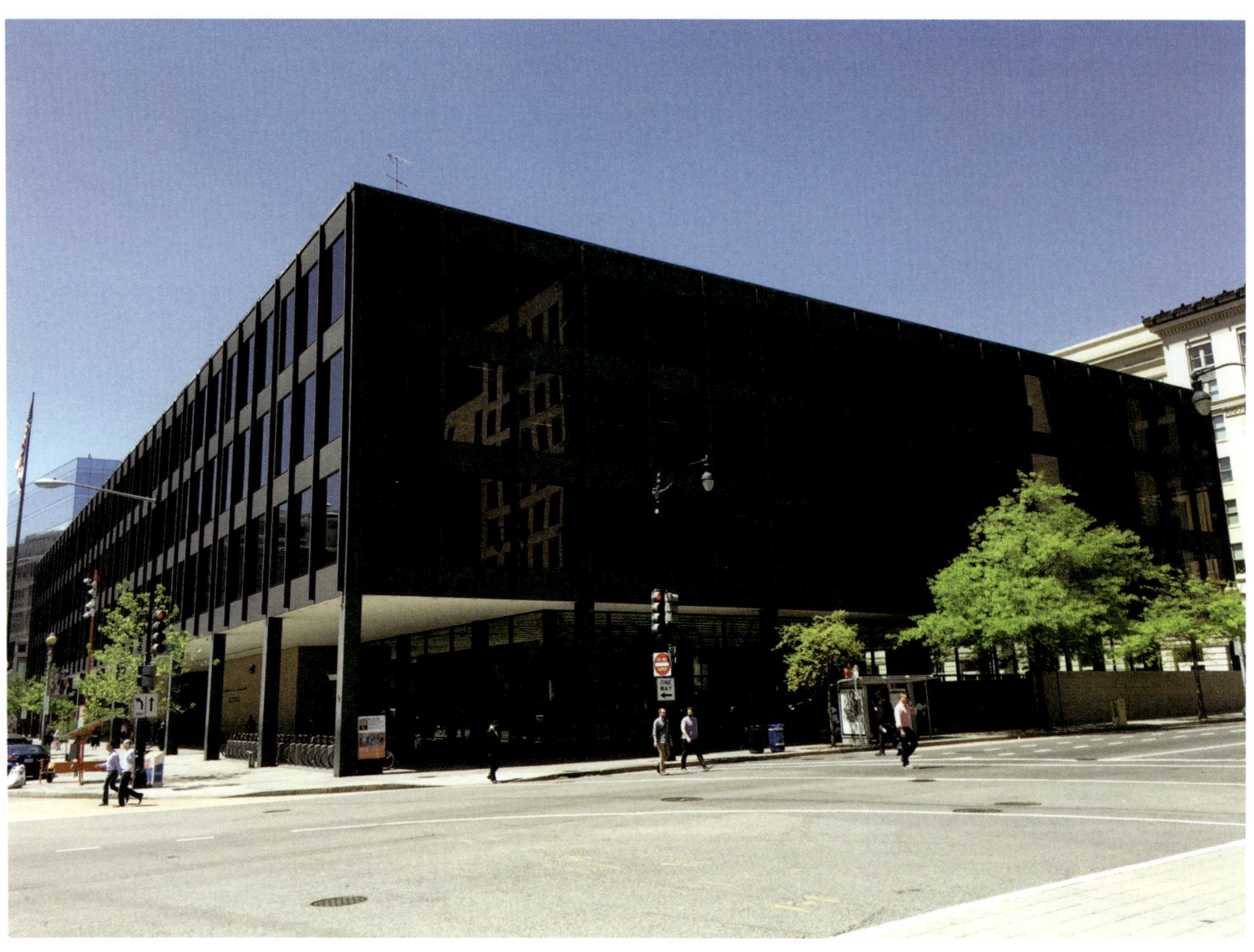

The District of Columbia library, by Mies van der Rohe
TOM MAYES/NATIONAL TRUST FOR HISTORIC PRESERVATION

Folk Art Museum building on East 53rd Street in New York by the Museum of Modern Art.[6] The potential loss was treated, without irony, as a preservation issue, even though the building was designed and constructed in 2001. Why? Because the building was widely recognized as an important work of architecture—of art—from the time it was built, and its potential loss is viewed by many as cultural iconoclasm, a loss to our civilization no different from destroying an important painting or sculpture. This controversy highlights the fact that preservation is about the present—about valuing things that matter now—not only about things of the past.

Although contemporary buildings may be valued as important pieces of architecture and art, age gives buildings something else—greater dimensions of meaning.

People have long recognized that there's something special that age imparts to buildings. John Ruskin wrote in the nineteenth century that old buildings were important because they were imbued with the spirit of the people who made them—"that

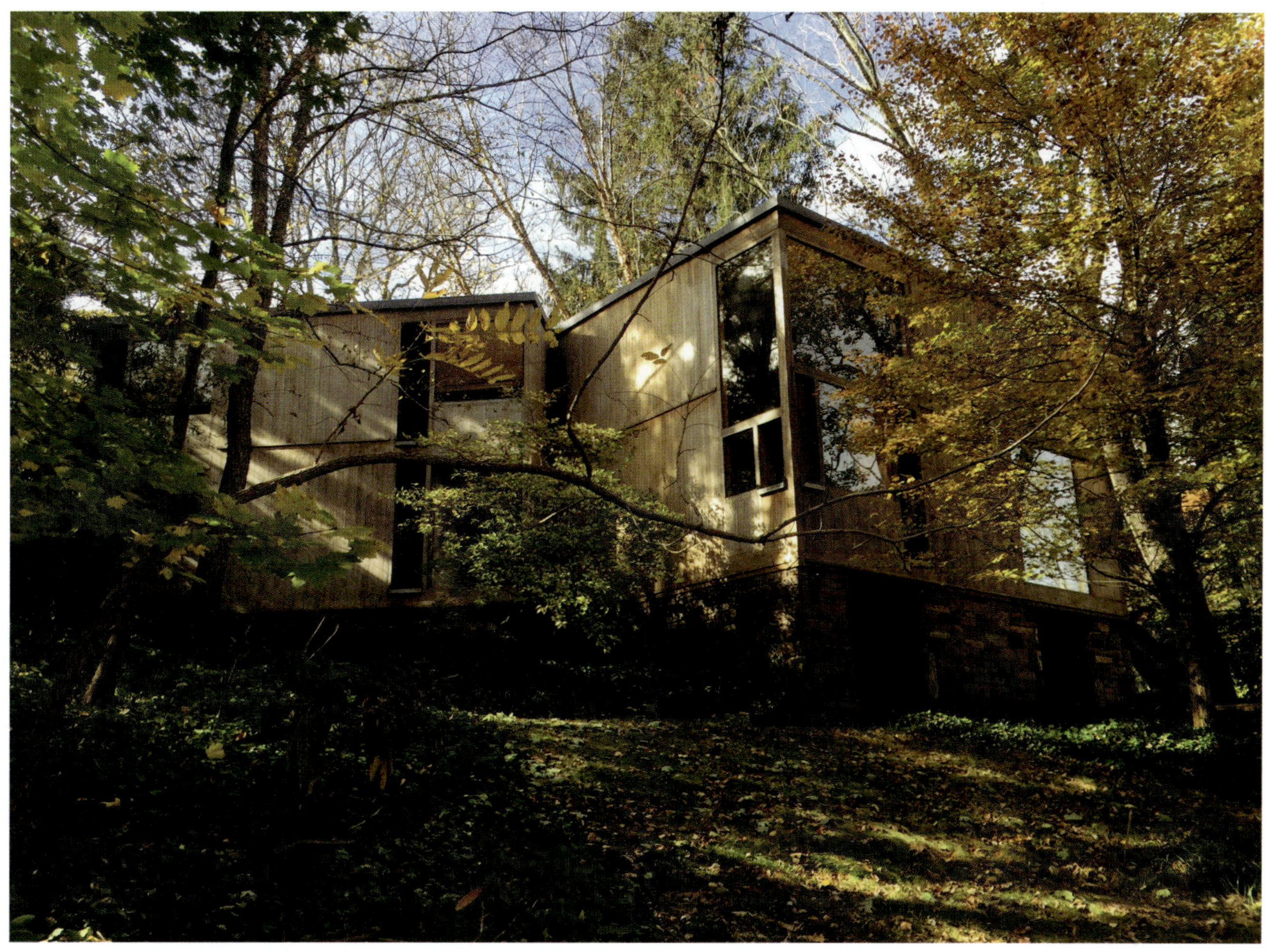

The Fisher/Kahn House in Hatboro, Pennsylvania, is a renowned residential design by Louis Kahn and is protected by an easement held by the National Trust
TOM MAYES/NATIONAL TRUST FOR HISTORIC PRESERVATION

spirit which is given only by the hand and eye of the workman"—and that they reflected the spirit of the age in which they were built.[7] This spirit is revealed in the specific workmanship and materials that the buildings are made from—the craftsmanship. Just as I appreciated the stair brackets at Jim Withers's old house, people appreciate the marks of the makers in buildings throughout the world. We have the exquisite craftsmanship of buildings from the arts and crafts movement—the Greene and Greene houses of Pasadena, for example. But we also find the mark of the builder's hand in the simple, visible plane marks on plain doors of log cabins. That sense of the maker's hand and the spirit imbued in the building is one of the irreplaceable things we lose every time a building comes down. We destroy a part of the spirit of our own civilization, irreplaceable clues to our understanding of ourselves.

We may not—we almost undoubtedly do not—know all the "spirit" embedded in old buildings. As the Finnish architect Juhani Pallasmaa wrote: "There is a tacit wisdom

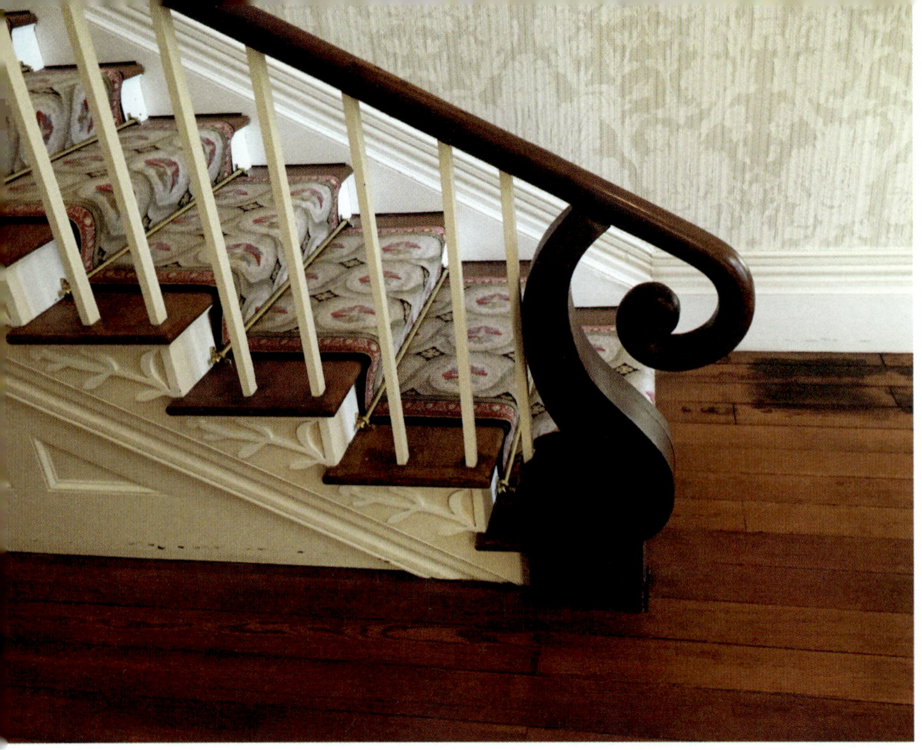

The newel post at Cedar Grove in southern Virginia is attributed to Thomas Day, a free black builder before the Civil War. The property is protected by an easement held by the National Trust.
TOM MAYES/NATIONAL TRUST FOR HISTORIC PRESERVATION

of architecture accumulated in history and tradition. But in today's panicked rush for the new, we rarely stop to listen to this wisdom."[8] Or, to use the example that the Washington, D.C., architect Andrew Singletary shared with me recently, an architect or planner raised in the 1960s suburbs is unlikely to be as aware of the ideal environmental siting of a farmhouse as a builder from the nineteenth century who was raised in that rural landscape. And when we lose that building, we lose the artifact of that knowledge.[9] Another example of this can be seen at the Wing Luke Museum in Seattle, where a light well that had been closed was reopened and now reestablishes light in the center of the building without the use of any ongoing energy consumption. In many early-twentieth-century apartment buildings in Washington, D.C., louvered doors with overhead transoms combated Washington's notoriously hot and sticky summers, though those are often not used anymore. This wisdom is increasingly appreciated in the recognition of the inherent sustainability of many older buildings, as documented by the research being done at the National Trust's Preservation Green Lab.[10]

Besides the embedded environmental wisdom, old buildings embed symbolic meaning and secret histories that may be revealed over time. What does a building say about the intentions of its builders at that time and how do we recognize it? We've become very familiar with the use of neoclassical orders, but few people recognize the meaning of the bulls' skulls and garlands that decorate buildings in every American city. Americans built neoclassical buildings to express democratic ideals, but we may be shocked to discover that our public buildings incorporate the symbols of pagan animal sacrifice (the bull or ox's skull represents the sacrificed animal, which was decorated with garlands as part of the ritual).[11] And we may not be aware of historic knowledge embedded in our architecture—the clues of past histories—from the tools hidden by slaves in the walls of plantation buildings, to the Hebrew lettering on a medieval building in Rome once used as a synagogue before the Jews were forced into the ghetto. All of this is lost when we lose an old building.

Pallasmaa wrote, "The significance of architecture is not in its form, but in its capacity to reveal deeper layers of existence."[12] Old buildings help us understand deeper layers of our existence, from the sometimes-thrilling experience of an architectural icon, to the mark of the people who made the places, to the symbolic and historic meanings that the places reveal. Architecture—with the mark of time—helps us become more aware of ourselves, our past ideals, our place in the long line of civilization, and the possibilities for a better future. It's the sense of harmony that I felt in Jim Withers's old house all those years ago, and it's the reason people all over the world love and revere old architecture.

NOTES

1. See, e.g., Alain de Botton, *The Architecture of Happiness* (London: Penguin Books, 2006).
2. Jukka Jokilehto, *A History of Architectural Conservation* (Oxford: Butterworth-Heinemann 1999).
3. Filippo Brunelleschi is said to have made four visits to Rome to study the architecture and technical solutions of the ancient Romans. Jokilehto, *A History*, 21.
4. Ashley Wilson, discussion with author, May 1, 2014.
5. Philip Kennicott, "Mecanoo, Martinez + Johnson to Renovate MLK Library," *Washington Post*, February 18, 2014.
6. Vanessa Quirk, "Glenn Lowry on American Folk Art Museum: The Decision Has Been Made" *Arc Daily*, January 29, 2014; Michael Kimmelman, "The Museum with a Bulldozer's Heart: MoMA's Plan to Demolish Folk Art Museum Lacks Vision," *New York Times*, January 13, 2014.
7. John Ruskin, *The Seven Lamps of Architecture* (New York: Dover Publications, 1989), 184.
8 Juhani Pallasmaa, *Encounters 1: Architectural Essays*, ed. Peter MacKeith (Helsinki, Finland: Rakennustieto Oy Publishing, 2012), 319.
9. Andrew Singletary, interview with author, April 26, 2014.
10. *The Greenest Building: Quantifying the Environmental Value of Building Reuse*, National Trust for Historic Preservation, 2011.
11. George L. Hersey, *The Lost Meaning of Classical Architecture* (Cambridge, MA: MIT, 1988), 44–45, 146.
12. Pallasmaa, *Encounters*, 317.

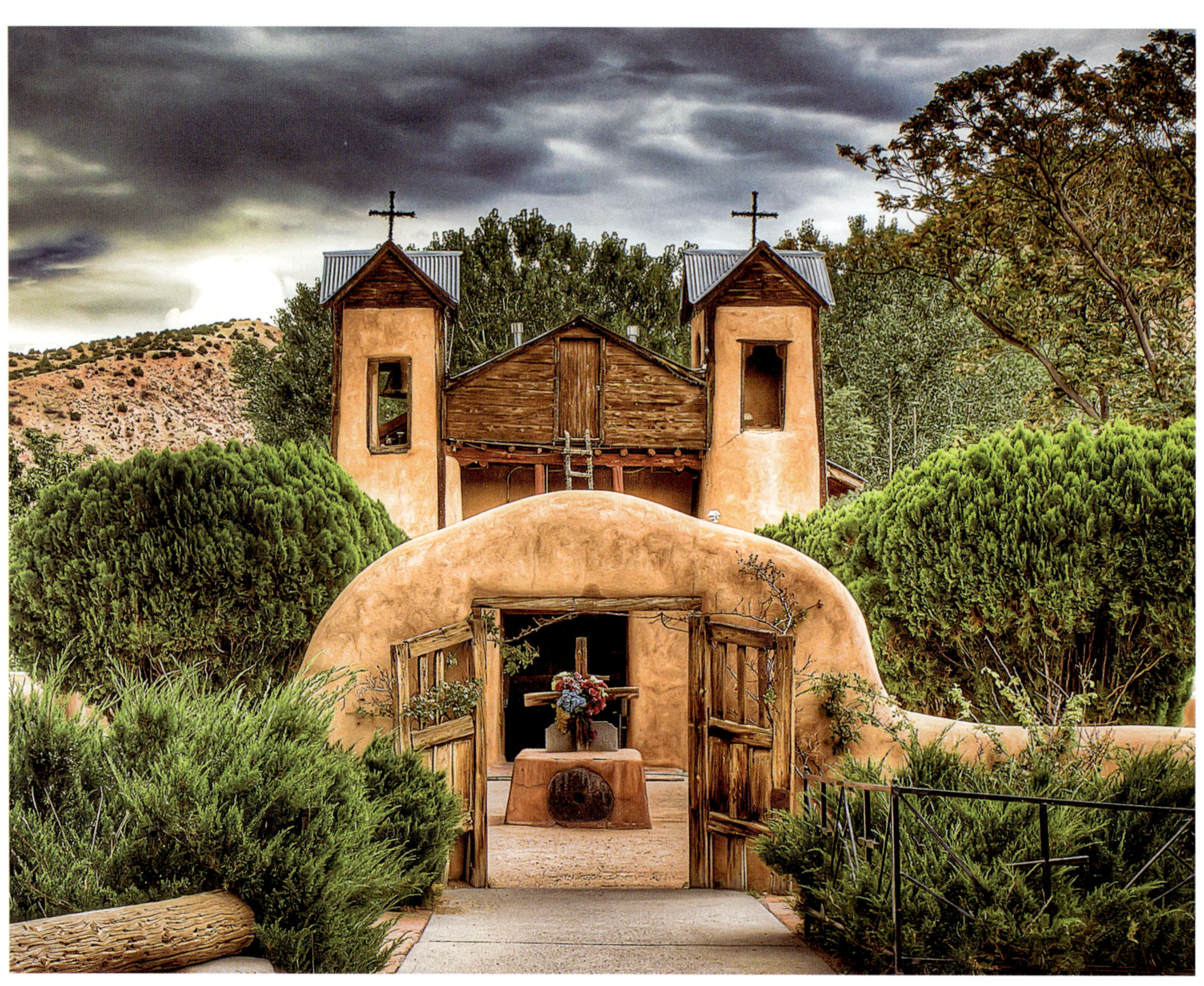

The Sanctuario de Chimayo in New Mexico is a place of pilgrimage
ANNA RUMIANTSEVA FINE ART

Sacred

Throughout the world, people revere OLD PLACES as sacred.

On my first visit to the Catholic pilgrimage site Santuario de Chimayo in New Mexico, like many people of many faiths (or of no faith at all), I was stunned into reverent silence by the palpable sense of sacredness at that old place. I don't know if it was the altitude, the impact of entering the dim, dusty chapel from the brilliantly sunlit skies of New Mexico, the lingering smell of incense and burning candles, the rhythmic voices of the pilgrims in prayer, the old paintings of Santos, or the sight of aluminum crutches lining the walls of the side chapel, left behind by those who believed themselves healed, but something touched me. I felt that I had come in contact with the sacred, even though I'm of a different faith. People all over the world find old places like the Santuario moving and actively seek to experience the feelings I had at that remarkable place. From the Wailing Wall of Jerusalem, the Ka'aba at Mecca, St. Peter's Basilica, Santiago de Compostela, to the Shrine at Ise in Japan, Varanasi in India, and Mount Taylor in New Mexico, sacred places have been revered for thousands of years by many different cultures. The age-old experience of visiting a sacred place remains so meaningful today that millions of people continue the tradition of pilgrimage, travelling to sacred places that have also become tourist destinations.[1]

Bob Jaeger, president of Partners for Sacred Places, explained to me that the word sacred is often interpreted as meaning set apart, separate, different, like a sanctuary. As Jaeger says, "these are places that are viewed as different, as set apart by the community—and there is something awesome in these places, something that lifts you up and takes you out of your normal life."[2] Martin Gray, a photographer for the National Geographic Society and author of *Sacred Earth*, listed different factors that he thinks cause people to perceive sacredness in places—visual beauty, geophysical characteristics, building materials, light and color, sound and music, aromatic substances, the awareness of centuries of ceremonial activity, collective belief, the power of ceremonial objects or relics, and others. Gray writes,

> I believe that the nature of a person's experience of a sacred site may be influenced by them having what Devereux [author of a book titled *Sacred Geography*] calls a "multi-mode" approach to the sites, that is, by experiencing the sites from the vantage points of both knowing and feeling, both mind and heart."[3]

Reading this, I was struck by how similar this explanation seems to be to my own experience at the Santuario de Chimayo—and at many other old places.[4]

Regardless of the source of the perception of sacredness, these places are also valued by those both inside and outside of the specific faith because of history, architecture, art, memory, identity, beauty—and broader senses of the sacred.[5] In reviewing the definitions of sacred places from a behavioral, emotional, or place-anchored perspective, the psychologists Daniel Levi and Sara Kocher wrote:

> Sacred places promote different types of emotional experiences. Religious tourists experience a "sense of God's presence" and respect for the spiritual values of the place, while even nonreligious visitors find sacred sites to be spiritually alive, feel a sense of peace or serenity, and find the place to be awe-inspiring.[6]

In short, old places that are considered sacred are treasured by the religious and the nonreligious. Why? Because these old places provide people with "restorative benefits that foster meditation and reflection and . . . a sense of peace or serenity,"[7] along with all the other benefits that old places provide—continuity, memory, identity, and beauty—that are psychologically and sociologically beneficial.

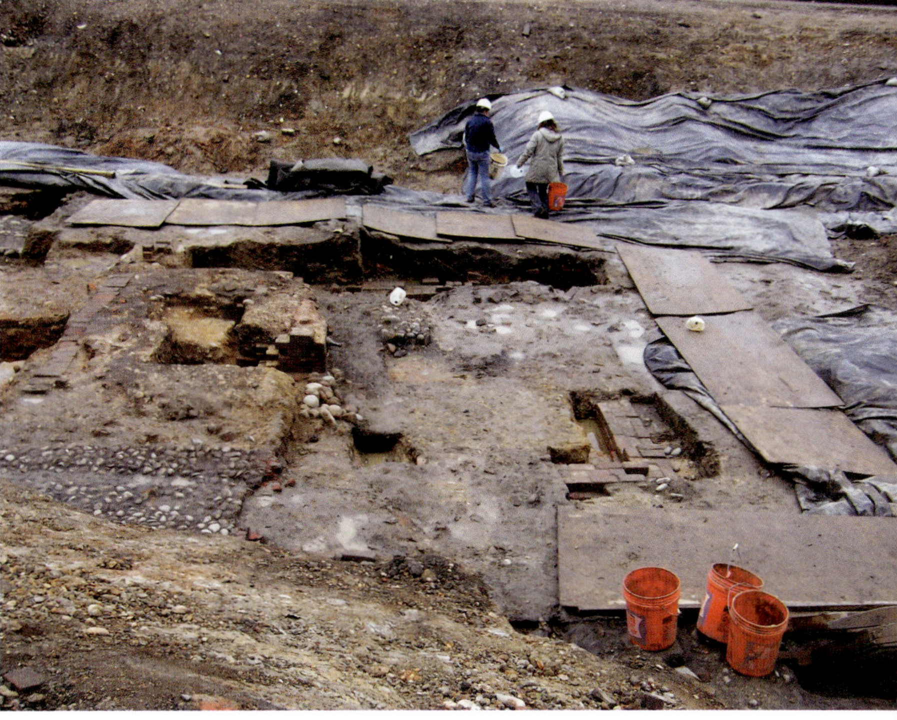

The site of Lumpkin's jail in Shockoe Bottom, Richmond, Virginia, was a center for slave trading and is considered by many to be a hallowed place
DAVID HERRING

There are also places that are revered and treated as nearly sacred because of their history, because of the difficult past they may represent, or because they serve as memorials or sites of conscience—places that are set apart, as Jaeger said. The World Trade Center site, Gettysburg, and the slave trading forts of western Africa all are made sacred—are sanctified—by the loss of life or freedom that occurred there. The International Coalition of Sites of Conscience encourages these sites to use their unique sense of sacredness to start discussions about difficult histories and to apply these difficult lessons of history to issues of today. Shockoe Bottom, in Richmond, Virginia, one of the largest slave-trading sites in America, was listed on the National Trust's list of eleven most endangered sites and then as a National Treasure. Shockoe Bottom is now revered because of the newly rediscovered history of human tragedies that occurred on the site—the humiliation of being bought and sold and separated from family, friends, and familiar places—and the resistance mounted by the people who endured these brutal acts. The very title of the National Heritage Area called "Journey through Hallowed Ground" conjures the sacredness of a region deemed hallowed for revolutionary patriots and the conflict and reunification of the Civil War. These sites remind us of the unique power of old places to be sites of memory, to provide a venue for the reexamination of history, and to spur activism to create a better future.

Partners for Sacred Places, the organization Bob Jaeger heads, encourages congregations of all faiths to understand the value of their historic churches and synagogues, both for the congregation and for the larger community, including recognizing these buildings as assets for the arts, food and nutrition, and a myriad of other community programs. Though these historic and architecturally significant buildings may be treated as sacred—or not—by their congregations, the work of Partners for Sacred Places reminds us that, in addition to providing the city or town where they are located a sense of history, identity, and continuity, they also serve in other ways. As beautiful and architecturally distinctive places, they are often primary tourist destinations—such as St. Michael's Church in Charleston, South Carolina, St. Patrick's Cathedral in New York, Touro Synagogue in Newport, Rhode Island, or Carmel Mission in California. Like sacred sites everywhere, these religious properties have a broader beneficial impact on their communities and have the capacity to inspire and "lift people out of their lives." And in this way alone, they fit into that broader understanding that Bob Jaeger explained to me, of sacred as places set apart by and for the community.

Most of the places I've noted above are well-known sites, recognized as sacred by many people. But as individuals, we may have our own personal sacred sites. The landscape architect Loretta Gargan spoke to me about a view from the Golden Gate Bridge to the Farallon Islands that she considers sacred because it reminds her of family members she has loved and lost.[8] For myself, I consider the country church cemetery where my mother, father, sister, aunts, uncles, and grandparents are buried, among their ancestors, under a cluster of old cedar trees, as sacred. I imagine many old cemeteries are sacred to other people.[9]

Of course, some old places are revered simply because of their age. Perhaps that's why people always want to know if a place is the oldest. There's something about the age that makes a place venerable, as Ruskin and others noted. This sacredness may resonate for people regardless of their specific faith. As my colleague Roberta Lane put it when talking to me about why old places matter, "I don't have a religious bone in my body, but sometimes I need to commune with old places."[10]

When old places are thought to be sacred, the sense of sacredness can be lost or diminished because of destruction or inappropriate activities or intrusions. Their very sacredness can cause them to be targets for destruction by groups that disapprove of different religious faiths, as with the destruction of the Bamiyan Buddhas. Sites can also be fought over when they are sacred to different religions, as we see in Jerusalem, which is sacred to the three Abrahamic faiths. Gentle souls everywhere protest the violent tendencies of religious extremism that leads to destruction, and it is a tragedy for civilization when a sacred old place is destroyed out of what I will simply call misguided religious fervor.

The very popularity of some sacred places can also diminish people's perception of a site as sacred. In a study about the perceived authenticity of sacred sites, the environmental psychologists Levi and Kocher found that although a site "perceived as containing historic architecture that was well preserved or maintained increased the feeling of sacredness," sites were viewed as inauthentic when they had "modern and nonreligious features, such as new buildings, sports places, housing, administration buildings, and modern technology."[11] Levi and Kocher and many other writers highlight common negative factors including "the presence of too many tourists and tourist-related commercial activities, and maintenance issues that showed signs of disrepair or created noise and other disruptions."[12] I imagine we've all had an experience like the one I had at Glastonbury Tor in England—a beautiful and special site degraded by shops full of badly molded metal dragons, baskets of crystals, and mass-produced dream catchers. Even the Santuario de Chimayo has been threatened by the possibility of increased tourism and development.

Despite the immense love and devotion that people show toward sacred places, in the professional preservation community, we tend to distance ourselves from talking directly about sacredness. Much official preservation work happens through government agencies that, following constitutional due process and establishment clause requirements, apply objective criteria in determining whether a site viewed as sacred meets the standards for designation on the National Register of Historic Places, a state register, or under a local ordinance. At the federal level, most places that are viewed as sacred are designated under the criteria for "traditional cultural properties," or TCPs as they are commonly called, which permit the consideration of sacredness from a historic perspective.[13] The New Mexico Supreme Court, in upholding the designation of Mount Taylor as a traditional cultural property, wrote, "Although these findings undoubtedly include a religious component, because religion is part of culture and history, the findings are nonetheless based primarily on historical evidence."[14]

Although we're comfortable acknowledging the fact that specific communities, particularly Native Americans, ascribe sacredness to a place and determining whether the place meets the requirements for designation as historic, we're often uncomfortable talking about sacred places directly or acknowledging that places may be sacred. Yet

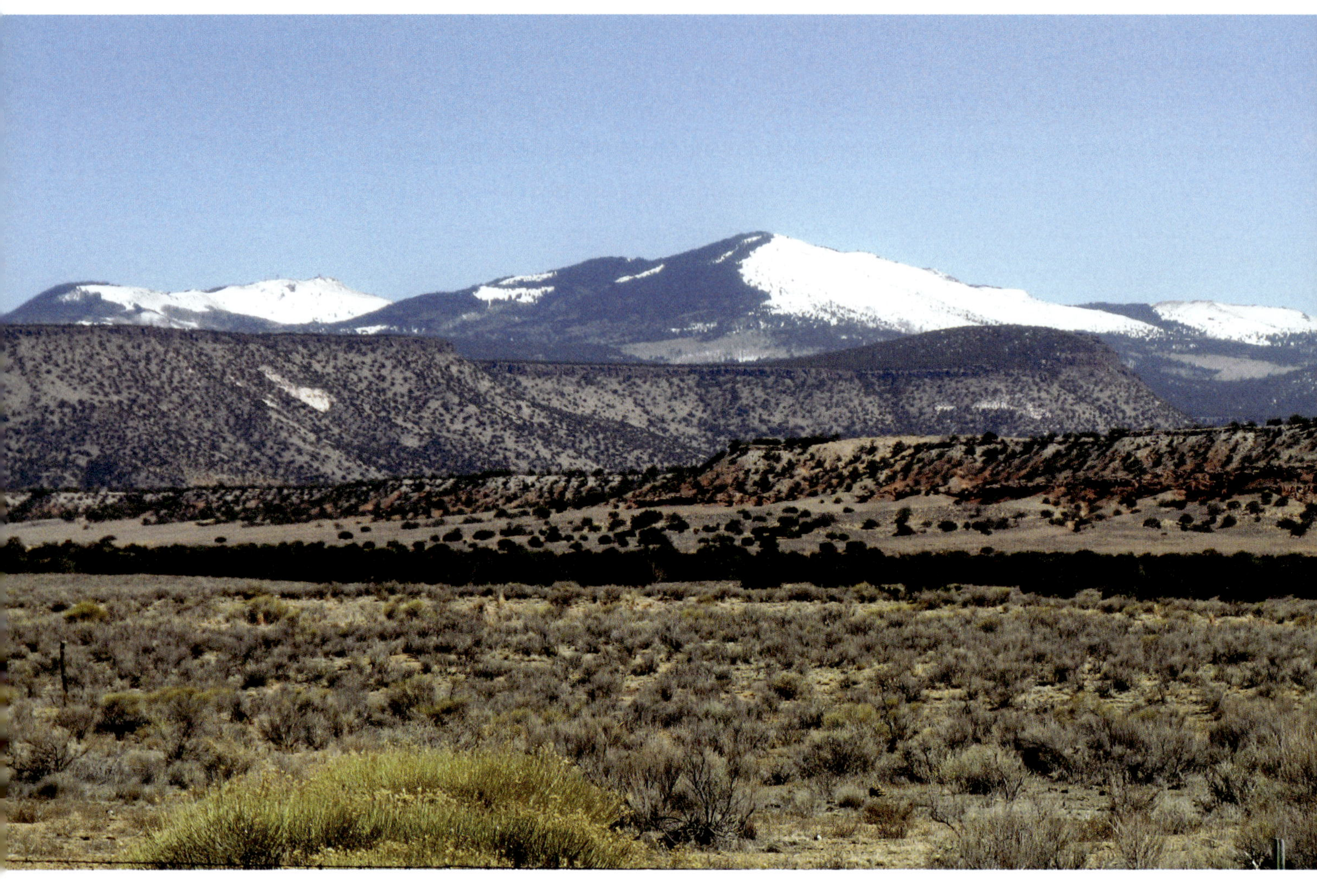

Mount Taylor, in New Mexico, is considered sacred by the Pueblo of Acoma and other Native Americans
THERESA PASQUAL

underlying the objective determination of historic are deeply held beliefs about the place, beliefs that resonate with many people. Here's a description of Mount Taylor from its determination of eligibility for the National Register:

> The Acoma refer to Mount Taylor as Kaweshtima, which means "a place of snow." The mountain is central to the Pueblo's belief system, and is a place where religious practitioners as well as the community as a whole have historically gone, and are known to go today, to perform ceremonial activities in accordance with traditional cultural practices that are important in maintaining the identity and cultural continuity of the community. The Acoma view the mountain as a living, breathing entity that encompasses all physical attributes such as the plants, ani-

> mals, stone, minerals and water, as well as air, clouds and rain, which are all believed to embody spiritual elements.[15]

Theresa Pasqual, the former tribal historic preservation officer of Acoma, says,

> In the United States, we're uncomfortable talking about particular beliefs. Yet to have a full and rich understanding of the sacredness of place, we have to look at the core values of the people. Our language does not have a word for *ownership*. We don't have a word for *preservation*. We have a word for *stewardship*. We have a word for *sacred*. Perhaps for preservation to be all-inclusive we need to talk about the sacred. It's the transmission of knowledge that is important—the stories, the songs. These give us a sense of who we are as a people and give us the understanding of sacred places in the landscape. Those values are the things that bind us together. We have to get over our uncomfortableness of talking about those core values or we won't have the rich understanding of place."[16]

Preservationists tend to be more comfortable grappling with old places as simply material objects or buildings rather than spiritual places. I was intrigued by an article in *The Getty* about a site in India called Sarnath, a site holy to Buddhists. Also an archaeological site, Sarnath remains a place of pilgrimage, and the article highlighted the challenges of honoring its history as a holy pilgrimage site while also maximizing its value as a historic archaeological site: "Candles and sheets of gold leaf are often stuck onto the stupas and architectural remains, despite signs discouraging it. These gestures are ones of respect and are not intended to mar the site, yet they do pose a concern for the long-term preservation of these remains."[17]

As the article highlights, although it's important to protect the site from damage, we have to be careful as preservationists not to let our preservation instincts prevent the ongoing use of these places—it's the ongoing use that causes people to continue to value them and that in fact gives them much of their power.

I understand why government agencies must apply objective criteria for what is historic. But for the rest of us, our reticence to talk about the sacredness of old places seems to cut us off from the potential power of these old places. Perhaps we should allow ourselves to give voice to the places that we really care about and consider sacred

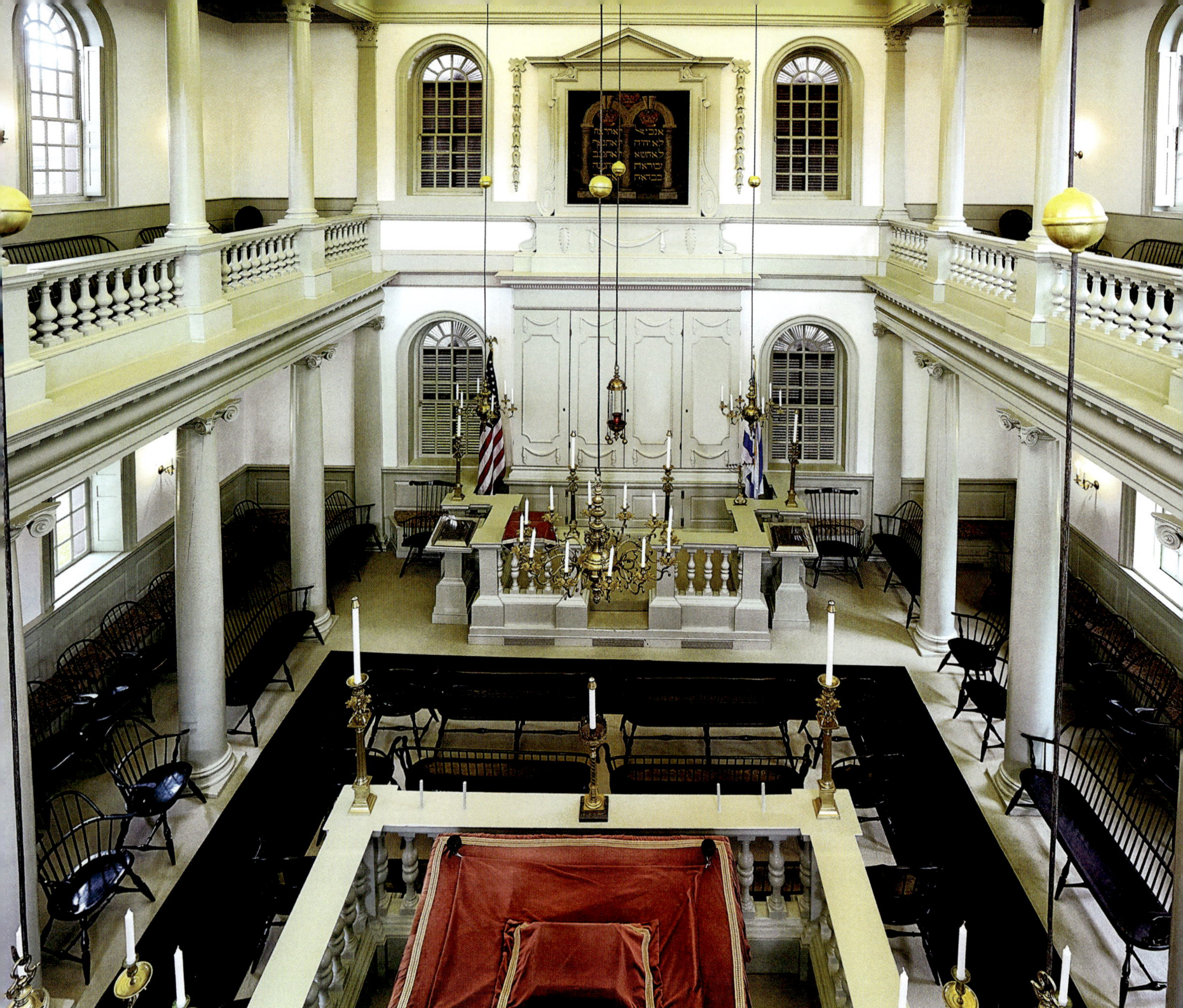

Touro Synagogue in Newport, Rhode Island, an active congregation, a place for learning about religious freedom, and a National Trust Historic Site operated by the Touro Synagogue Foundation
STANLEY GOLDBERG

in our own way. After all, these places have the capacity to provide deep spiritual and psychological benefits; for me, this is really what preservation is all about—making our present and future lives better.

Like many people who visit Rome, my husband Rod and I feel compelled to make a pilgrimage to the Church of Santa Maria and the Martyrs, better known as the Pantheon, sacred to the Catholic Church, once sacred to the Romans as the temple to all the gods, and I think, sacred to architects, architectural historians, and everyday people like Rod and me who care about old places. Entering that round, domed, marbled space, aware of the deep and long history, seeing the signs of age in the wear on the stone, and looking up at that great oculus open to the sky like an enormous eye, well, it feels like a place set apart, a special place, sacred in the many ways that we find old places sacred.

NOTES

1. See Alliance of Religions and Conservation, accessed February 7, 2018, www.arcworld.org.
2. Robert Jaeger, interview with author, June 25, 2014.
3. Martin Gray, "Sacred and Magical Places," *Sacred Sites*, accessed February 7, 2018, www.sacredsites.com. See also Martin Gray, *Sacred Earth: Places of Peace and Power* (New York: Sterling, 2007).
4. Note also that the factors are similar to the explanation given by architectural theorists about the experience of architecture, referred to generally as "atmospheres." See Peter Zumthor, *Atmospheres* (Basel, Switzerland: Birkhauser, 2006).
5. Some congregations may not consider their building sacred, but only as a meeting house for the congregation. In addition, there may be conflicts between the religious beliefs and the preservation of historic buildings, such as when a congregation wishes to remove iconography that is inconsistent with religious beliefs or to demolish a building altogether.
6. Daniel Levi and Sara Kocher, "Perception of Sacredness at Heritage Religious Sites," *Environment & Behavior* 45, no. 7 (2012): 912–30, 917.
7. Levi and Kocher, "Perception of Sacredness," 917, citing T. Herzog, P. Ouellette, J. Rolens, and A. Koenigs, "House of Worship As Restorative Environments," *Environment & Behavior* 42 (2010): 395–419.
8. Loretta Gargan, interview with author, June 11, 2014.
9. Note that the National Register does not generally designate cemeteries unless they are significant for other reasons, though they are definitely places "set apart."
10. Discussion at National Trust field staff meeting, June 11, 2013.
11. Levi and Kocher, "Perception of Sacredness," 923.
12. Levi and Kocher, "Perception of Sacredness," 925.
13. Patricia L. Parker and Thomas F. King, "Guidelines for Evaluating and Documenting Traditional Cultural Properties," National Park Service, 1990; rev. 1992, 1998. Commonly referred to as Bulletin 38. For legal issues involved in the designation of historic religious buildings, see, e.g., *Preserving Historic Religious Properties*, Massachusetts Preservation Coalition and the National Trust for Historic Preservation, June 2005.
14. *Rayellen Resources, Inc. v. New Mexico Cultural Properties Review Committee*, slip op. 17 (NM Sup. Ct., Feb. 6, 2014).
15. Cynthia Buttery Benedict and Erin Hudson, "Mt. Taylor Traditional Cultural Property Determination of Eligibility for the National Register of Historic Places," February 4, 2008, 17. The idea that all aspects of Mount Taylor—plant, animal, and stone—are a living being seems to touch on other recent theories of ecology, on the vibrancy of matter, and on theories of the numinous (the idea of spirits inhabiting places or things), concepts that underlie preservation philosophy and that could be explored more.
16. Theresa Pasqual, interview with author, June 26, 2014.
17. James Cuno, "Holy Site, Historic Site: The Challenge of Sarnath," *The Getty*, Spring 2014, J. Paul Getty Trust.

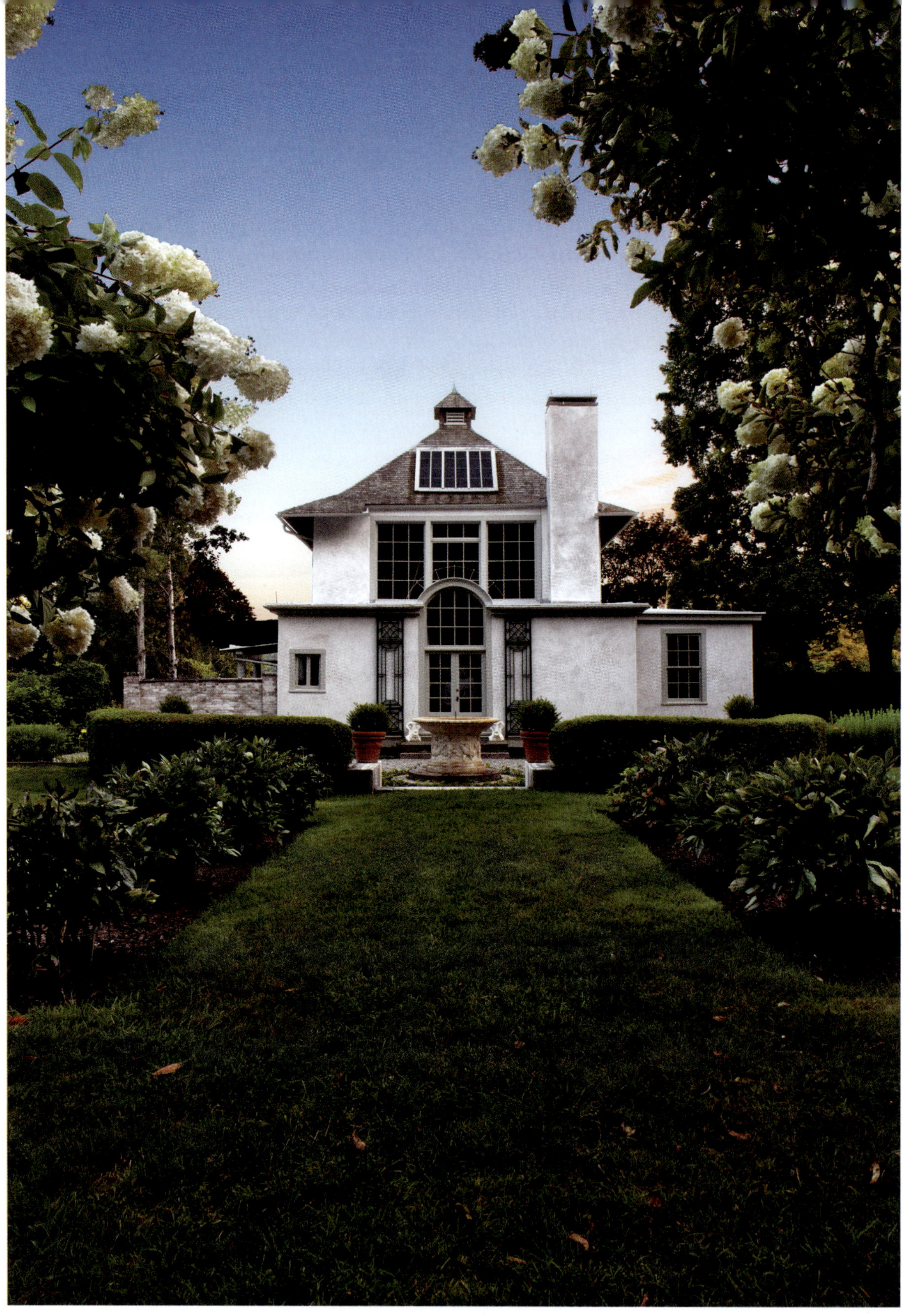

The studio of Daniel Chester French in Stockbridge, Massachusetts, the sculptor of the Seated Lincoln in the Lincoln Memorial, continues as a place of creativity as a National Trust historic site
MICHAEL LAVIN FLOWER

Creativity

Richard Florida, in his studies and writings on the rise of the creative class, noted that the creative class is drawn to certain types of places, and he's tried to identify the qualities of places that are attractive to creative people. One of the key ingredients of creative places, according to Florida, is authenticity. Florida says:

> Authenticity—and in *real* buildings, *real* people, *real* history—is key. A place that's full of chain stores, chain restaurants, and chain nightclubs is seen as inauthentic. Not only do those venues look pretty much the same everywhere, but they also offer the same experiences you could have anywhere.[1]

Although Florida may have been one of the first to articulate the attraction that creative people have to certain places (which, by the way, he also says is a key measure

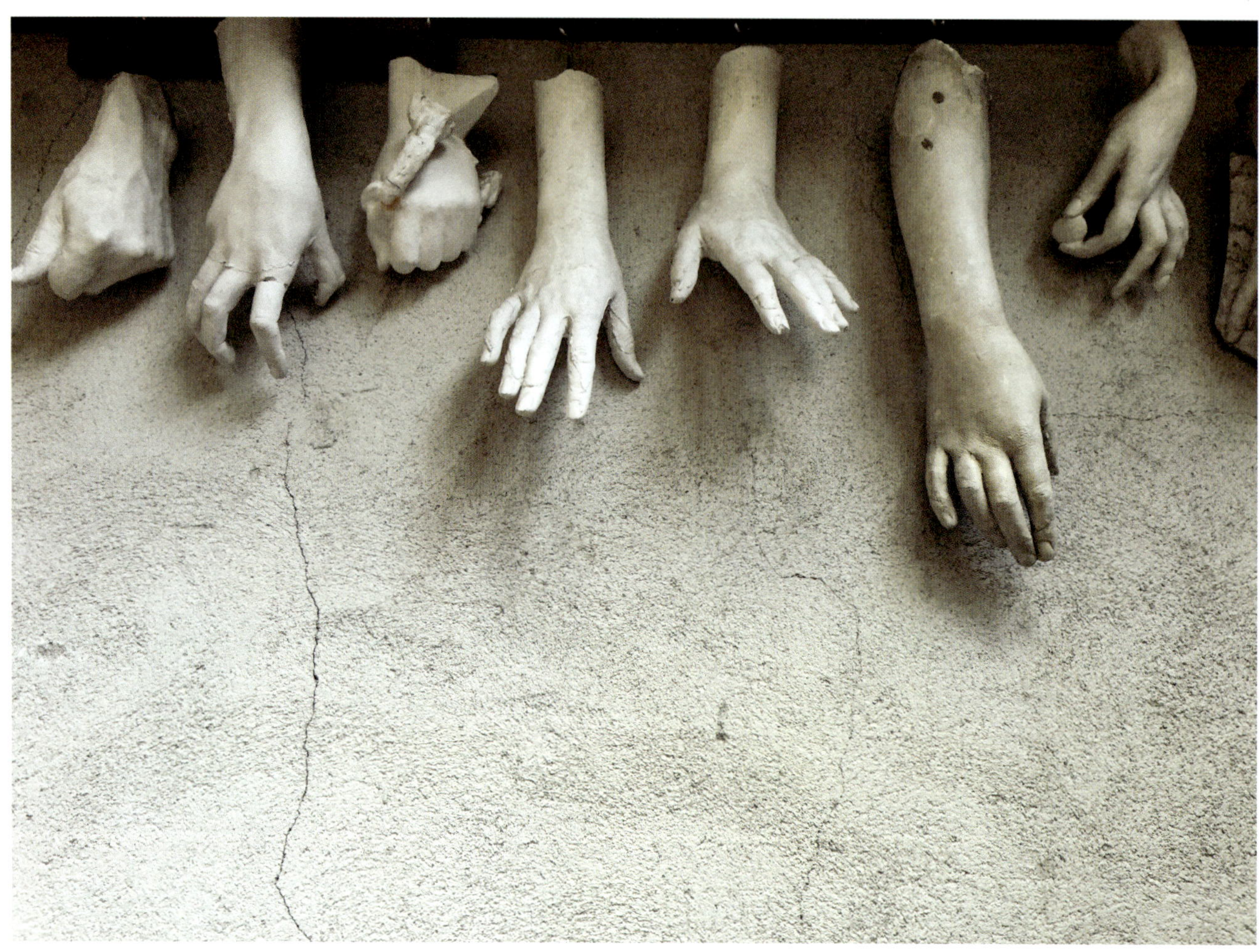

The interior of the Daniel Chester French's studio
TOM MAYES/NATIONAL TRUST FOR HISTORIC PRESERVATION

of the possible success of a city in the future), it's not a new concept. Many of the people who started the preservation movement in America were artists and writers, such as the people from the Charleston Renaissance, who were key to beginning the preservation movement in Charleston. We find this overlap throughout the country. Artists' colonies are often historic places that become tourist attractions, like Carmel, Provincetown, Ogunquit, Greenwich Village, and increasingly, to many people's surprise, Brooklyn and Detroit. All were places that creative people were drawn to because they were distinctive and interesting (and at one time cheap)—and because other creative people were there.

These places of creativity draw other people who want to connect to the power of creativity. Just as people once travelled on pilgrimages to visit the relics of saints, they now go to visit the places where creative people worked, dreamed, and struggled.

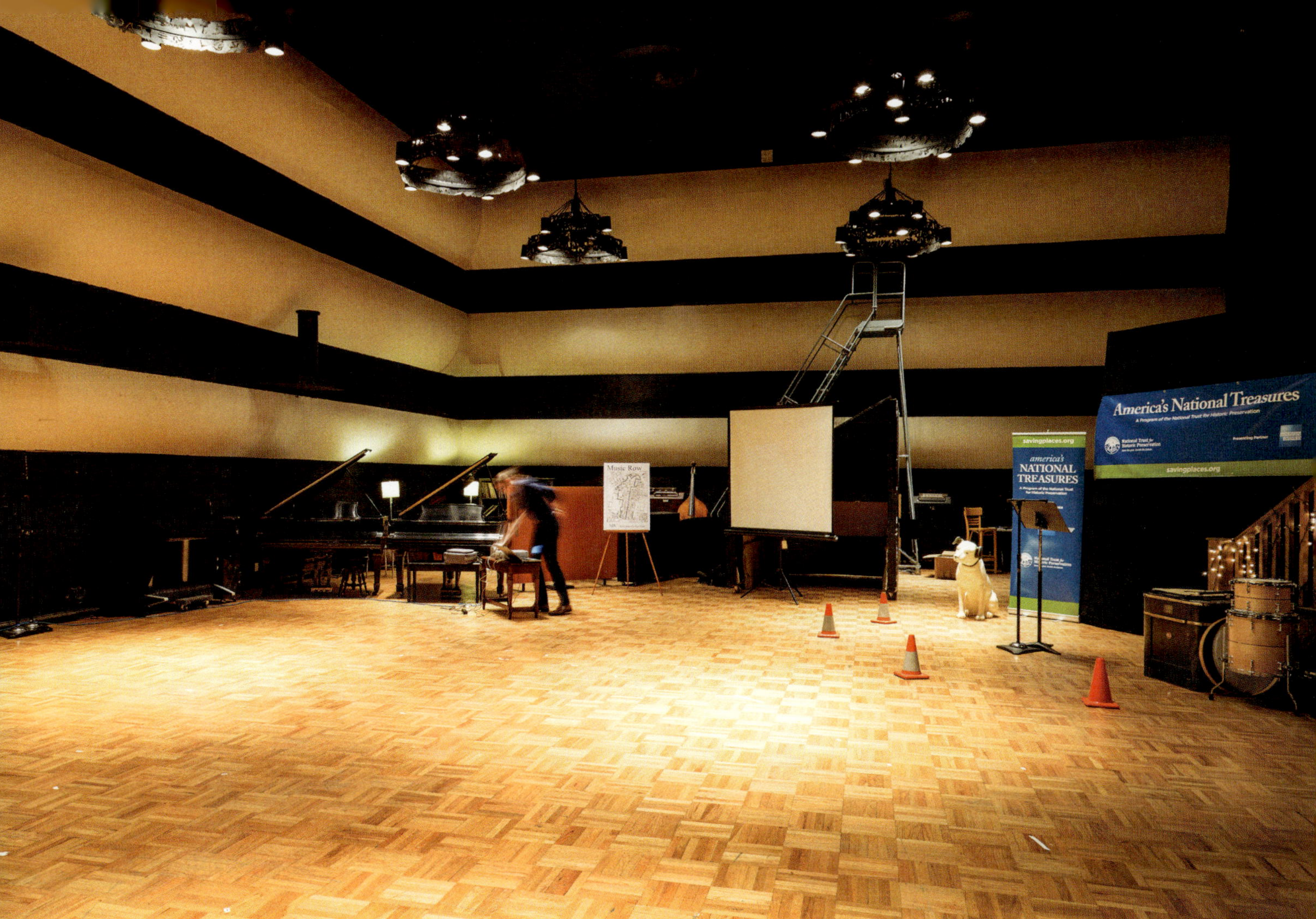

RCA Studio A, in Nashville, Tennessee, was saved through the efforts of the musician Ben Folds and philanthropist Aubrey Preston so that the studio can continue to be a place for creating music
RICK SMITH

The National Trust operates a network of Artists Homes and Studios to help these sites strengthen their programs and operations. From Mark Twain's house in Hartford, Donald Judd's loft building in Manhattan, Jackson Pollock's house on Long Island, to William Faulkner's Rowan Oak, these places attract people who want to connect with the creative power of art and artists.[2]

I was delighted to connect, through Facebook (and my network of friends from Chapel Hill), with the musician Ben Folds, who was trying to save the historic RCA Studio A in Nashville. Ben and a host of other artists, including Dolly Parton and even Elvis himself, recorded in the studio, producing hit after hit. Ben has an ear not only for music, but also for how to talk about why this old place matters to him as a songwriter and musician. Here's what he has to say about Studio A:

> take a moment to stand in silence between the grand walls of RCA Studio A and feel the history and the echoes of the Nashville sound that changed the world. . . . Listen firsthand to the stories from those

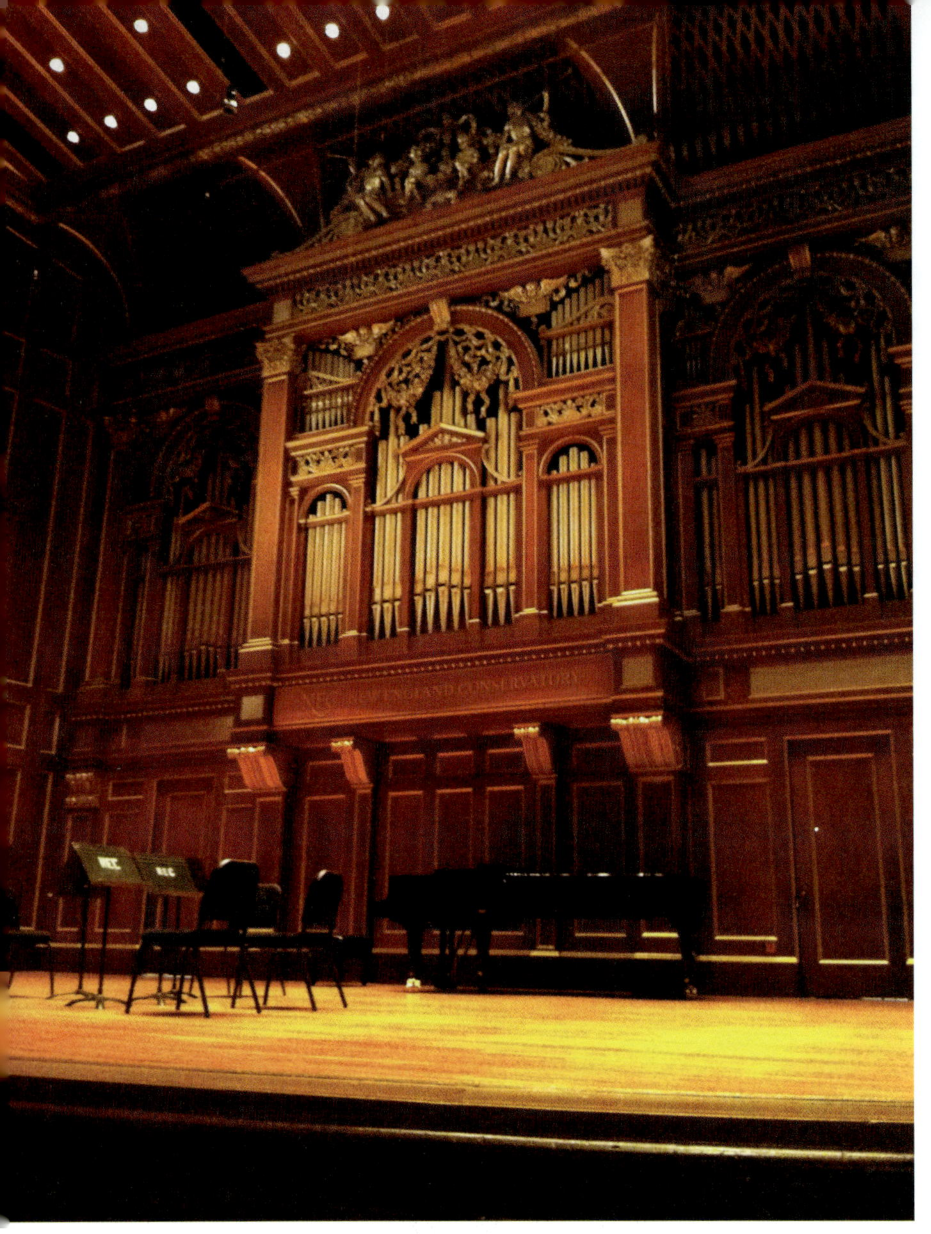

Jordan Hall, in Boston, Massachusetts, a national historic landmark, home of the New England Conservatory, and the site of the premiere of Eric Nathan's "Why Old Places Matter"
TOM MAYES/NATIONAL TRUST FOR HISTORIC PRESERVATION

among us who made the countless hit records in this studio—the artists, musicians, engineers, producers, writers who built this rich music legacy note by note, brick by brick.[3]

Ben's words capture the essence of why certain places matter to creative people—the distinctive characteristics of the space itself—in this case the acoustics—and the more intangible sense that comes from the legacy of all the people—Dolly and Elvis and others—who have created music in the space. Although Ben has had to leave RCA Studio A because the new landlord has jacked up the rent, he's continuing his efforts to save the place—and he is speaking out about why this place of creativity is so important to him.[4]

At the American Academy, I was privileged to interview the novelist Peter Bognanni, who talked about what a difference one particular old place meant to him on his journey to become a novelist. Peter studied at the Iowa Writer's Workshop at the University of Iowa, which has produced famous writers for decades. Peter shared with me the way the Dey House, the old Victorian where the writers meet, seemed to create an environment that gave him *permission* to write—that the writers who had been there before seemed to imbue the place with the possibility that he too could write, that it was possible for him. The legacy of a place dedicated to writing and talking about writing and the ongoing use of the place by writers nurtured his sense that he too could do it.[5]

There are many reasons that old places foster creativity—this is just a taste—but as you listen to Ben's music and read Peter's books, consider the fact that their creativity was nurtured by old places—and think of the places that inspire you to create.[6]

NOTES

1. Richard Florida, "What Draws Creative People? Quality of Place," UrbanLand, October 11, 2012, https://urbanland.uli.org/industry-sectors/what-draws-creative-people-quality-of-place.
2. For more information on the National Trust's Historic Artists Homes and Studios program, see "Welcome to HAHS: Witness Creativity," Historic Artists' Homes and Studios, accessed February 8, 2018, https://artistshomes.org.
3. Ben Folds, Open Letter, June 24, 2014, republished in "Ben Folds' Open Letter: RCA Studio A to Be Sold," *Music Row*, June 24, 2014.
4. RCA Studio A was successfully saved through an acquisition and continues as an active recording studio. The threat to RCA Studio A became a rallying cry for the preservation of music row in Nashville, and Music Row was designated as a National Treasure by the National Trust. See "Nashville's Music Row," National Trust for Historic Preservation, accessed February 8, 2018, https://savingplaces.org/places/nashvilles-music-row/updates/national-treasure-designation-officially-announced-in-nashville#.WnxyPUly6Uk.
5. Peter Bognanni, interview with author, December 16, 2013.
6. Listen also to Eric Nathan, "Why Old Places Matter," which was inspired by the old church Santa Sabina in Rome. https://youtu.be/dtc9gsrTWns. Eric Nathan Music, accessed February 22, 2018, www.ericnathanmusic.com/news.

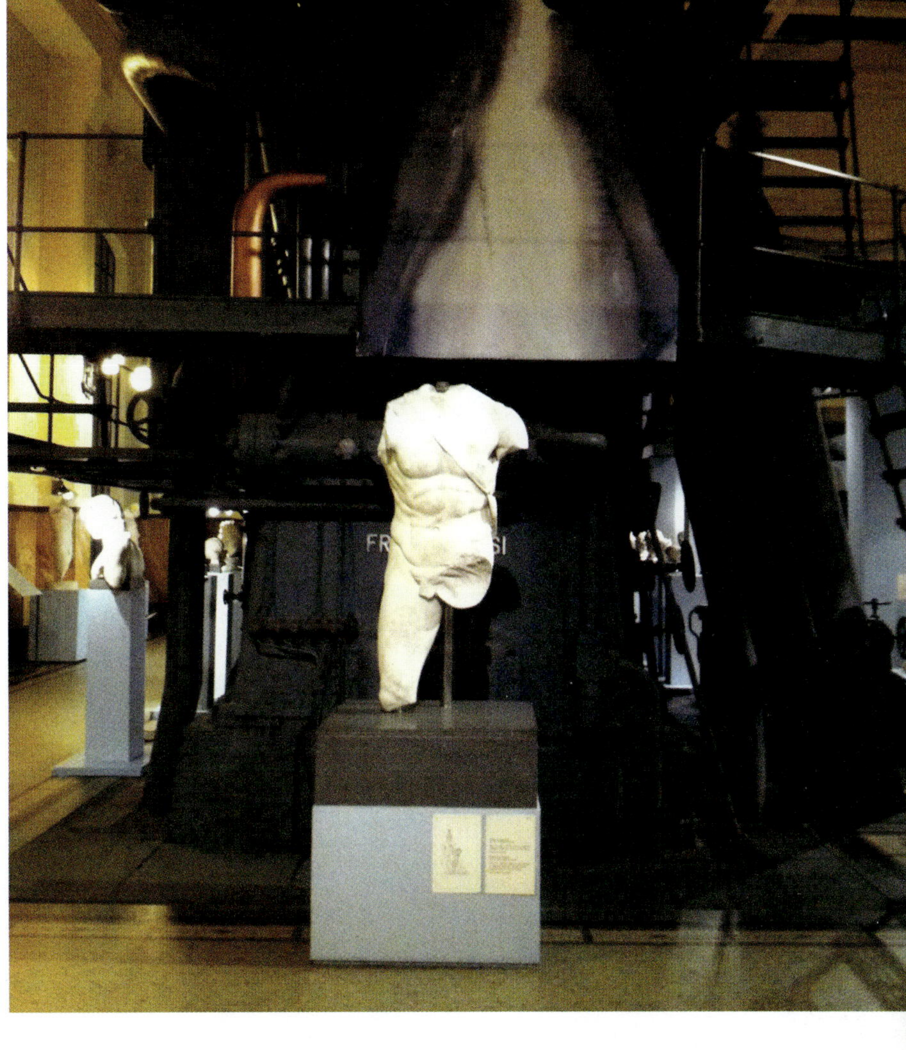

Museo Centrale Montemartini in Rome with an installation of Patricia Cronin's exhibit, Machines, Gods, and Ghosts
TOM MAYES/NATIONAL TRUST FOR HISTORIC PRESERVATION

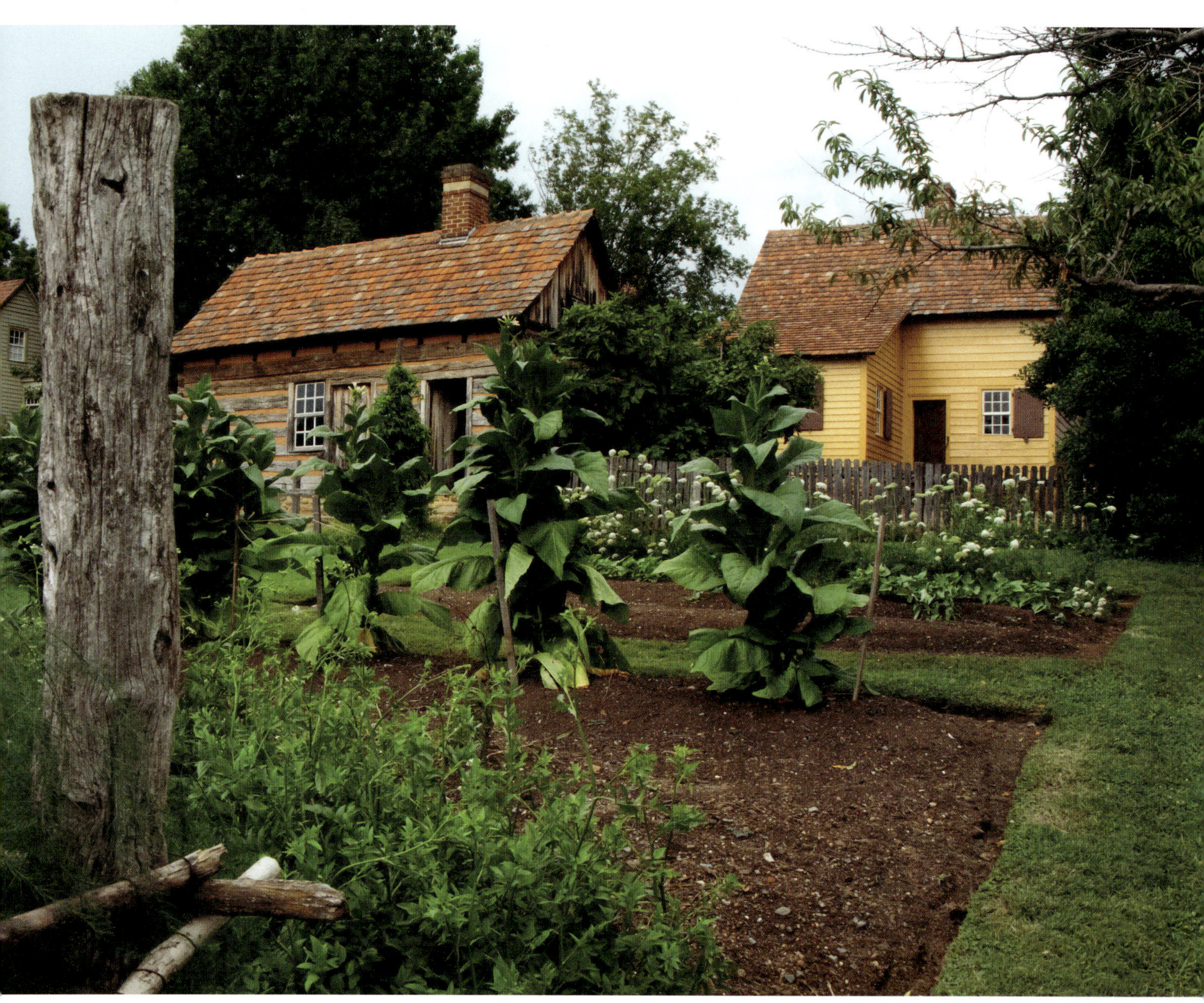

Old Salem in North Carolina has interpeted Moravian history to generations of visitors
PHOTOGRAPH COURTESY OF OLD SALEM MUSEUMS & GARDENS, WINSTON-SALEM, NC.

Learning

People learn from OLD PLACES, and they learn information that is not accessible to them in any other way.

Like most people, when I think about learning at old places, I immediately think about visits to historic sites as a schoolchild, places such as Old Salem in my home state of North Carolina, where I remember a woman singing a Moravian song a cappella in a vaulted and plastered room and the taste of the sugar cake served at the Moravian love feast afterward. This experience fixed in me an awareness of the long-standing tradition of religious diversity, tolerance, and freedom in our country. These types of visceral experiences at old places facilitate our potential to understand—and to remember—complex ideas, and they are available every day at hundreds of historic sites around the country.

Historic sites like Old Salem have an express educational mission, and such sites have developed interpretive programs that are designed to teach history using the old place as the educational tool.[1] In the earlier chapter on history, I emphasized that history can be understood at the real place where history actually happened in a way that it can't be understood through documents and books alone. Education is a traditional role

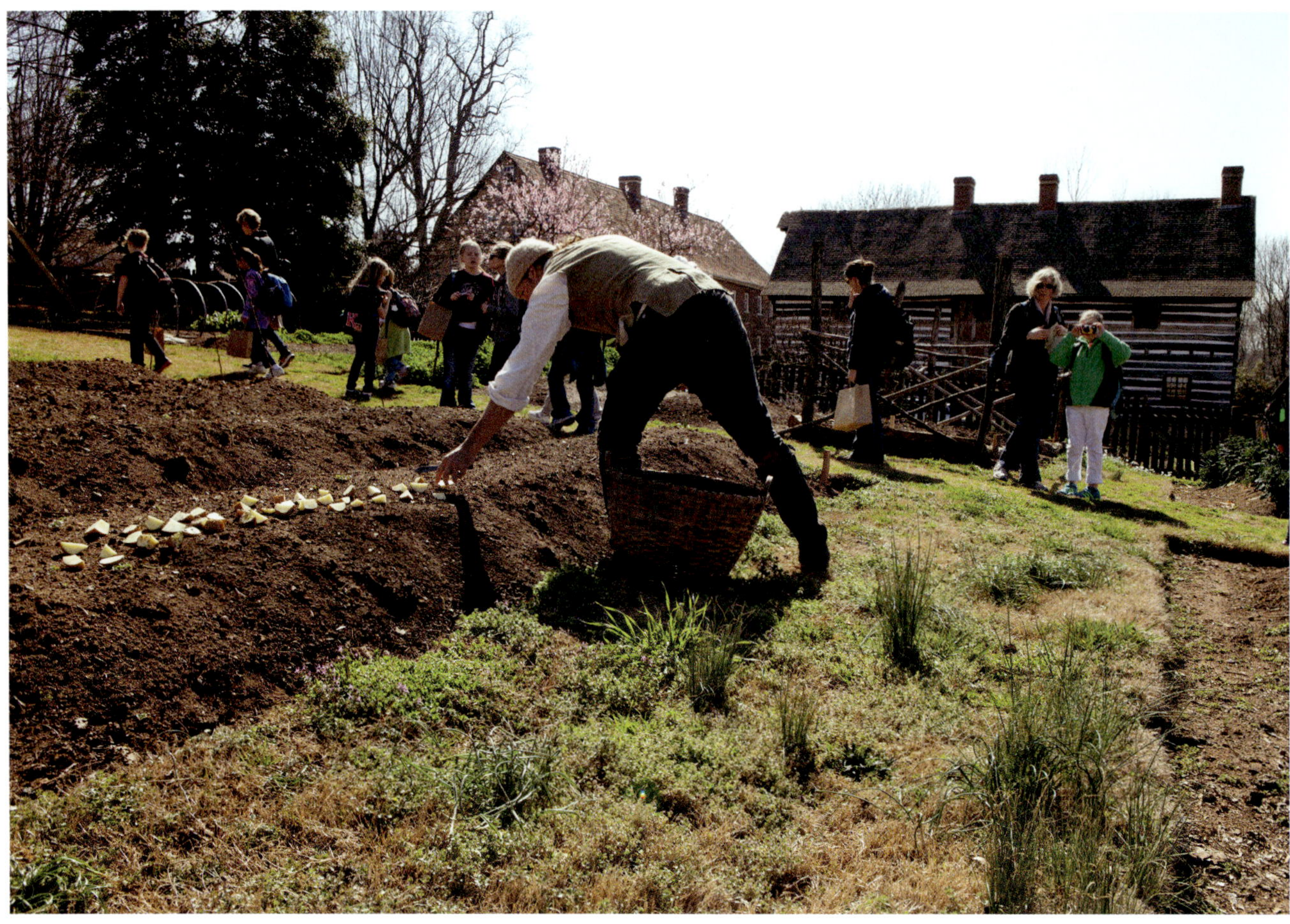

A group of visitors with an interpreter planting in a garden at Old Salem
PHOTOGRAPH COURTESY OF OLD SALEM MUSEUMS & GARDENS, WINSTON-SALEM, NC.

for historic preservation and one of the main reasons expressed for why historic preservation is supported through laws and public policy. This traditional and invaluable—and undervalued—educational activity continues to be a primary reason for valuing and saving old places.[2]

As Callie Hawkins, associate director of programs at President Lincoln's Cottage at Soldier's Home National Monument put it:

> Educators at historic sites put considerable time and effort into planning programs that reinforce local and national learning standards. These standards-based programs demonstrate to classroom teachers that time spent out of the classroom is time well spent. Most importantly, though, this type of informal learning environment helps cultivate in students a deep appreciation of how the past informs the present and shapes the future beyond what any textbook could achieve.[3]

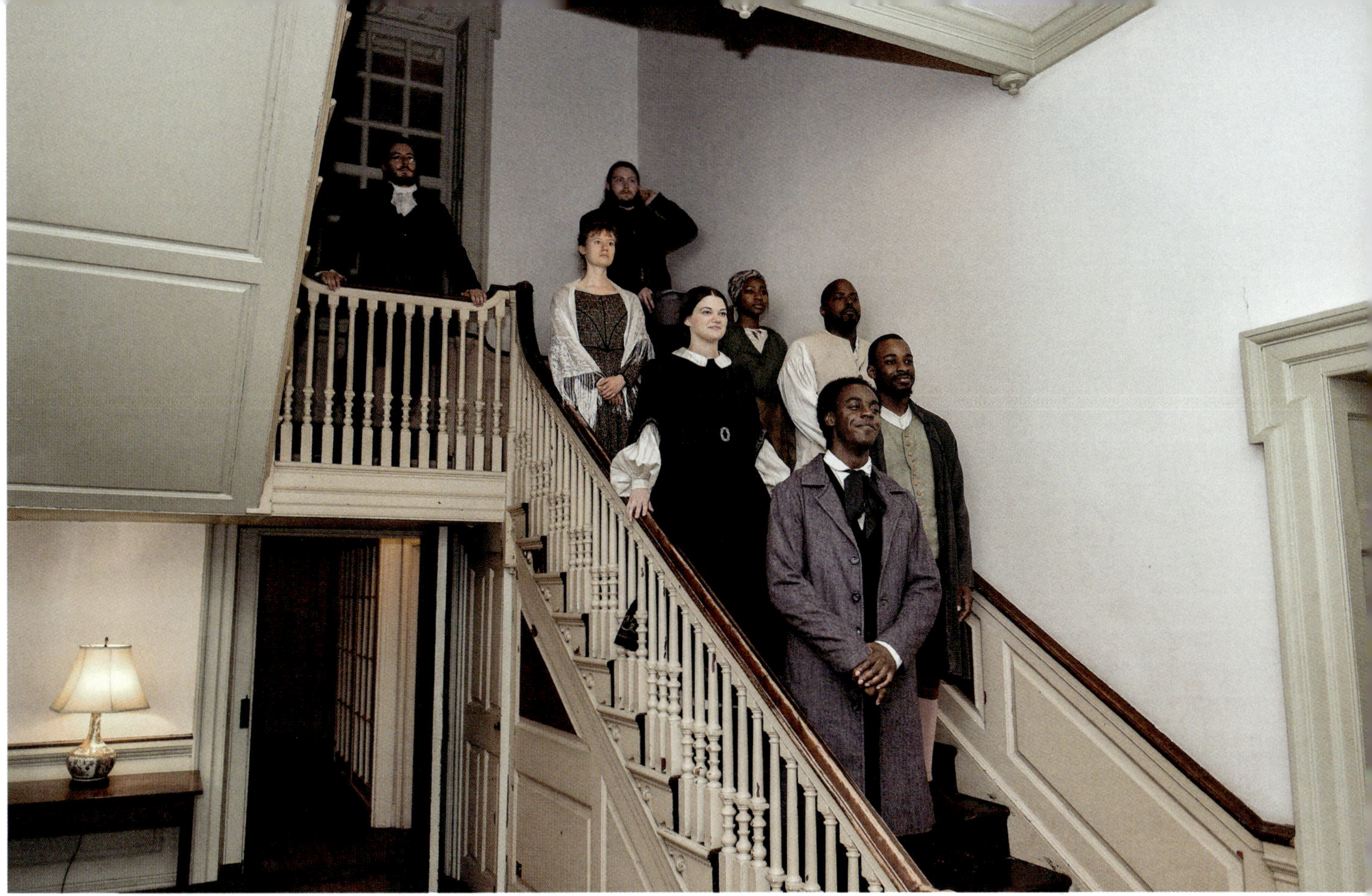

Cliveden, in the Germantown area of Philadelphia, Pennsylvania, where a contemporary play, "Liberty to Go to See" interprets concepts of freedom across generations
JUSTUS HENRY/SSM PHOTOGRAPHY

In addition to traditional educational programs, there are also other less obvious ways that we learn at and through old places. First, old places foster lifelong learning. As the website for the National Council on Public History states:

> Those who don't always remember their high school and college history classes fondly are often the same people who spend holidays, vacations, and their spare time seeking out history by choice: making pilgrimages to battlefields and memorials, visiting museums, watching television documentaries, volunteering with historical societies, participating in a community history project, and researching family histories.[4]

And it's not just history that we're learning. Different places present different topics and issues. At Touro Synagogue in Newport, Rhode Island, we learn about religious freedom. At Montpelier, in Virginia, we learn about the principles of the Constitution. At the Lower East Side Tenement Museum in New York, we learn about the experience of being an emigrant. At the Glass House, in Connecticut, we learn about architecture and design. And we don't just learn about these issues as something in the past, something only about history, but rather how these issues are being discussed, developed, debated, and prodded into the future today.

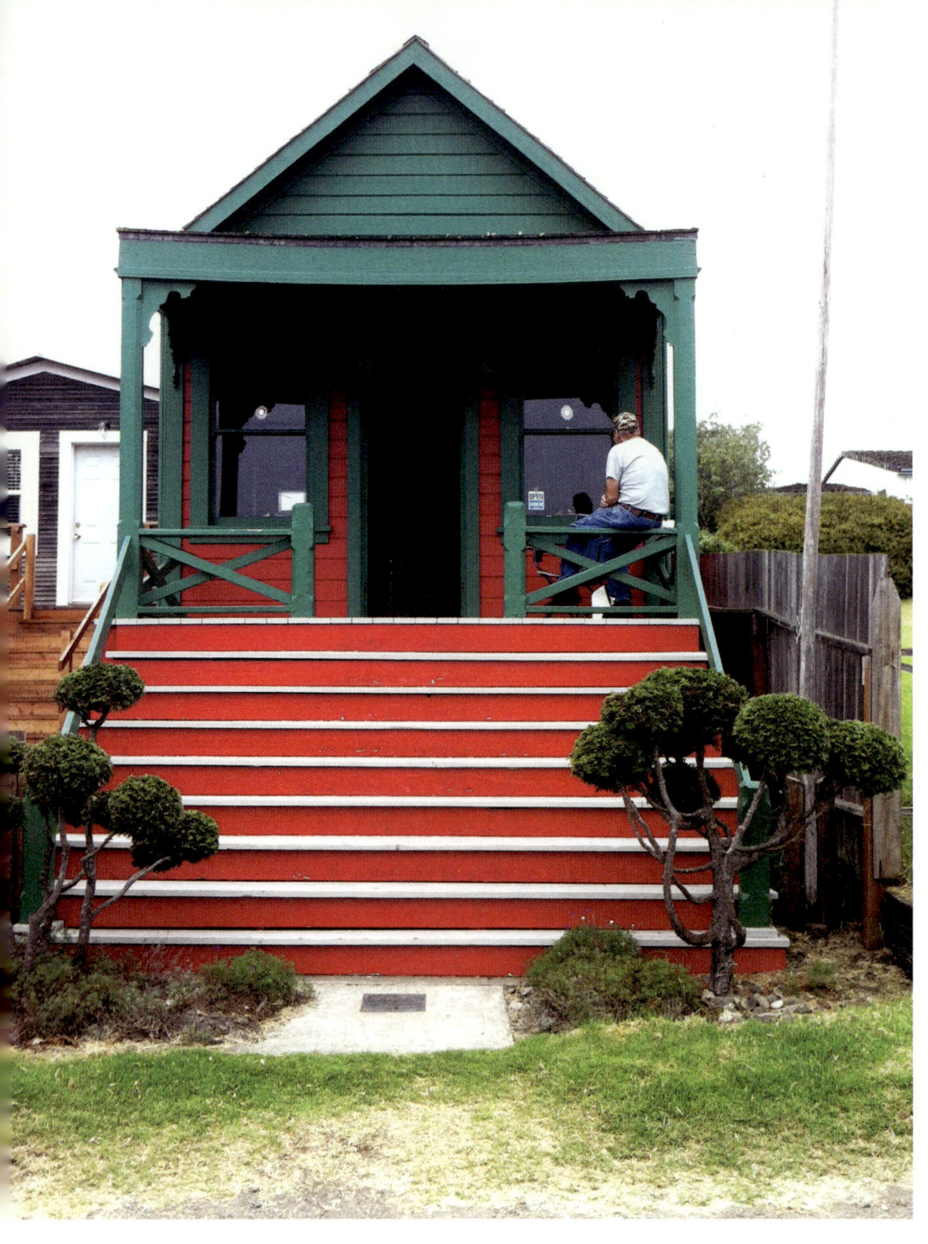

The Kwan Tai Temple, in Mendocino, California, built by Chinese immigrants in 1854
TOM MAYES/NATIONAL TRUST FOR HISTORIC PRESERVATION

Without exactly paying attention to it, we also absorb information about people and how they lived—what they ate, how they worked, how they made money, how they lost money, how they coupled, raised their families, and lived and died. And in learning about others from the past, we learn about ourselves.

Recently I visited the Kwan Tai Temple, a Taoist temple built in 1854 by Chinese immigrants in Mendocino, California. One of the women who saved this old place and who opens it to the public, Loretta Hee-McCoard, talked to me and some friends as we sat on the simple redwood benches along the walls, gazing around at Chinese calligraphy, ancient and fragile lanterns, the aged and crackled paint on the altar, and a thousand other telling details. A descendant of one of the people who founded the temple, Loretta told us that this red and green building was the only intact physical reminder that Chinese people were in Mendocino as early as 1854. It struck me that this building, simply by its continuing presence, is testament to the fact that the Chinese were here. The idea that "we were here" seems a perfect example of what people learn from old places, and one that is deeply affirming.

I've primarily mentioned historic sites that are open to the public where people go expressly to learn. But we also learn from old places that are not open to the public expressly to fulfill an educational mission. I treasure a visit that I made with my mother and my aunt to a distant cousin in South Carolina who lived in the house my great-something-grandfather built in 1792. Although added onto many times, at its heart, the house was a simple log cabin, handmade by this great-great himself, probably with the help of the people in the community in which he lived. I'd heard about this house most of my life, but nothing prepared me for actually being there. I was bowled over by the simplicity of the place, the unpainted plank walls, the small stair leading to a loft, the hand-planed mantel around the fireplace. Those earlier Mayeses had come and gone through that short plank door. I'd always wondered who they were, and being in this place where they had lived helped me get a sense of who they might have been in a way that nothing else could. I left that day deeply satisfied. I hadn't found that my ancestors were rich or powerful or important, but that they were self-reliant people who could plane a molding for their own mantel. It felt like I had found out something about who I was.

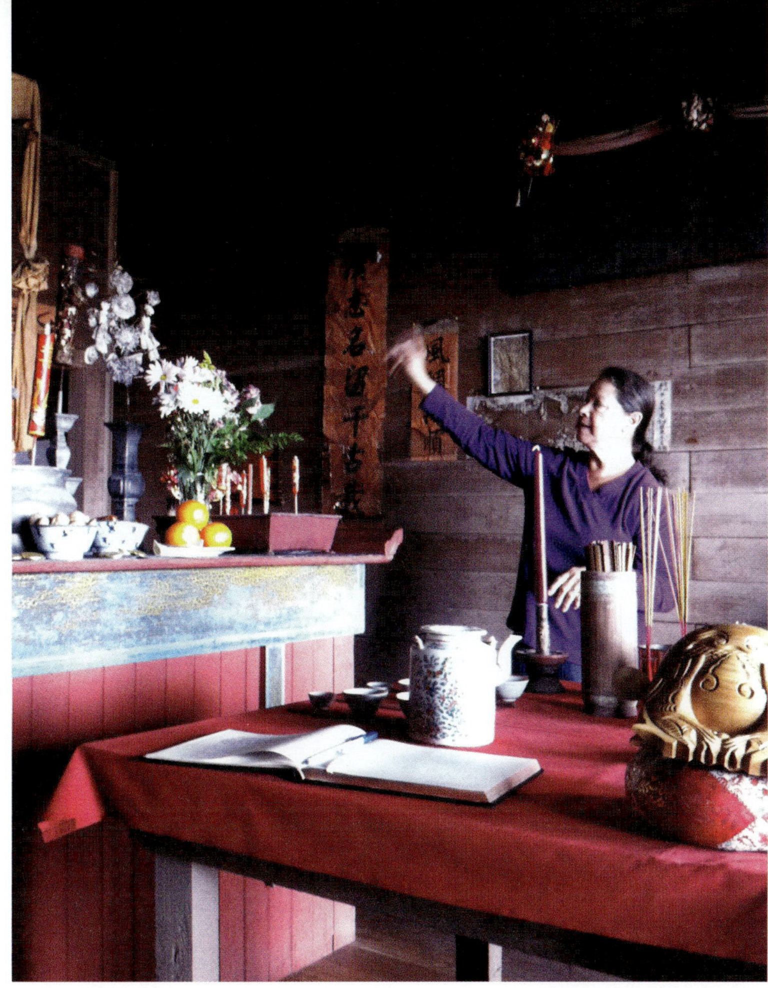

A descendant of one of the original founders of the Kwan Tai Temple explains the significance of the interior
TOM MAYES/NATIONAL TRUST FOR HISTORIC PRESERVATION

There are endless facts, concepts, and ideas that people learn from old places. Happily, the capacity to learn from old places is all around us today, more than ever before, and in a much more open and democratic way. Through mobile apps such as NextExitHistory, cellphone tours, Wikipedia, mapping apps, and simple Google searches, we have the capacity to learn about virtually any old place where we might find ourselves. And there are an endless variety of themes, from crime history to LGBT history, architecture, and even city planning. People now have access to information about old places wherever they are, and they can access it when and how they want. I hope they use these tools and learn something that surprises and delights them.

NOTES

1. See also the National Park Service program for "Teaching with Historic Places," National Park Service, accessed February 8, 2018, www.nps.gov/subjects/teachingwithhistoricplaces/index.htm.
2. There are a number of organizations that support the teaching of history and other topics through the use of old places, such as the National Council on Public History (www.ncph.org) and the American Association for State and Local History (www.aaslh.org).
3. Callie Hawkins, e-mail to author, September 22, 2013.
4. "What Is Public History?" National Council on Public History, accessed September 21, 2014, http://ncph.org/cms/what-is-public-history.

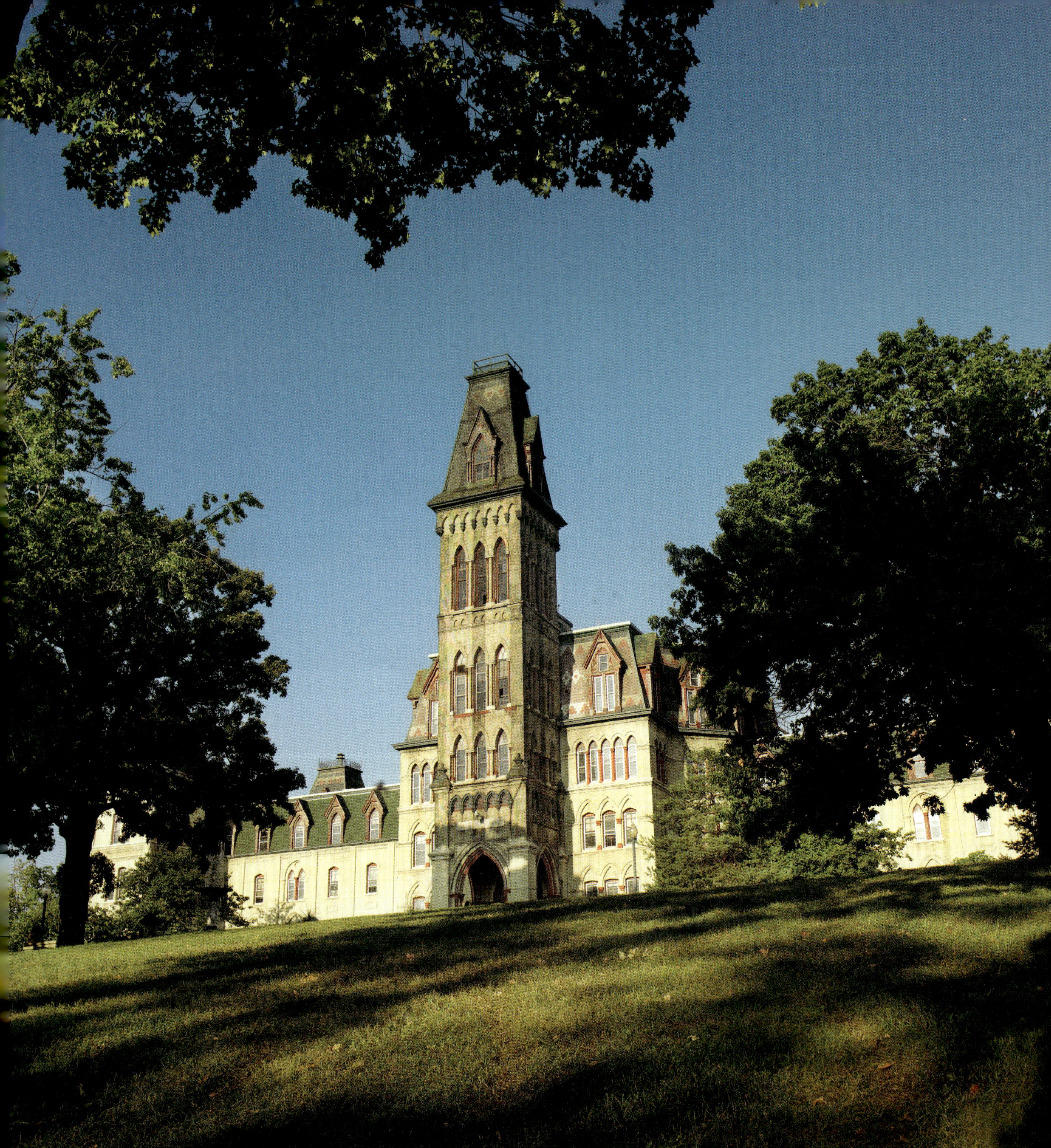

Reusing existing buildings with character is likely to be more long lasting and therefore sustainable, such as at Old Main at the Milwaukee Soldiers Home, a National Treasure

MATTHEW GILSON

Sustainability

Keeping and using old places is one of the most environmentally sound things a person or community can do—more than building or buying anything new that claims to be "green." As Carl Elefante of Quinn-Evans Architects brilliantly said, "the greenest building is . . . one that is already built."[1] Yet it's my perception that society at large doesn't yet fully acknowledge the "green" values of keeping and reusing existing buildings and communities—in fact, old buildings are often viewed as throwaways and teardowns. Fortunately, a reuse ethic seems to be growing, and the benefits of reusing existing buildings and communities are becoming recognized more widely.

In this essay, I hope to summarize some of the key takeaways from the work by the National Trust's Preservation Green Lab, the Urban Land Institute, the Green Building Council, Smart Growth America, and others[2] in the hope that it will give people a brief look at the reasons that keeping and reusing old buildings and communities is green. But I also want to suggest that old places should themselves be viewed as part of the ecology we hope to sustain.

Here's my quick summary of the reasons the continued use of old buildings and communities is environmentally sound.

Avoided impact. Reusing old buildings avoids the environmental impacts of the extraction, processing, and transportation of new materials and the construction processes. As a Preservation Green Lab report, *The Greenest Building: Quantifying the Environmental Value of Building Reuse*, states:

> Building reuse almost always yields fewer environmental impacts than new construction when comparing buildings of similar size and functionality. . . . It takes 10 to 80 years for a new building that is 30 percent more efficient than an average-performing existing building to overcome, through efficient operations, the negative climate change impacts related to the construction process.[3]

Land conservation. Continuing to use existing buildings and communities avoids or minimizes the use of forests, farms, wildlife habitat, and open space for new construction. As SmartGrowthAmerica states:

> Reusing already developed land . . . preserves open spaces that are home to wildlife. Habitat loss is the main threat to 80 percent of the threatened and endangered species in the United States, but building within an existing community, rather than outside of town on a wild greenfield, helps preserve wildlife habitat, protect air and water quality and foster the strong economic growth that's only possible in dense development.[4]

Embodied energy. Old buildings and communities embody the energy and carbon that was devoted to produce them—the wood and coal used to fire the bricks, smelt the tin, forge the nails, saw and transport the timber. Although some critics argue that the concept of "embodied energy" doesn't result in any positive impacts today or in the future, it remains true that it would be incredibly wasteful to discard these materials and their historical energy and haul them to a landfill, adding to the environmental impact of demolition.[5]

Operating energy. Many old buildings, because of the way they are designed, already use less operating energy than new buildings. Again, from the Preservation Green Lab:

Building owners, developers, policy makers, and green-building experts often assume that it is preferable to build a new, energy-efficient building than to retrofit an older building to the same level of efficiency. . . , [yet] data from the U.S. Energy Information Administration demonstrates that commercial buildings constructed before 1920 use less energy, per square foot, than buildings from any other decade of construction.[6]

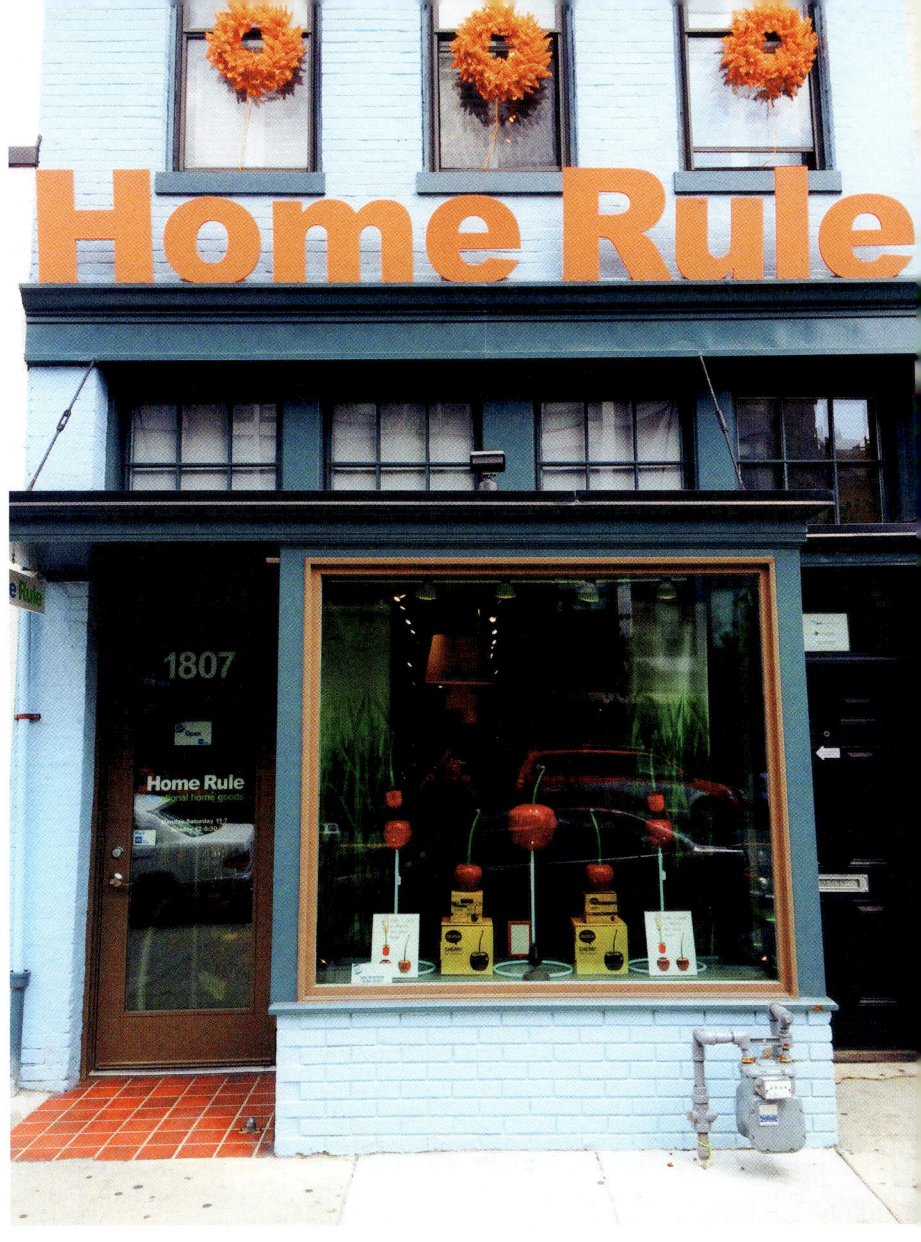

The nineteenth-century building housing Home Rule, a housewares store in Washington, D.C., benefits from natural light from the historic transom windows
ROD GLOVER

Although this is not true for all older buildings, many old buildings are inherently green.

Passive design. Older buildings were often designed to take advantage of naturally occurring energy, like the light well at the Wing Luke Museum mentioned in the earlier chapter on architecture or the transom windows in Main Street commercial buildings, like the one at my husband's store, HomeRule, on 14th Street in Washington, D.C. Many designers are recognizing anew the inherent passive sustainable designs incorporated in older buildings. I'm reminded of a 1970s study of the farmhouses of the New River Valley in North Carolina. These farmhouses developed organically in response to the climate to take advantage of the landscape for warmth in the winter, coolness in the summer, and the gravity flow of water to the springhouses.

Transportation and density. Older communities are often on existing transportation corridors, have greater density, and are close to workplaces so that fuel consumption from cars is minimized. This has long been recognized as one of the benefits of the reuse of existing built communities because of the benefits for land conservation, and it is one of the key principles of smart growth.[7]

All of these reasons—farmland conservation, habitat preservation, open-space preservation, reduced fuel consumption, avoidance of adverse impacts from the extraction and transportation of new materials, avoidance of new landfill material, positive environmental passive design, and others—add up to a powerful rationale to continue to use, reuse, and strengthen existing buildings and communities. The benefits of reusing existing buildings are now recognized by the Green Building Council in the credits awarded for reuse in the LEED certification calculation (although these may not adequately reflect the full environmental value of reuse).[8]

But there are more deeply philosophical ecological reasons to keep, maintain, and reuse old places. First, older communities are organic systems developed over time with their own distinctive cultures. They are themselves irreplaceable if everchanging parts of our environment. Choosing not to continue to maintain and strengthen them essentially condemns a distinctive and unique community to a form of extinction. One aspect of this is captured by the writer and architect Kimberley Mok: "Building 'green' isn't just about using the latest and greatest technologies—it can also be about preserving time-honored, local building traditions that respect regional cultures and have been proven to be climatically appropriate over the centuries."[9]

Second, the building materials and craftsmanship also deserve respect, not only because of the environmental cost of extracting, transporting, making, and installing them, but also because of the fact that some of the materials and craftsmanship will never exist again. The floor of my little river cabin in West Virginia is made of chestnut from before the die-off of the chestnut trees. Like heart pine windows, wide pumpkin pine floorboards, old growth redwood siding, and a host of other building elements, these materials may never be available again. Yet people who offered to buy the cabin before us planned to scrap it, seeing it as a teardown. It seems to me that throwing old floorboards and siding away is not only disrespectful to the materials and to the humans who labored to saw, plane, groove, and install them, but inherently inconsistent with the very idea of sustainability.

In trying to envision a world that is more environmentally sustainable, I hope for a world where we are more appreciative of the communities, buildings, and things that already exist and that we continue to use them so that we're not constantly tearing buildings down and throwing things away. Unthinking consumerism—including some allegedly "green" consumerism—contributes to many of our environmental problems, including stoking climate change. Although I may not be much of a consumer, I am a

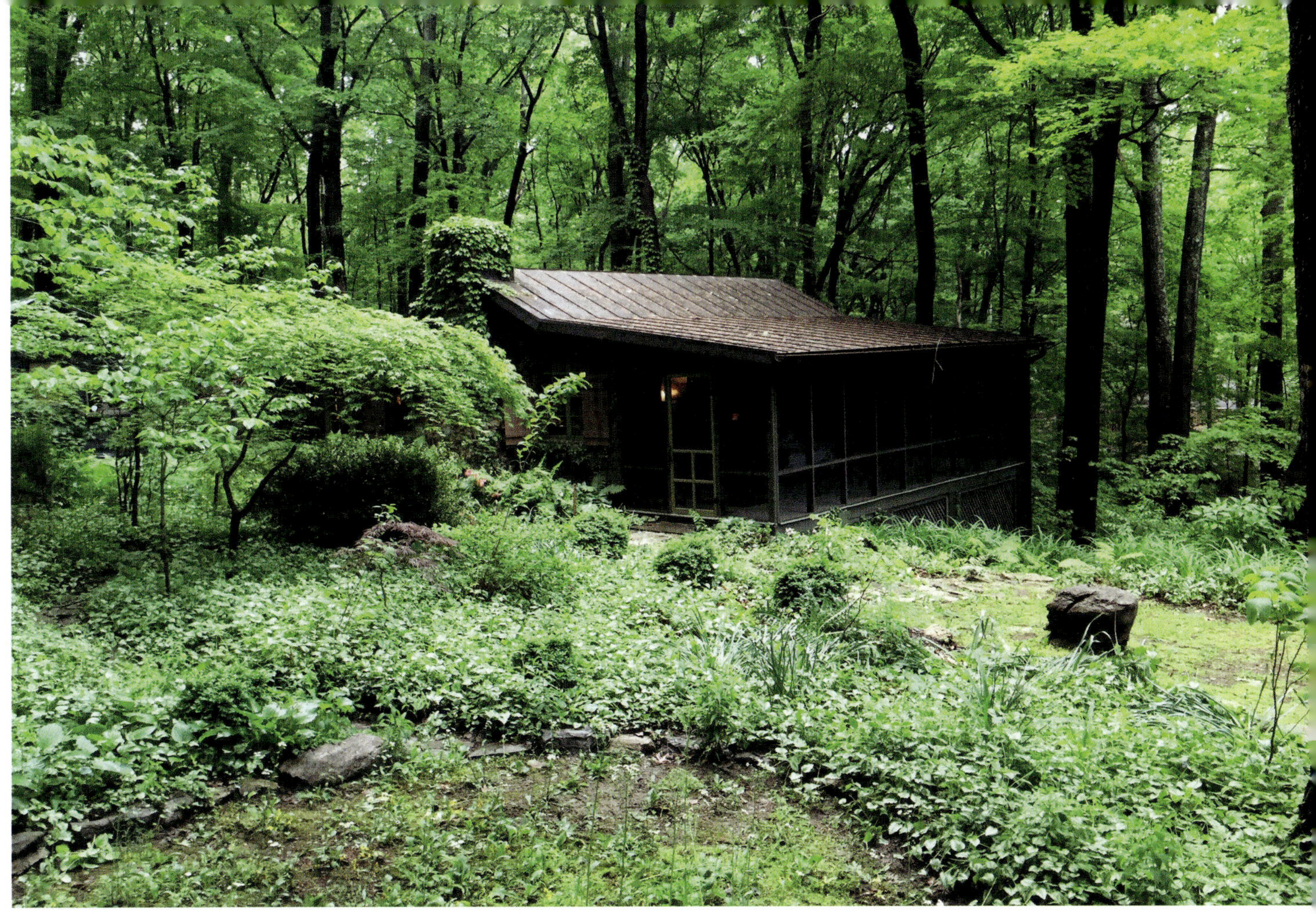

This 1950s cabin in West Virginia could have been a teardown, a wasteful loss of irreplacable building materials, such as old chestnut
TOM MAYES/NATIONAL TRUST FOR HISTORIC PRESERVATION

materialist. I value buildings and the meaning they have for us. I value objects and the meanings they have for me. The political theorist Jane Bennett, in her book *Vibrant Matter* notes the way objects seem to call to us and advocates for a rethinking of our relationship with objects and materials as a way of shifting our political ecology. As the website Cultivating Alternatives summarized the idea, "Bennett thinks that if we paid attention to the aliveness of matter, we wouldn't be so careless with our stuff."[10] Being "careless with our stuff" contributes to a throwaway mentality that is environmentally damaging.

Something about Bennett's theory about things resonates with me, and I imagine with others who see meaning in our existing built environment and who have a respect for materials, buildings, and practices that have preceded us. Some people have questioned whether our current view of sustainability may be too narrowly measured by a limited assessment of carbon footprint and may not adequately take into account other factors, including the factor of time. Scott Doyon, principal of Placemakers, in his post on considering soul as a part of green building practice, states:

> If you tear down a storied and graceful historic building—hand-built and rooted in tradition, in which generations of people have crisscrossed into

and through each other's lives—and replace it with a high-performance, modular gizmo-green equivalent, how much embedded energy is lost if you also count the loss of soul?[11]

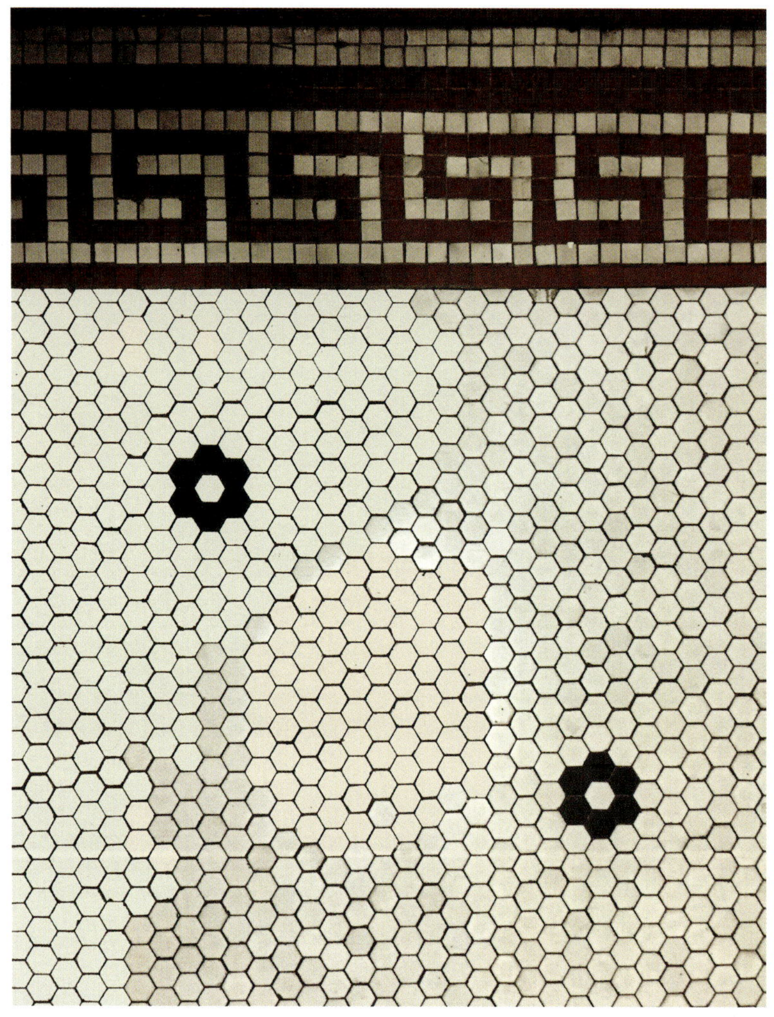

The tile floor of Rutland Courts, a Harry Wardman building in Washington, D.C. The floor has been in continuous use since 1917.
TOM MAYES/NATIONAL TRUST FOR HISTORIC PRESERVATION

Doyon goes on to ask whether a place that has no "soul" has the longevity necessary for it to be truly sustainable over time.

As I noted earlier, I'm delighted to see the current turn toward reuse, recycling of materials, and appreciation for old places. Some of the projects I've seen seem to reflect an idea from a quote I found in Jean Carroon's book *Sustainable Preservation: Greening Existing Buildings*: "The reuse and salvage in the project infuses it with a sense of connection, history and narrative. Every detail comes alive with a story of origins, disposal, and re-birth."[12]

I hope people become more aware of the fact that reusing not just materials, but whole existing buildings is good for the soul and the environment.

I suspect that the current low level of recognition of the green qualities of existing buildings and communities is partly because, as Carl Elefante has identified, we are "drunk on the new and now" and therefore can't even see the obvious benefits of the old.[13] We are blanketed with advertisements for green products. The building industry is primarily interested in developing new communities. Although I support the development of green products and green communities, the predominance of those voices should not blind us to the reality that simply continuing to use the existing buildings, communities, and things that we already have is one of the most environmentally sound (and soulful and sustainably long-lasting) things that we can do. As Jim Lindberg, senior director of the Preservation Green Lab said to me, "There is intelligence as well as energy embodied in our older buildings and neighborhoods. These places have so much to teach us about adaptation, sustainability, and resilience."[14]

NOTES

1. Carl Elefante, "The Greenest Building Is . . . One That Is Already Built," *Forum Journal*, 21, no. 4 (Summer 2007).
2. Please refer to the materials from these organizations for the full reports and studies. See also the fall 2010 *Forum Journal*: *Bridging Land Conservation and Historic Preservation* 25, no. 1.
3. The analysis of older buildings uses life cycle assessment to determine the environmental impact of a building over time. *The Greenest Building: Quantifying the Environmental Value of Building Reuse*, 2011, 14–15.
4. "Smart Growth Protects Natural Habitat," Smart Growth America, accessed October 25, 2015, www.smart growthamerica.org/issues/environment/smart-growth-protects-natural-habitat.
5. See *The Greenest Building*, 20.
6. *The Greenest Building*, 18.
7. I take note of the argument made by Ed Glaeser in *Triumph of the City* (New York: Penguin Press, 2011) and others who advocate for replacing current older and historic buildings with high-rise buildings to increase density in urban areas. Fortunately, in addition to the voices crying out about the loss of livability, character, history, identity, and memory that this would entail, more recent studies show that the avoided fuel impacts are better in areas where buildings are comparable to older and historic buildings, or approximately three to six stories tall, and that the environmental benefits are not better with densities that are greater. See Lloyd Alter, "Is There a 'Goldilocks Density'—Not Too High, Not Too Low, but Just Right?" November 1, 2011, accessed October 22, 2014, www.treehugger.com/slideshows/urban-design/is-there-goldi-locks-density-not-too-high-not-too-low-just-right. See also F. Kaid Benfield, *People Habitat* (Washington, DC: People Habitat Communications, 2014).
8. See "LEED Is Green Building," United States Green Building Council, accessed February 8, 2018, https://new.usgbc.org/leed.
9. Kimberley Mok, "Cool but Endangered Conical Houses Get Preservation Treatment in Indonesia," Treehugger, accessed October 23, 2014, www.treehugger.com/green-architecture/yori-antar-mbaru-niang-preservation-worok-flores-island-indonesia.html.
10. Nick Montgomery, "Summary: *Vibrant Matter* by Jane Bennet," Cultivating Alternatives, accessed October 28, 2014, cultivatingalter-natives.com/2013/11/28/summary-vibrant-matter-by-jane-bennett.
11. Scott Doyon, "Let's Get Metaphysical: Considering the Value of Soul in Redevelopment," Placemakers, accessed October 28, 2014, www.placemakers.com/2014/08/11/lets-get-metaphysical.
12. Leger Wanaselja, "Architecture," in *Sustainable Preservation Greening Existing Buildings*, ed. Jean Carroon (Hoboken, NJ: John Wiley & Sons, 2010), 252.
13. Elefante, "The Greenest Bulding," 37.
14. James Lindberg, e-mail to author, October 28, 2014.

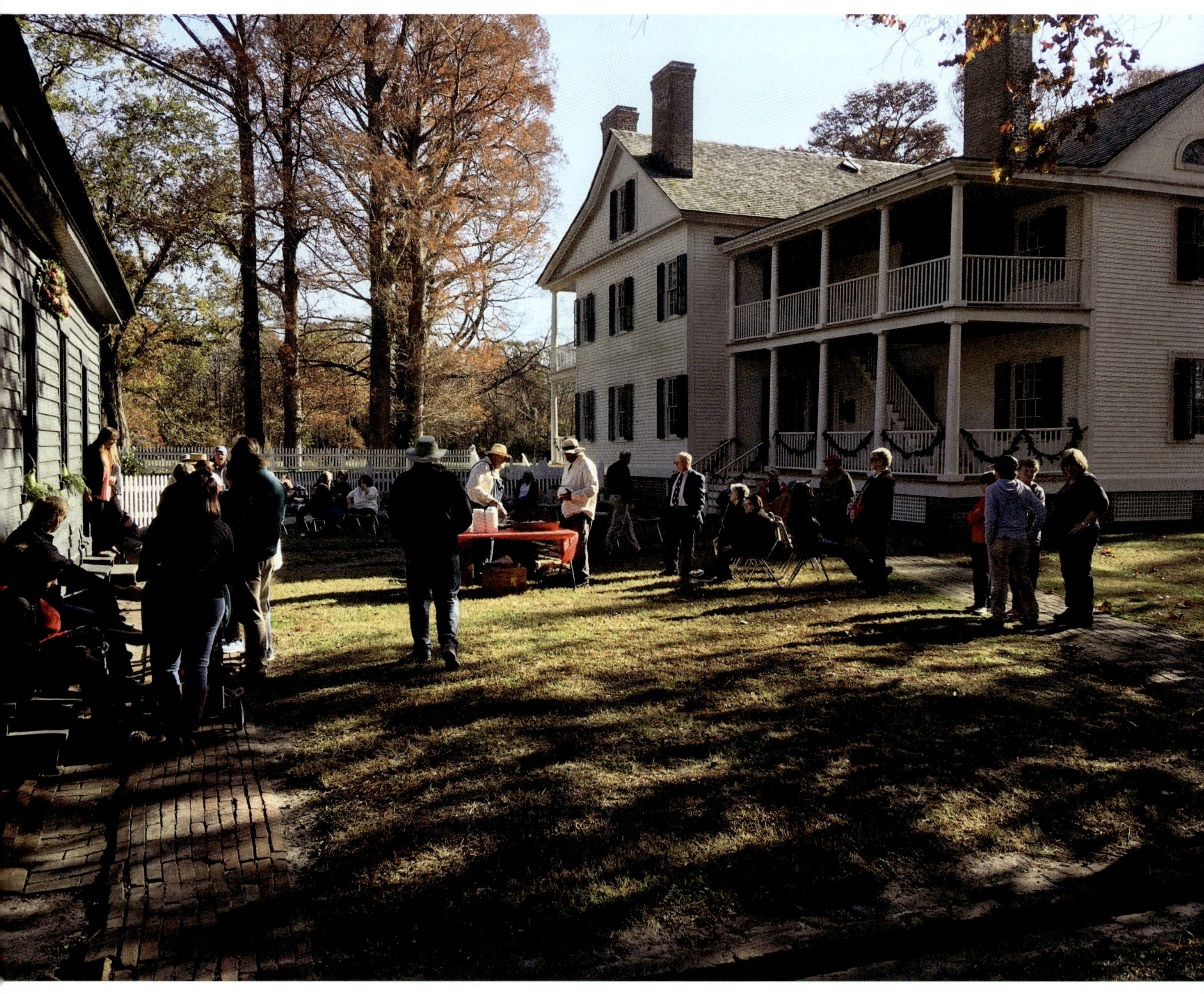

Open house event in front of the Collins House at Somerset Place

PHOTO COURTESY OF NORTH CAROLINA DEPARTMENT OF NATURAL AND CULTURAL RESOURCES

Ancestors

OLD PLACES connect us to our ancestors.

Old places connect us to our ancestors, and our ancestors connect us to old places, giving us a sense of belonging and identity. Whether our ancestors came through Ellis Island and lived on the Lower East Side, traveled through the middle passage of the slave trade to a cabin in eastern North Carolina, lived here all along in pueblos and villages throughout America, or arrived on the Mayflower and lived in eighteenth-century mansions in Salem, Massachusetts, the old places where our ancestors lived tell us about ourselves.

There is an enormous interest in genealogy in the United States today, as we can see with the popularity of Ancestry.com, *Finding Your Roots*, *Who Do You Think You Are?* and other television and online programs and applications. People of all backgrounds are devoted to finding out who—and where—they came from and discovering, recovering, or forging new ties between themselves and their ancestors. Ancestry.com states that based on a 2005 poll by Market Strategies Inc., 73 percent of all Americans are interested in their family history.[1] In searching for their family's past, the *where* is important

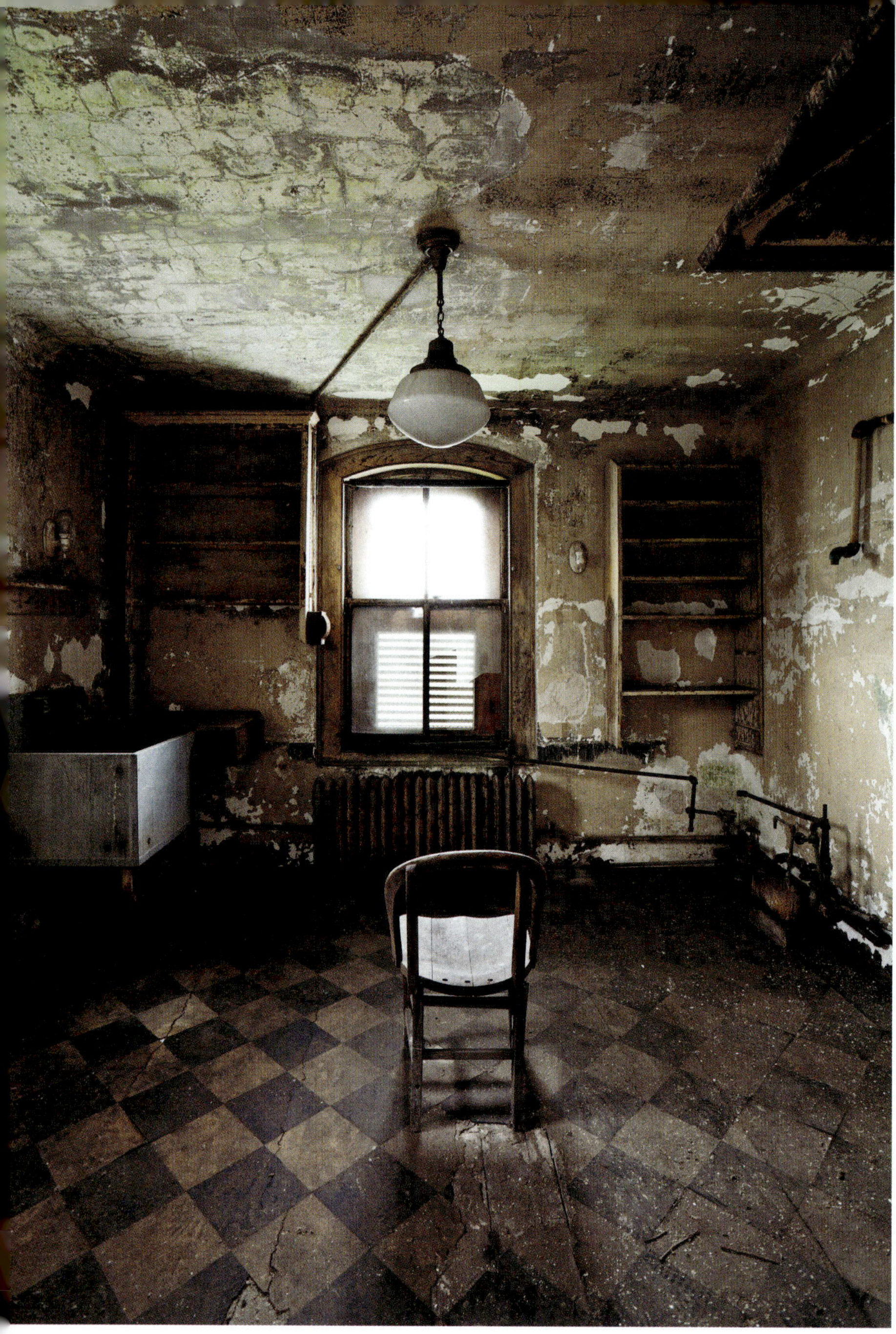

A room at Ellis Island, which was the port of entry for the ancestors of many Americans
CLARA DALY

to people, and being able to experience the *where* is often deeply moving. Here's the way people describe the experience of visiting the old places where their ancestors lived, worked, worshiped, fought, died, and were buried.

The musician Trace Adkins, in the Civil War Trust's magazine, said: "I was able to look across the battlefield and see it the way it looked when my great-great-grandfather was there. Words cannot describe what a spiritual moment that was for me, and it was only possible because of the preservation of that hallowed ground."[2]

Dorothy Spruill Redford, who wrote *Somerset Homecoming* about her path through genealogy to Somerset Plantation in North Carolina wrote:

> People need that, they need tangibility. They need something they can touch, that they can hold, look at, point to. Why that's so important I don't know, but it's honest-to-god necessary for people to feel something with their fingers, not just with their minds. The past is that way—the house you used to live in, the tree you used to climb, the doll you used to take to bed. These are all tactile triggers that fire the emotions in a way mere memories can never do. The day I first stepped onto the ground of Somerset, I felt a tangibility more intense than all the documents and records I'd collected.[3]

There has always been a strong tie between interest in genealogy and interest in historic preservation. Many people involved in early preservation efforts were motivated by

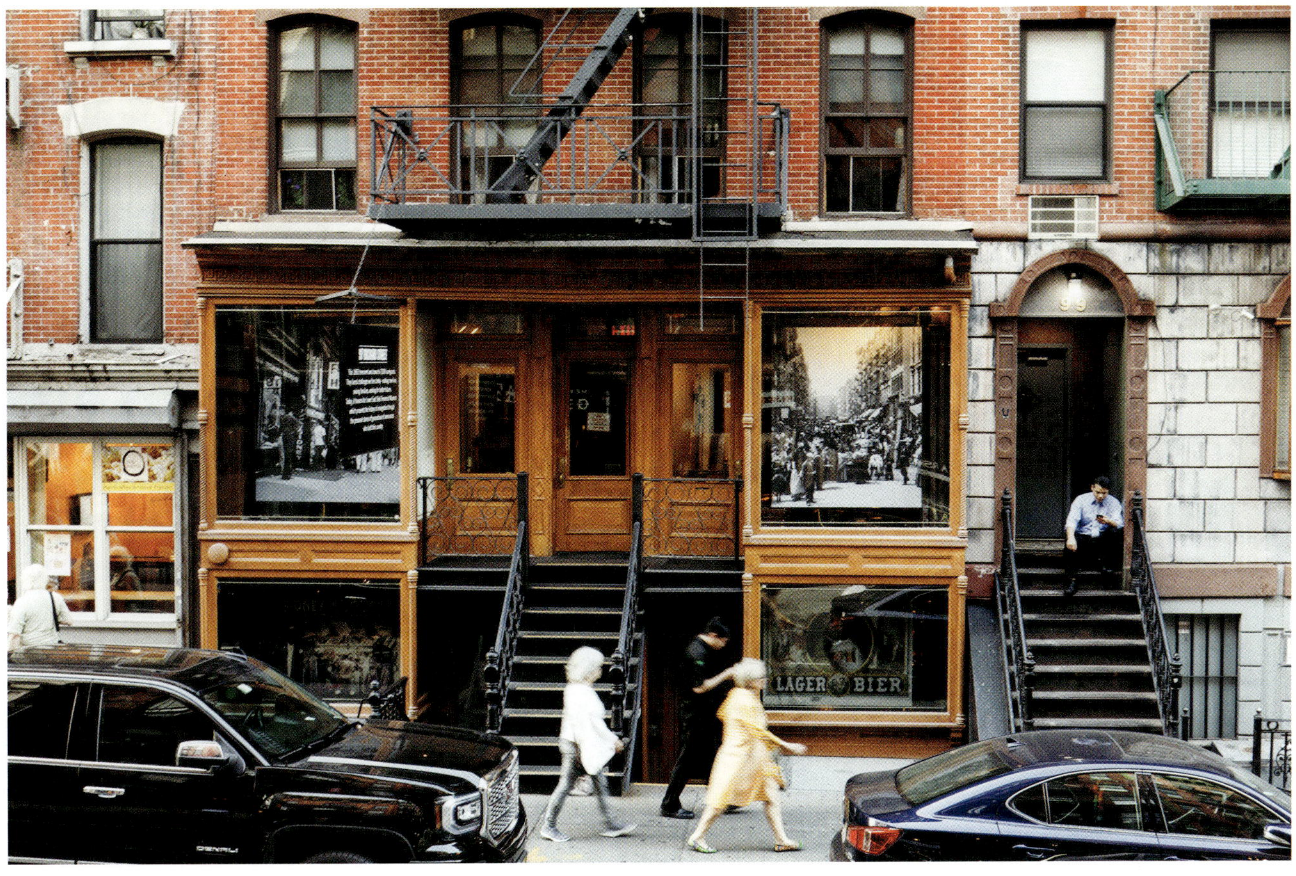

The Lower East Side Tenement Museum, a National Trust historic site, which fosters relationships with the descendants of the people who lived there
TRAVIS ROOZEE

the desire to preserve the places where their ancestors lived.[4] This motivation honored the achievements of those ancestors and reinforced the strong sense of identification between people and those achievements. For example, membership in the Daughters of the American Revolution (DAR) is based on a genealogical tie to someone who fought in the American Revolution, and part of DAR's mission is to preserve sites of American history. DAR continues to preserve and support historic sites throughout the United States.[5]

Today, genealogy is appealing to people of all backgrounds, yet I don't think the field was always as welcoming as it is today. Many may still feel that genealogy is tainted by the reality that people have used it to establish a sense of superiority over other people. For example, descendants of someone who came over on the Mayflower might distinguish themselves from those whose ancestors came to America later, like the Germans, Irish, or Eastern Europeans who came in the mid-to-late nineteenth century. Like certain aspects of our preservation history, genealogy was used to distinguish and exclude people and therefore told only a selective part of the American story. I think that's

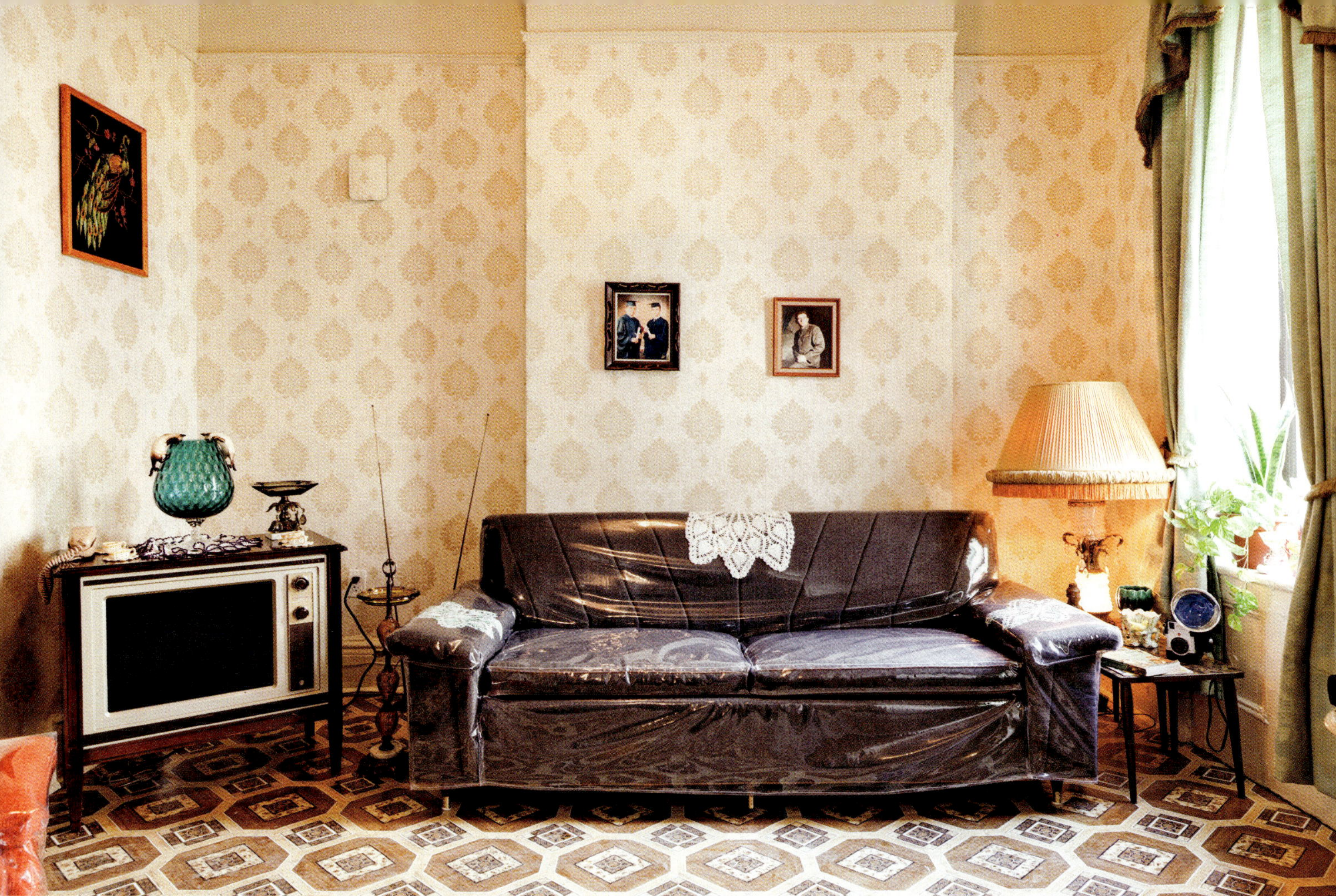

An interior at the Lower East Side Tenement Museum
TRAVIS ROOZEE

why preservationists haven't always felt very comfortable in recent years fostering the connections between family history and the preservation of old places. Yet the field of genealogy has changed dramatically in the years since *Roots* aired in 1977 and is now embraced by people of all backgrounds. It seems to me that it may be time for people who care about old places to welcome and foster the connections that family history can forge between people and old places.

I asked Brock Bierman, senior director at Ancestry.com, about the connections between people's search for their ancestors and old places. Brock is an enthusiastic proponent of the power that genealogical research and knowledge can unlock. Here's his take on the connection between finding your ancestors and old places:

> It's very important for you to not only know who your ancestors were, but also where your ancestors were from. Where did they come from? How did they end up where they did? People want to know the journey—the journey is as important as the family history. It gives you roots, it gives you an association with where you're from, how you're connected not only to your local community, but to the very country

you live in, and to the society you belong to. It makes you feel very appreciative of the sacrifices they made, but also a sense of pride—that your ancestors helped build this country.[6]

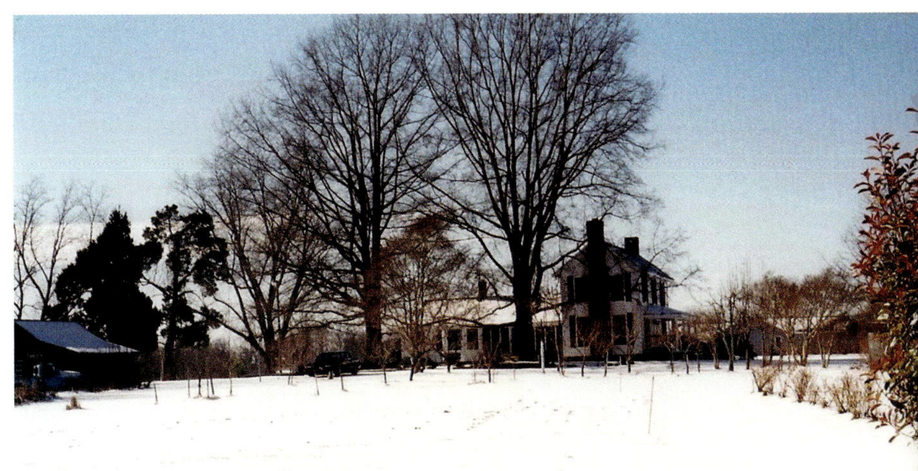

My great-grandparents' house, now lost
COURTESY OF MICHAEL MAYES

Others also have noted that many of our ancestors may not have been the building owners or the people written about in the history books but nonetheless were the actual builders of America. The Somerset Plantation website tells the story of an elderly black gentleman visiting this plantation site:

> What had been unnamed before was pride in the craftsmanship and skill his ancestors brought to the place and left there. What had been unrecognized was his tangible connection or place in the history of America: his inherent and historic value. Regardless of the circumstances under which they labored, the existence of the plantation house symbolized all that his ancestors created and at that moment in time, instantly connected him, in a culturally affirming way, to his past.[7]

If people listen to what the genealogical record actually says and follow that to the places of their ancestors, they can learn a far more interesting, deeper, and nuanced story of their own past and the past of America as a whole. As I've written about why old places matter, I've also written about my own family's connections to place—a log cabin in South Carolina, a frame farmhouse in North Carolina, a country Presbyterian church. These were places I knew well throughout my life. But through genealogical research, I discovered to my surprise that an early ancestor, Bartholomew Thompson, was not only a farmer, as I had assumed, but an ironworker at a place called Vesuvius Furnace. The site of Vesuvius Furnace and the house of the owners still survive in Lincoln County, North Carolina. The original owners are well documented, but the workers, like my ancestor, are not. Yet this place remains as a tangible link to Bartholomew Thompson's life—a physical, tangible, textured, 3-D document. I now feel a tie not only to that place and to Bartholomew Thompson, but to iron workers and iron furnaces everywhere.

Brock pointed me to recent studies that talk about the impact of knowing where your family is from. A study released in 2014 draws a correlation between interest in family history—a group defined as "family history enthusiasts"—and community involvement. The study concludes that people who explore family history—including travelling to a cemetery, church, or a particular area specifically for the purpose of learning about their ancestors—perform more volunteer work, are more active in voting and/or public affairs, belong to more civic or veterans organizations (including preservation organizations), and contribute more to charitable causes than other people.[8]

More strikingly to me, a study by Emory University in 2010 found that "children who know stories about relatives who came before them show higher levels of emotional well-being" and "family stories provide a sense of identity through time, and help children understand who they are in the world."[9] Though I haven't seen studies that specifically examine the role that old places play in these family stories, I'm struck by the similarity to the sense of identity, continuity, and memory that old places play in our lives more generally. Those values show up in the way people talk about being in places where their ancestors lived, worked, and died.

Earlier when I wrote about what we learn from old places, I described a visit with Loretta Hee-McCoard at the Kwan Tai Temple, which her ancestors built in Mendocino, California, in 1854. Its continuing presence is testament to the fact that the Chinese were here, that Loretta Hee-McCoard's people have been here all along. Dorothy Redford from Somerset emphasizes the same idea: "The need to belong. That's what this was all about. Not just my need, but the need of our entire people, whose destiny was out of our hands for so long, and who are still struggling to shape our identity, our sense of place in a society that was not of our making.[10]

Old places that connect us to our ancestors provide an exceptional experience for people—an experience that is deeply beneficial. The Petersburg Battlefield National Park website says:

> The most important aspect of a National Park Service site is the "power of place." This manifests itself at Petersburg National Battlefield in visitors asking about where their ancestor may have stood, fought, and/

> or died. There is no substitute for the emotions of a connection made across 150 years while walking over the same hallowed ground.[11]

I hope everyone has the experience of journeying to places where their ancestors lived, worked, *built*, and died. Think about the power that might be unleashed by reconnecting old places with people searching for their ancestors.

NOTES

1. "Americans' Fascination with Family History Is Rapidly Growing," Ancestry, accessed December 22, 2014, http://corporate.ancestry.com/press/press-releases/2005/06/americans-fascination-with-family-history-is-rapidly-growing.
2. "Trace Adkins Forges Links to the Past," *Hallowed Ground*, Summer 2013, Civil War Trust, accessed December 22, 2014, www.civilwar.org/aboutus/heroes-of-preservation/trace-adkins-forges-links-to.html.
3. Dorothy Spruill Redford, *Somerset Homecoming: Recovering a Lost Heritage* (New York: Doubleday, 1988), 209–10.
4. Robert R. Weyeneth, "Ancestral Architecture," in *Giving Preservation a History*, ed. Max Page and Randall Mason (New York: Routledge, 2004), 275.
5. Daughters of the American Revolution, accessed December 13, 2014, www.dar.org.
6. Brock Bierman, interview with author, December 19, 2014.
7. "Somerset Homecomings," NC Historic Sites, accessed February 8, 2018, www.nchistoricsites.org/somerset/homecoming.htm.
8. Odum Institute for Research in Social Science, University of North Carolina at Chapel Hill, "Family History Research and Community Involvement," September 26, 2014. Accessed February 8, 2018, www.ancestrycdn.com/aa-k12/236/assets/Ancestry-Final-Report-Oct14.pdf.
9. R. Fivush, M. Duke, and J. Bohanek, "Do You Know . . . The Power of Family History in Adolescent Identity and Wellbeing," *Journal of Family Life* 2010, accessed December 21, 2014, www.journalof familylife.org/ doyouknow.html#.
10. Redford, *Somerset Homecoming*, 236.
11. "Personal Connections," National Park Service, February 8, 2018, www.nps.gov/pete/learn/history culture/reserch.htm.

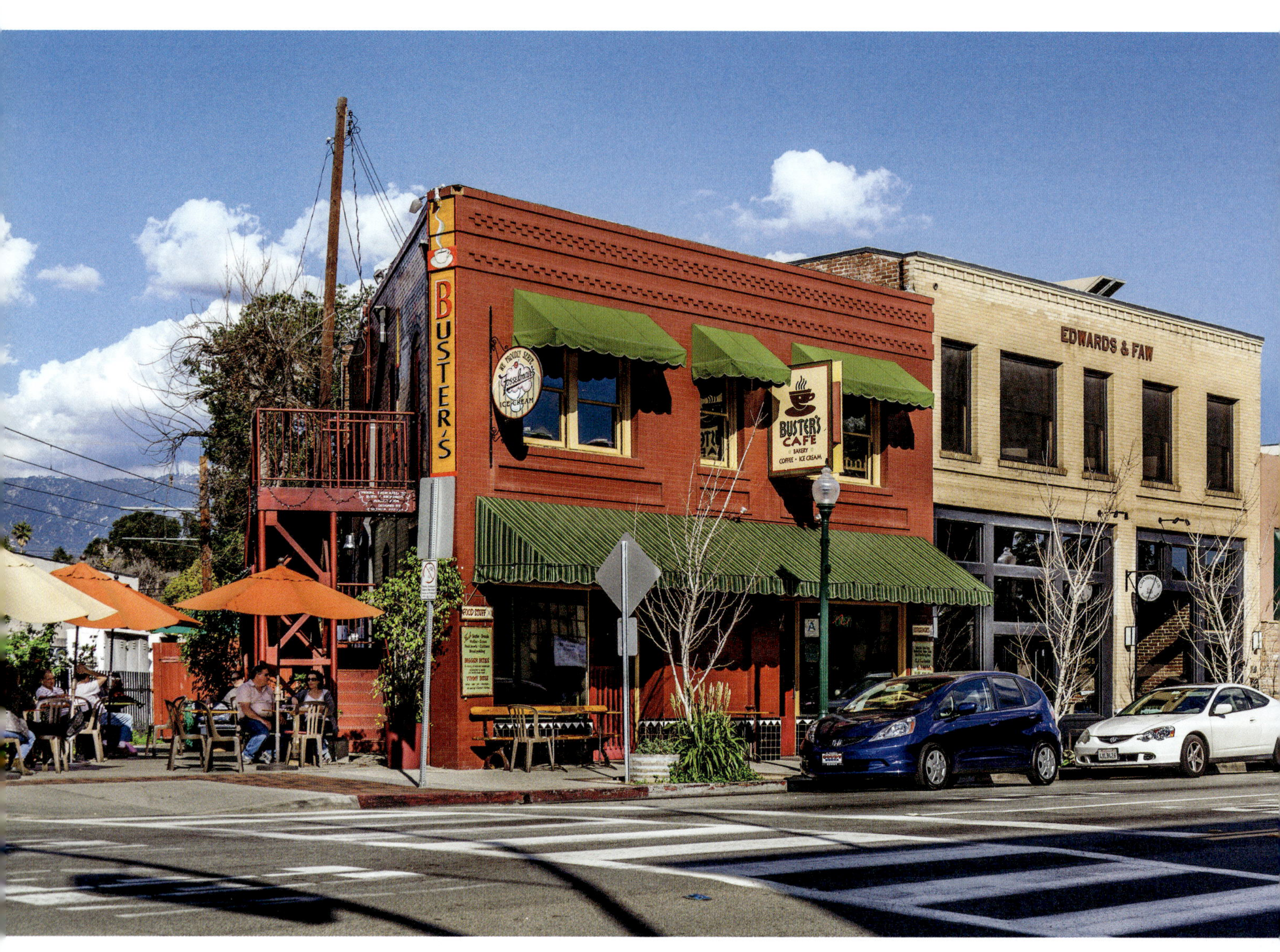

A vibrant area of South Pasadena, California, which was threatened by highway construction
BARRY SCHWARTZ

Community

OLD PLACES foster community.

One of the first people I interviewed about why old places matter was Dennis Hockman, editor-in-chief of *Preservation* magazine, who lives in an old neighborhood near Baltimore, Maryland. Dennis told me that one reason old places matter is because of community. Dennis described a cluster of ideas about how old places foster community, from a shared sense of place, to the storytelling that happens in old neighborhoods, to the way people meet and gather on common ground. "People matter more than buildings, than things," Dennis told me, "but the spirit of the people—the heartbeat of the community—is in the old things."[1]

We see how old places foster community in the way many old neighborhoods seem to have their own personalities,[2] in the way Main Streets and historic post offices act as the daily gathering place for people,[3] and in the way people in some old towns seem to be able to run into exactly the person they need to see exactly when they need to see them. People are proud of where they live. They identify with where they live. They are able to run their lives efficiently where they live. They feel connected and interconnected and *embedded* where they live. And when they leave, they may feel *homesick*, as I was when I first left the Ramah community near Huntersville, North Carolina, to go to the University of North Carolina in Chapel Hill. I missed not only my family and our farm, but the whole familiar, interconnected web of people and place that made up Ramah, from the taste of pound cake at dinners at our old, white frame church, to the cedar trees that lined the barbed wire fences at Mr. Ed Barnhardt's farm.

But how do old places, old buildings, old cities and towns foster community? What particular role do old places play? The writer Wendell Berry says, "A community is the mental and spiritual condition of knowing that the place is shared."[4] The architectural critic Paul Goldberger said,

> In an age in which we travel from private houses in little enclosed metal boxes on wheels into private office cubicles and then back again . . . there is precious little sense of shared experience in our lives or at least precious few times in which shared experience is expressed in terms of a common physical place.[5]

Old communities are often the places where people share a common space, a common experience, and a shared sense of what the space means to them. People in a community share a sense of its identity and character, which is often represented by the old places that serve as community landmarks. In 2014, graduate student Sandra Shannon conducted a survey asking people about their preferences for old and new buildings. In reviewing the results, Shannon concluded with the idea of "most people believing that historic resources are community assets and preservation is an important community service, even in comparison to other services considered important, such as economic development and public landscaping."[6]

A great example of the way old places foster community is how we experience post offices. Local post offices, often architecturally distinctive and in the center of town, serve as both meeting places and community landmarks.[7] That's one reason people fight so fiercely to keep historic post offices. A recent newspaper article from Milton, Tennessee, captured the reasons that old post offices help give a sense of community:

> Resident Michelle Eastman said, "The history is great, but the convenience of it being here is better."

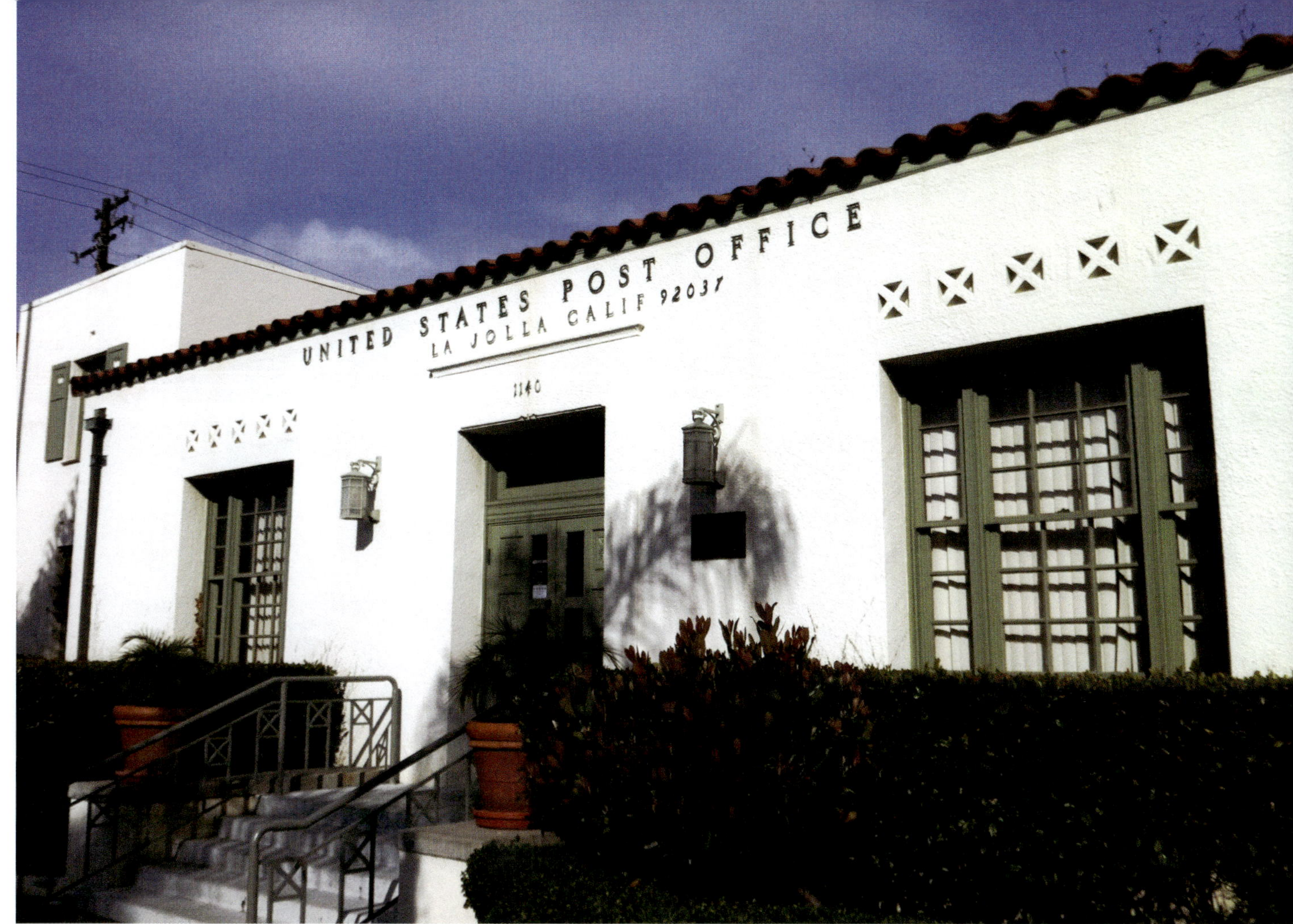

The post office building in La Jolla, California, which continues to serve as a meeting place for residents
ADRIAN FINE/NATIONAL TRUST FOR HISTORIC PRESERVATION

> "While Milton's strong families are still in place, the symbols they feel make the community are at risk of going away. In turn, the town and its leaders are willing to fight to try to keep its longtime identity in place."

"When you don't have a gathering place to go to, you start to lose your identity."[8]

Post offices are but one of the many old places that foster community. Schools, churches, town squares, parks, streets, blocks of houses, all of these allow people to share a place. In planning lingo, these may be referred to as "community assets." The planner Jeffrey Soule wrote about how communities can "map" these shared assets:

> A key way to engage the community and gather specific data regarding how people use space and ultimately what they value, cultural mapping starts by asking the question "Where are the places in your community that are important to you?"
>
> This is first done as a list-making exercise to identify the places within a community that people value: local meeting places, locations

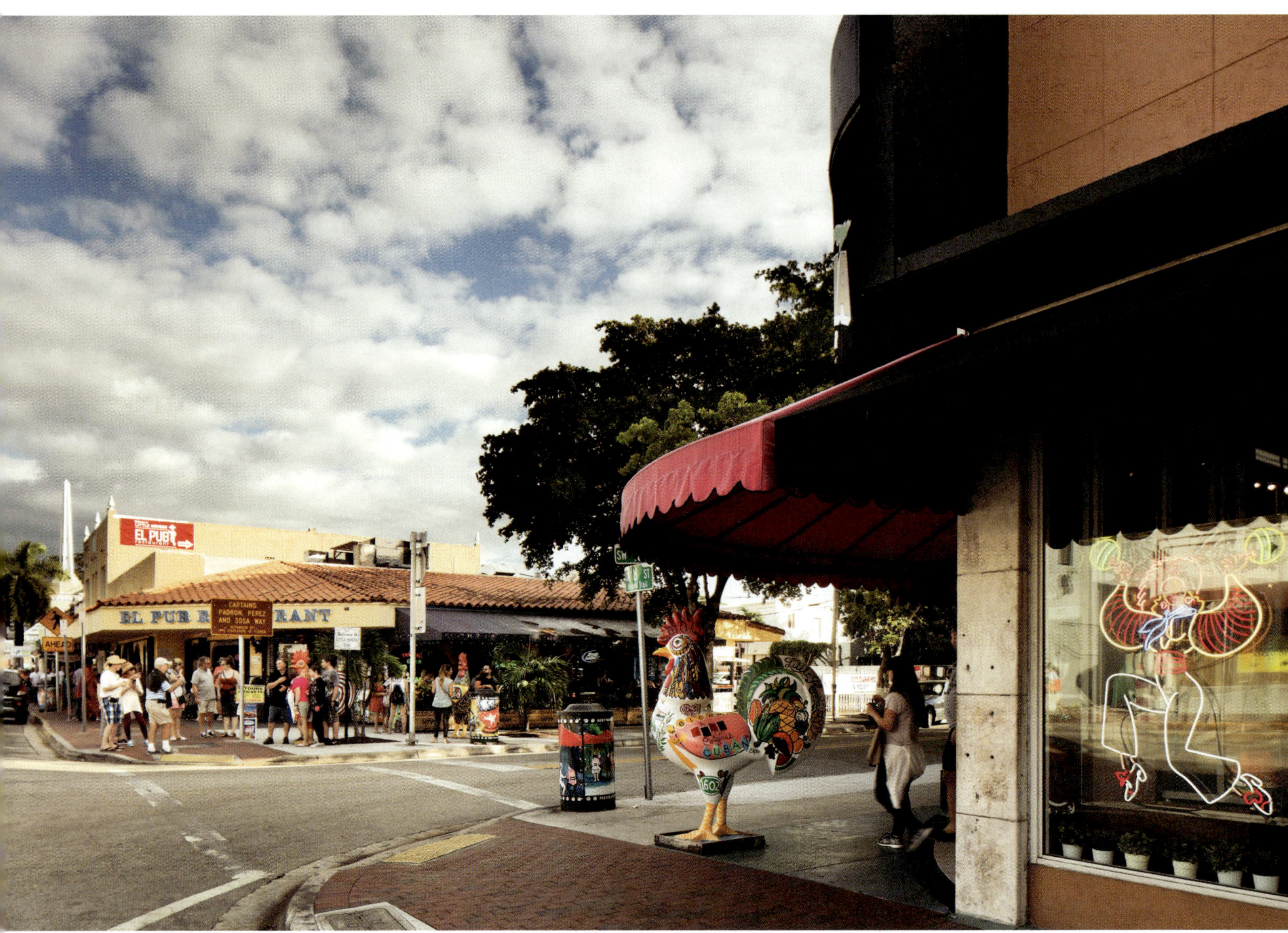

Little Havana in Miami, Florida, is a living community
STEVEN BROOKE STUDIOS

> which serve to build community cohesion, spiritual sites, places of visual quality, and others. Participants then go out into the community and actually map where these values and activities are found. . . . After the site visits, the group then goes through a process to discuss the values that these places represent and determine the threats to maintaining that place in the community.[9]

In an older community, many of these community assets are already established and the conditions that foster community already exist. The old buildings, streets, and

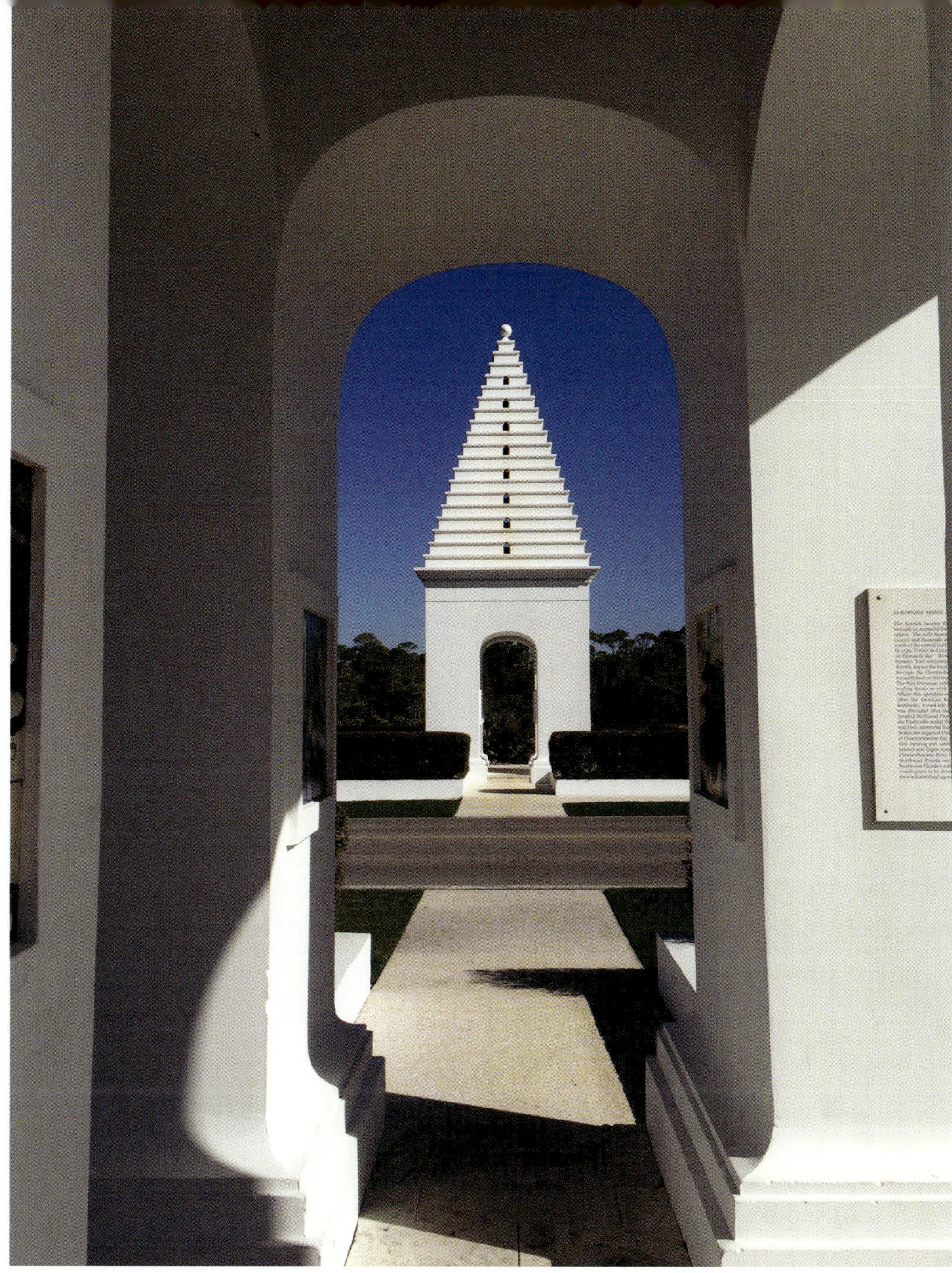

The gatehouses of Alys Beach, a new urbanist development on the Florida panhandle
TOM MAYES/NATIONAL TRUST FOR HISTORIC PRESERVATION

parks may already be designed for walkability and interaction. These places may already have gathered stories over time, from the memory of the quirky family who lived in the house on the corner, to recollections about the crotchety old man who warned the kids off his lawn, to reminiscences about schools that generations of families attended. These buildings, streets, and even trees serve as landmarks for telling stories that give people a sense of something shared—something lived together. The experience of living, working, shopping, exercising, worshipping, and playing in and around these old places builds a sense of shared community, and it is a sense of community that transcends generations.

For more than two decades, planners, academics, preservationists and everyday people have lamented the way sprawl has destroyed the American landscape, diminished the distinctiveness of places, and eviscerated the vitality of older towns and cities, essentially destroying community. New urbanists promote *placemaking*—the design of new places to foster a distinctiveness of place and a sense of community.[10] Developers of new places advertise walkability, design (front porches, alleys, garages behind the houses), open space, squares, and a mix of retail, residential, and workplaces (the very things that many old places already have) that are intended to allow people to interact with each other, to avoid getting in their cars, and therefore to create the conditions that foster community.[11]

I applaud these efforts. Yet something critically important is often overlooked, and that is the idea that the development of a real community takes *time*. Community develops through the interaction between people and place over *time*. We cannot build a community—we can only foster the conditions in which communities can grow and thrive. Community occurs in the organic interaction between people and place. Over time, these communities typically develop with a diversity of ages, incomes, and ethnicities. Charles Wolfe, in *Urbanism without Effort*, suggests that real urbanism is best when it is recognized where it already exists and has developed organically. "I believe the best urbanism is often the urbanism we already have, and that understanding the organic nature of this 'urbanism without effort' is key."[12] Old places have by their very nature developed organically and, in many cases, have already developed the attributes that foster community.

Yet not all old places are successful communities. Some old neighborhoods are unsafe, undervalued, and (for the moment) undesirable on the real estate market and do not provide their residents with adequate economic, educational, or other opportunities. In these undervalued neighborhoods, a focus on old places as community assets can play a role in turning these communities around so that they are increasingly valued by their residents and by newcomers. In fact, one of the factors that points to the possibility of improvement for a community—and an argument for the investment of public and private resources—is the presence of old places that give the community a sense of shared history, identity, and memory. The Preservation Green Lab of the National Trust has studied neighborhoods in Philadelphia and Baltimore to identify the areas that are likely to be successful if government programs invest in them. A key factor is the presence of older, smaller buildings.[13]

The flip side of the coin is also true. If older, smaller buildings can foster success, the loss of old places can lead to a lost sense of community. Former National Trust president Richard Moe wrote in *Changing Places*:

> Like individuals, a community can fall victim to amnesia, can lose the memory of what it was, and thereby lose touch with what it is and what it was meant to be. The loss of community memory happens most frequently and most dramatically in the destruction of familiar landmarks that are themselves familiar reminders of who we were, what we believed, and where we were headed.[14]

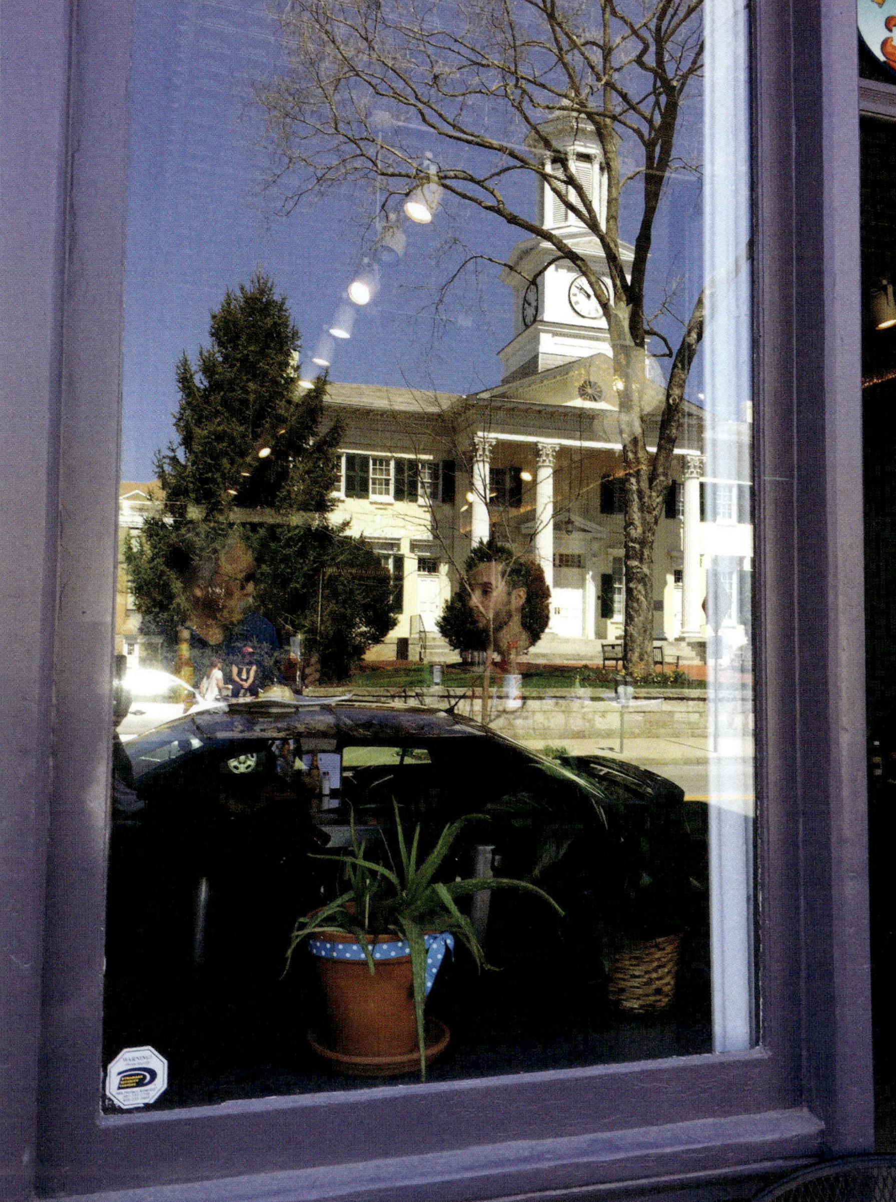

The original building of Shepherd University, in Shepherdstown, West Virginia, an important landmark and gathering place
TOM MAYES/NATIONAL TRUST FOR HISTORIC PRESERVATION

The loss of familiar landmarks means the loss of a community asset that may be most helpful in reversing the decline of a community, and it may diminish the identity that remaining residents share.

Old places foster community by giving people a sense of shared identity through landmarks, history, memory, and stories; by having the attributes that foster community, such as distinctive character and walkability; and by serving as shared places where people meet and gather. In her report about historic preservation, Sandra Shannon wrote,

> community satisfaction has been found to be significantly associated with a person's overall quality of life. Its effect on quality of life is second only to marital satisfaction. It might be easy to brush off preference as something that is a low priority to people in the grand scheme of things, but it appears to actually matter to people in a deep way,

and from a planning standpoint, this humanistic element should be an important consideration.[15]

If community is "shared experience . . . expressed in terms of a common physical place," old places are crucial. Old places are where people, time, and place intertwine to form community.

NOTES

1. Dennis Hockman, interview with author, May 10, 2013.
2. Just ask people from Takoma Park, an old town near Washington, D.C., or Georgetown, D.C., or the neighborhood of Capitol Hill. Each has a distinct personality.
3. See Save the Post Office, accessed February 28, 2015, www.savethepostoffice.com.
4. Wendell Berry, *The Long-Legged House* (Berkeley, CA: Counterpoint Press, 2012), Google e-book, 61.
5. Paul Goldberger, "Cities, Time and Architecture," A speech for the Nelson-Atkins Museum, Kansas City, MO, 2007.
6. Sandra Shannon, "A Survey of the Public: Preference for Old and New Buildings, Attitudes about Historic Preservation, and Preservation-Related Engagement" (master's thesis, University of Southern California, December 2014), 99–100.
7. For more on the important role that post offices play, see Save the Post Office, accessed February 28, 2015, www.savethepostoffice.com. Professor Steve Hutkins, who operates the website, emphasizes the meeting place aspect of post offices, as well as their historic and artistic significance.
8. Brian Wilson, "Milton Residents Fight to Keep Milton's Community Identity," Rutherford County Tennessee Historical Society, accessed February 15, 2015, http://rutherfordtnhistory.org/milton-residents-fight-to-keep-miltons-community-identity.
9. Jeffrey Soule, "Using the Historic Urban Landscape Approach: Context and Culture As a Framework," Sustaining Places, American Planning Association, accessed March 8, 2015, http://blogs.planning.org/sustainability/2014/11/20/using-the-historic-urban-landscape-approach-context-and-culture-as-a-framework/?utm_source=rss&utm_medium=rss&utm_campaign=using-the-historic-urban-landscape-approach-context-and-culture-as-a-framework. For more on communities defining their identity, see William Hatcher, "Building and Selling Community Identity," *PATimes*, accessed March 2, 2015, https://patimes.org/building-selling-community-identity.
10. See "The Charter of the New Urbanism," which includes the statement, "We stand for the restoration of existing urban centers and towns within coherent metropolitan regions, the reconfiguration of sprawling suburbs into communities of real neighborhoods and diverse districts, the conservation of natural environments, and the preservation of our built legacy." Congress for the New Urbanism, accessed February 8, 2018, www.cnu.org/who-we-are/charter-new-urbanism.
11. In the rush to focus on the excitement of new places, planners and government officials often have not paid sufficient attention to the real communities—the older places that already exist, which may not be as architecturally sophisticated or aesthetically pleasing. Yet community may exist there. One of the conundrums of the interaction between the preservation field and the smart growth movement

is that the smart growth movement did not seem to acknowledge the reality that many older suburbs function very well and are successful communities where people love to live.

12. Charles R. Wolfe, *Urbanism without Effort* (Washington, DC: Island Press E-ssentials, 2013), Kindle locations 426–29.
13. "Older, Smaller, Better," Preservation Green Lab, National Trust for Historic Preservation, accessed February 18, 2018, https://savingplaces.org/stories/preservation-tips-tools-older-smaller-better-new-findings-preservation-green-lab#.WosvcUly7oo.
14. Richard Moe and Carter Wilkie, *Changing Places: Rebuilding Community in the Age of Sprawl* (New York: Henry Holt, 1997), 261.
15. Shannon, "A Survey of the Public," 102.

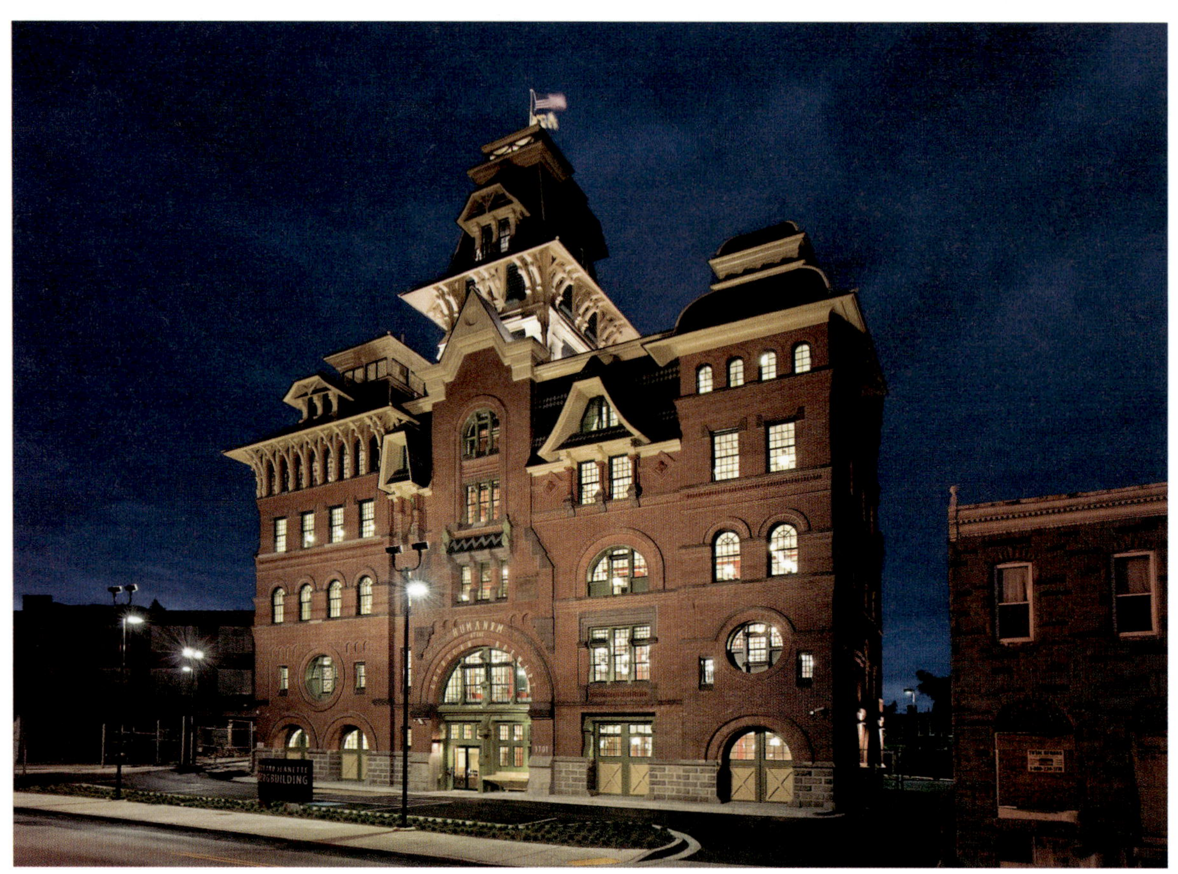

The American Brewery building in Baltimore, Maryland, a project of the National Trust Community Investment Corporation
PAUL BURK

Economics

OLD PLACES support a sound, sustainable, and vibrant economy.

In writing this series of essays about why old places matter, I have intentionally saved the discussion of how old places support a sustainable and vibrant economy for last. Why? Because the other fundamental reasons for keeping, using, reusing, and preserving old places are given short shrift, and professional preservationists often jump right to the argument that saving old places is economically beneficial, assuming that the economic argument is the only one that decision makers want to hear. It seems to me that starting a discussion about the importance of saving an old place with the economic rationale immediately positions people who care about old places on the defensive, as if old places are worth keeping only for economic reasons. And often the economic justification is assessed by narrow and limited economic measurements that don't fully take the broader economic—and other—values of old places into account.[1]

Old places are deeply beneficial to people because of the way they give us a sense of continuity, identity, and belonging; because they inspire us with awe, beauty, and sacredness; because they tell us about history, ancestry, and learning; and because they foster healthy, sustainable communities. Not all of these "nonuse values" can be fully measured economically (yet)—although increasingly, people are trying. Keeping and using old places is good for people for those reasons, even if the historic places can't fully pay for themselves or if they require subsidies or other public support. Fortunately, there seems to be a growing desire to measure and weigh "nonuse values," as economists call these not easily measurable values.[2]

As Randall Mason, chair of the graduate program in historic preservation at the University of Pennsylvania, wrote in a study on preservation and economics for the Brookings Institution in 2005,

> Historic preservation is organized primarily to sustain and create cultural values, like historical associations, senses of place, cultural symbolism, the aesthetic and artistic qualities of architecture, and the like. Studying the economics of this (or any other part of the cultural sector) amounts to calculating the incalculable, or pricing the priceless. Economic analyses can easily determine partial or proxy values for the full value of historic preservation, but what do these tell us? Are they sufficient or even useful?[3]

That we must justify saving the old places that give us a sense of belonging and identity by showing that they support our economy is a sign of just how wholly commercial our American society is.

But justify we must. Although I don't think we should lead with the economic rationales, we still need to have them in the toolbox for those who won't accept the other reasons why old places are beneficial. Fortunately, as Donovan Rypkema, real estate consultant and principal of PlaceEconomics puts it,

> The good news is historic preservation is good for the economy. In the last 15 years dozens of studies have been conducted throughout the United States, by different analysts, using different methodologies. But the results of those studies are remarkably consistent—historic preservation is good for the local economy. From this large and growing body of research, the positive impact of historic preservation on the economy has been documented in six broad areas: (1) jobs, (2) property values,

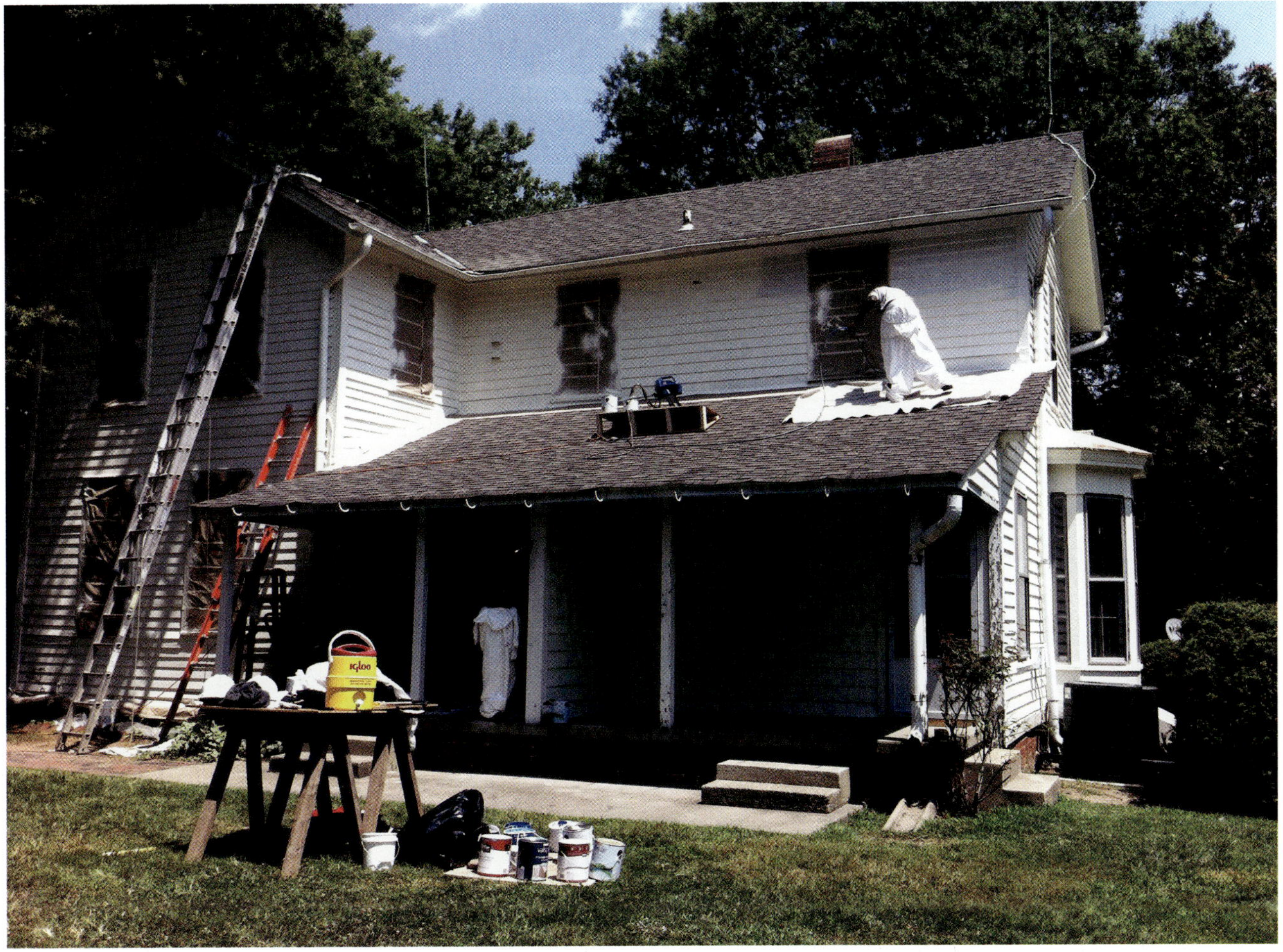

A HOPE (hands-on preservation experience) crew of the National Trust working at Grandview, a house on the grounds of the National Trust Historic Site, Woodlawn Plantation
TOM MAYES/NATIONAL TRUST FOR HISTORIC PRESERVATION

(3) heritage tourism, (4) environmental impact, (5) social impact, and (6) downtown revitalization.[4]

Although I won't follow Rypkema's list of six reasons exactly (the National Trust's website lists twelve),[5] here's a quick review of six key reasons that keeping and reusing old places is good for the economy.

1. *Jobs, income, state and local taxes.* Rehabilitation of older buildings produces higher paying jobs than new construction, and the money tends to stay in the local economy. Because rehabilitation of historic buildings generally requires a higher skill set, wages produced with rehabilitation generally are higher and remain in the local economy more. As the fiscal year 2012 annual report on the economic impact of the rehabilitation tax credit states:

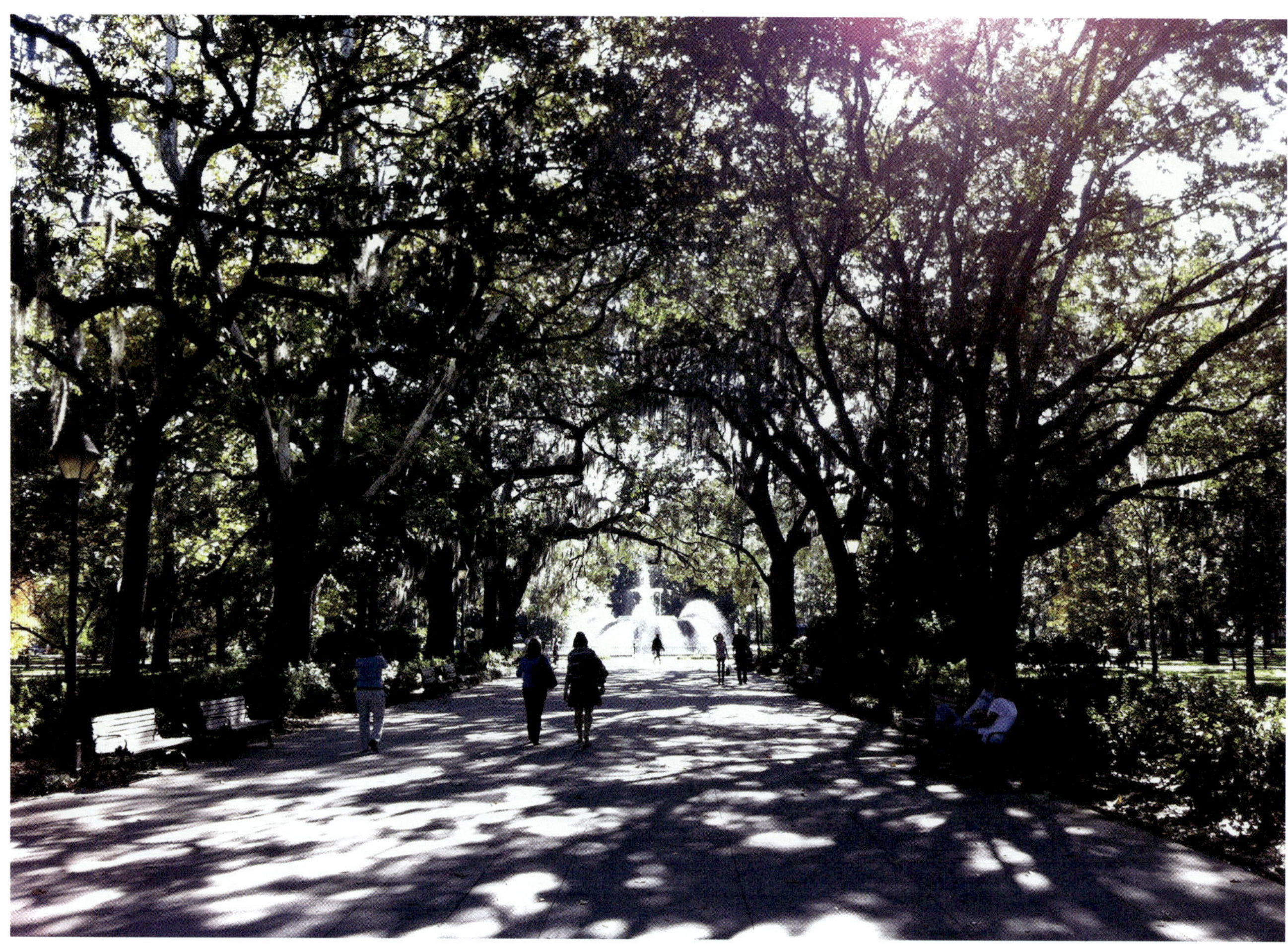

Savannah, Georgia, draws tourists because of the beauty and charm of its historic parks, buildings, and streetscapes
TOM MAYES/NATIONAL TRUST FOR HISTORIC PRESERVATION

Numerous studies conducted by Rutgers University have shown that in many parts of the country, a $1 million investment in historic rehabilitation yields markedly better effects on employment, income, GSP, and state and local taxes than an equal investment in new construction or many other economic activities (e.g., manufacturing or services).[6]

2. *Heritage tourism*. Whether people go to old places to experience the awe of the sacred or transcendental beauty, for incomparable opportunities to learn, to spur their imaginations, or simply to experience a place that has maintained a sense of distinctiveness, old places are destinations for tourism and have been so for millennia. The economic benefits of heritage tourism are unparalleled. As Donovan Rypkema has said, "Wherever heritage tourism has been evaluated, this basic tendency is observed: heritage visitors stay longer, spend more

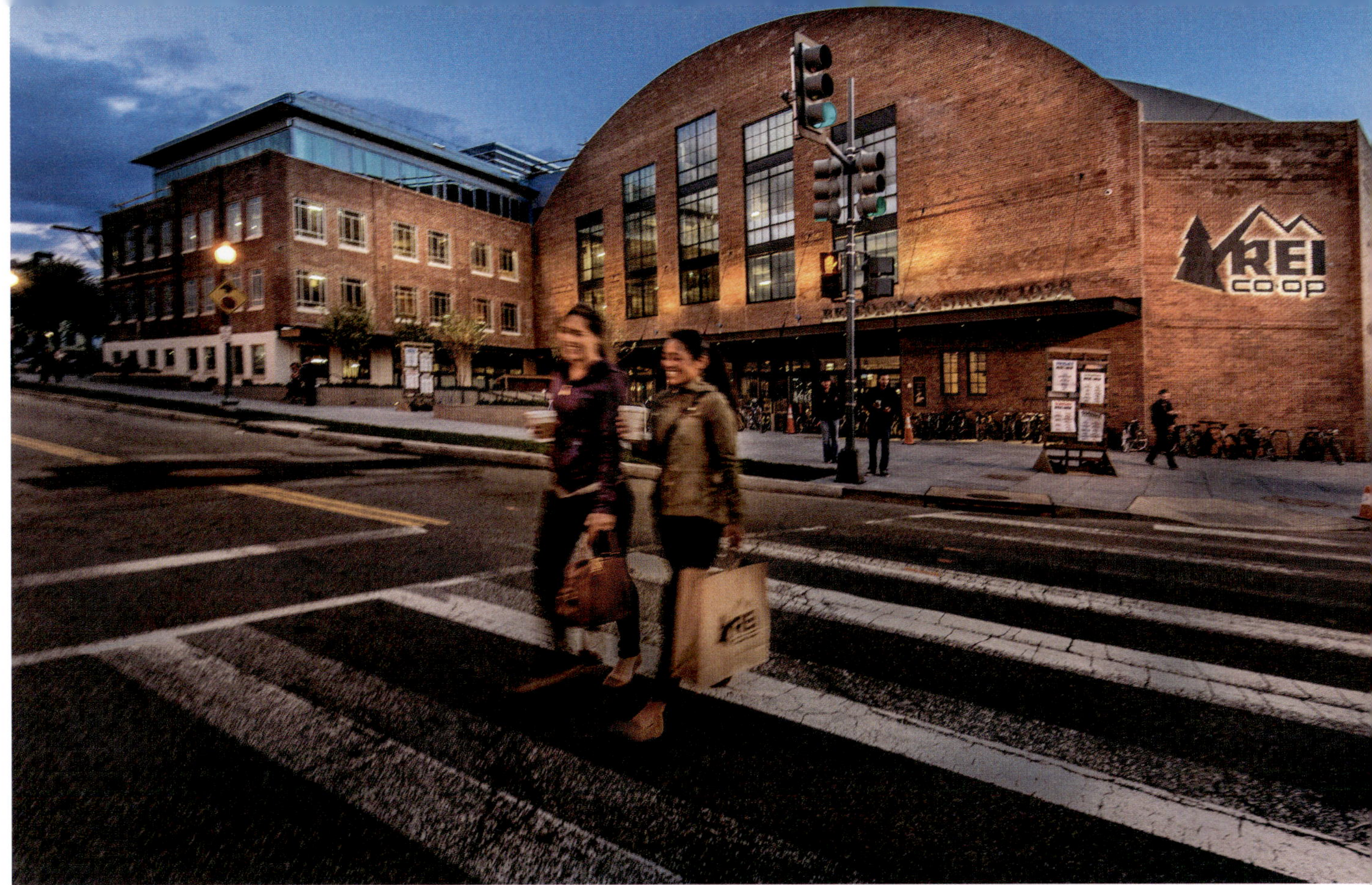

The Uline Arena, in Washington, D.C., was recently rehabilitated and reused
SAM KITTNER

per day, and, therefore, have a significantly greater per trip economic impact."[7] The World Bank report, *The Economics of Uniqueness*, emphasizes that heritage tourism is an important economic development strategy, particularly because "tourism development . . . requires less capital, infrastructure, and skilled labor."[8] And there's the sustainable benefit—for everyone—of saving a community's sense of history, distinctiveness, and identity.

3. *Revitalization.* For decades, older communities have used their historic buildings and streetscapes as assets for revitalization, providing a greater diversity of income and cultural background in neighborhoods, increasing property values, increasing job opportunities.[9] As the website for the Main Street program says, "the cumulative success . . . of the Main Street programs on the local level has earned a reputation as one of the most powerful economic revitalization tools in the nation."[10]
4. *Attracting talent and investment.* According to *The Economics of Uniqueness*, heritage-related projects "contribute to urban livability, attracting talent, and providing an enabling environment for job creation." As Richard Florida and others have emphasized, creative people are the talent that drives the new economy, and creative people are attracted to places that have authenticity. Businesses located in places that are perceived as good places to live, with a sense of

authenticity, have an edge in attracting talent and investment. Or as the World Bank report puts it: "heritage is a differentiator that attracts talent to cities."[11]

5. *Property values.* One of the main purposes cited in preservation statutes as a rationale for historic preservation is that it stabilizes and supports property values. Studies throughout the United States show that this is generally true, with property values in historic districts rising more consistently than in areas that are not historic districts. In addition, studies show that historic districts maintain their value during times of real estate devaluation, such as the recent recession, and recover more rapidly.[12]
6. *Business incubation.* As the Preservation Green Lab report *Older, Smaller, Better* recently concluded, older smaller buildings are critical to the incubation of small businesses, which are the primary job creators in the U.S. economy.[13]

This is the briefest summary of some of the economic benefits of old places, yet it makes a powerful and forward-looking case for the economic benefits of keeping and reusing old places. Scores of studies and reports provide both backup and caveats for these conclusions and can be found from a wide variety of sources.[14] Combined with the many other benefits—the benefits that are hard to measure economically, which are deeply beneficial for people—keeping and retaining old places seems like a no-brainer.

I object to the notion that everything in life has to be reduced to an economic equation, but imagine if these studies could capture the full *value* of the benefits old places give people—the sense of identity and belonging, the awe of beauty, the creativity and imagination? The valuation would be, as Randall Mason put it, "calculating the incalculable, or pricing the priceless."

NOTES

1. For insightful discussions of the limits, opportunities, and current innovations in measuring the economics of preservation, see Guido Licciardi and Rana Amirtahmasebi, eds., *The Economics of Uniqueness* (Washington, DC: World Bank, 2012).
2. The fact that the rehabilitation tax credit was retained in the tax act enacted in late 2017 may be evidence of how much the economic and other values are recognized by the public and by Congress. See Shaw Sprague, "Determined Advocacy Preserves the Historic Tax Credit," National Trust for Historic Preservation, December 20, 2017, https://savingplaces.org/stories/determined-advocacy-preserves-the-historic-tax-credit#.WpMThUly74g.
3. Randall Mason, *Economics and Historic Preservation: A Guide and Review of the Literature* (Washington, DC: Brookings Institution, 2005), 8, accessed March 29, 2015, www.brookings.edu/research/reports/2005/09/metropolitanpolicy-mason.

4. Caroline Cheong, Donovan Rypkema, and Randall Mason, "Measuring the Economics of Preservation: Recent Findings," Advisory Council on Historic Preservation, June 2011, 1.
5. "12 Economic Benefits of Historic Preservation," National Trust for Historic Preservation, accessed April 8, 2015, my.preservation nation.org/site/DocServer/Economic_Benefits_of_HP_April_2011.pdf?docID=9023.
6. "Annual Report on the Economic Impact of the Federal Historic Tax Credit for FY 2013," National Park Service and Rutgers University, Edward J. Bloustein School of Planning and Public Policy, 2013, accessed April 5, 2015, www.nps.gov/tps/tax-incentives/taxdocs/economic-impact-2013.pdf, 7. See also the 2016 annual report, "Annual Report on the Economic Impact of the Federal Historic Tax Credit for FY 2016," National Park Service, accessed February 25, 2018, www.nps.gov/tps/tax-incentives/taxdocs/economic-impact-2016.pdf.
7. Donovan Rypkema, "The Economics of Historic Preservation," keynote address, Alexandria Historic Preservation Conference and Town Meeting, May 5, 2007.
8. Licciardi and Amirtahmasebi, *The Economics of Uniqueness*, 183.
9. I recognize and acknowledge the concern that revitalization strategies may result in gentrification, the displacement of existing residents because of increased rents or property taxes. Although the complex topic is outside the scope of this brief essay, it deserves additional attention, and it has and will continue to be addressed and studied. For an introduction, see Donovan Rypkema's "Heritage Conservation and Property Values," in *The Economics of Uniqueness*, ed. Guido Licciardi and Rana Amirtahmasebi (Washington, DC: World Bank, 2012), 125–38.
10. The National Main Street Center conducts research to document this by annually collecting statistical information on the preservation, revitalization, and economic activities in local Main Street programs throughout the country. These estimates are based on cumulative statistics gathered from 1980 to December 31, 2016, for all designated Main Street communities nationwide.

    Dollars reinvested (total reinvestment in physical improvements from public and private sources): $74.73 billion
    Number of building rehabilitations: 276,790
    Net gain in jobs: 614,716
    Net gain in businesses: 138,303
    Reinvestment Ratio: $26.43: $1

    "Reinvestment on the Rise," Main Street America, accessed February 18, 2018, www.mainstreet.org/mainstreetimpact.
11. Rypkema, "Heritage Conservation and Property Values," xxiii.
12. See several studies at www.placeeconomics.com. Accessed February 8, 2018.
13. "Older, Smaller, Better," accessed February 18, 2018, http://forum.savingplaces.org/connect/community-home/librarydocuments/viewdocument?DocumentKey=83ebde9b-8a23-458c-a70f-c66b46b6f714, 31–34.
14. A good beginning point, which will refer to other studies, is Cheong, Rypkema, and Mason's "Measuring the Economics of Preservation" and Randall Mason's *Economics and Historic Preservation*.

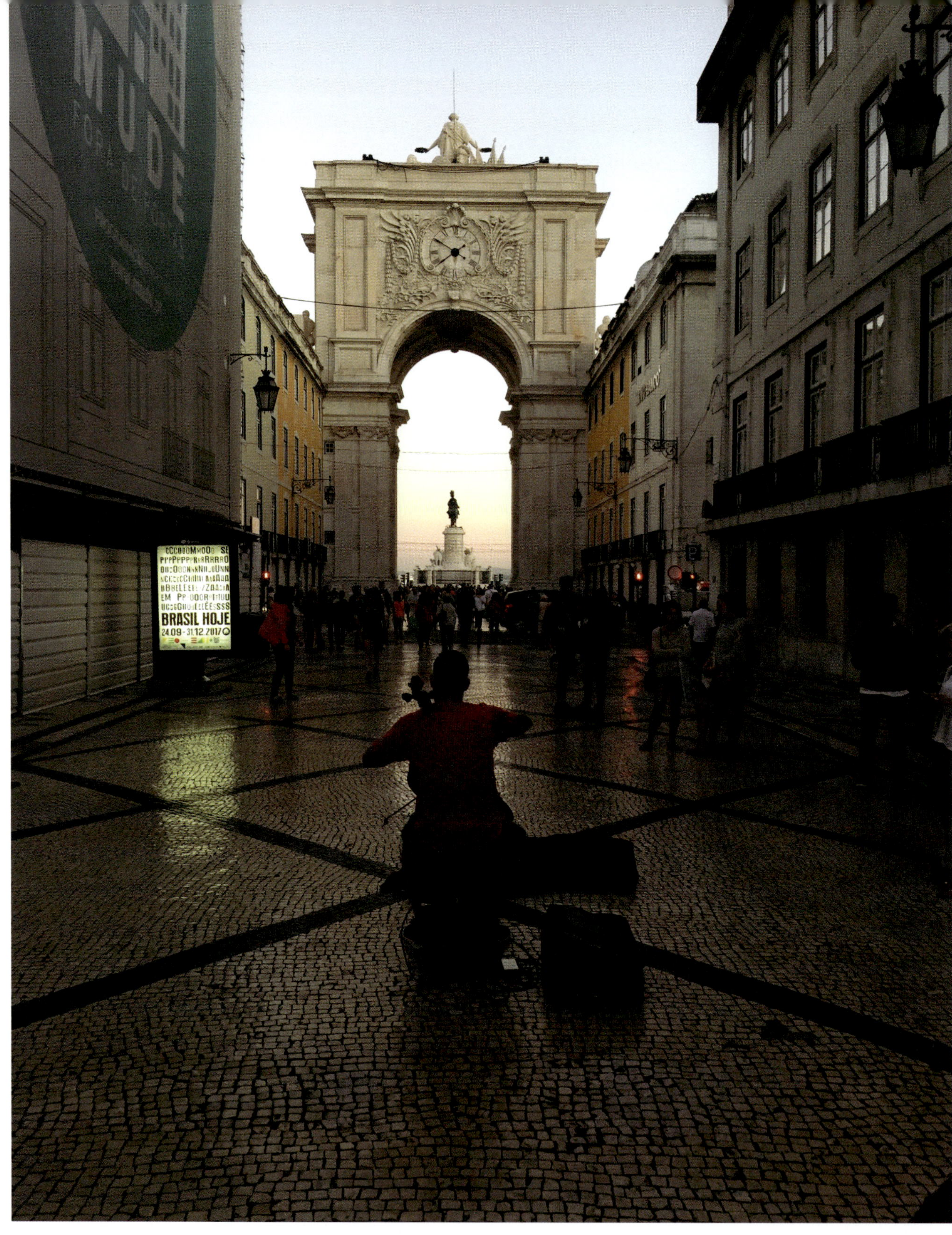

A street in Lisbon, Portugal, leading to the main square, the Praca do Comercio
TOM MAYES/NATIONAL TRUST FOR HISTORIC PRESERVATION

Epilogue

OLD PLACES matter.

Even as a dedicated and lifelong preservationist, researching and writing these essays led me to a surprising conclusion: old places are more important to people—and for more reasons—than I'd thought. The feelings of continuity, memory, and identity from old places gives us a sense of who we are. The experience of beauty and the awe of the sacred at old places deepens our connections to a broader world and fosters a sense of empathy with others. Knowing the places where our ancestors are from gives people a deep sense of belonging. Learning history at the places where history happened is a viscerally memorable experience that stays with us for the rest of our lives. The simple act of continuing to use an existing place is one of the most effective things people can do for a more sustainable world. Old places inspire creativity and foster a flourishing economy. The bottom line is that old places matter for more reasons than we generally assume. As such, the preservation of old places is not just something "nice" to do; it provides profound material, emotional, sociological, and spiritual benefits for all.

I said in the introduction that this collection of essays was a journey. When I began, I hoped to help provide people with ideas, words, and phrases to express their deeply held feelings about the old places that ground them in their lives. Although the essays in this book highlight some of the more profound impacts these places have on us, I've always said that there may be as many reasons why places matter as there are people and places. The relationship between people and old places is so encompassing that all we may be able to hope for are glimpses of the larger intertwined codependent relationship.

Nonetheless, like all journeys, there were discoveries along the way. Some of these glimpses seemed to point to a broader understanding of why places matter, as well as ideas that I think are worth more thought and reflection. Here are a few discoveries and directions from my viewpoint.

Preservation is a vast field. First, preservation is a much larger field than its traditional boundaries suggest, so we should listen to both intentional and "accidental" preservationists about why old places matter to them.[1] Everyday people—mayors, shop owners, housing advocates, planners, developers, brewers, philosophers, historians, architects, politicians, environmentalists, sustainability experts, environmental psychologists, sociologists, neighborhood advocates, artists, writers, composers—all have their own profound connections to the old places around us, filtered through their own experiences and pursuits. The field of historic preservation could become larger still—more diverse, more influential, and, perhaps most importantly, more responsive to the human needs that can be served by old places—if we listen to and collaborate with these many other voices.

Preservation is for people. Listening to people from all walks of life talk about why they care about old places led me to a different way of thinking about preservation. Perhaps most simply, I came to realize that we save old places not for the old places themselves, but for what they can do for people. This idea, which I heard reinforced by many different voices when the National Trust hosted listening sessions throughout the country in 2016 about the future of preservation, became the central focus of the National Trust's guidebook for the next fifty years: *Preservation for People: A Vision for the Future.*[2] Though this idea may seem obvious to those who are not practicing professionals in historic preservation, it represents a profound philosophical shift for the field. It encourages us to see through the bricks and mortar of an old place to focus on how these places help people flourish.

Old places support well-being. The cluster of ideas about continuity, identity, and memory seems to lie at the heart of why old places matter so deeply to people. In thinking about these ideas, it became apparent that old places support people's mental and emotional health. Although people may have recognized this idea intuitively throughout history, the preservation field is only beginning to study the relationship between our work and mental and emotional health.[3] It is my hope that we continue to forge connections with health scholars and practitioners and deepen our understanding of the role of old places in supporting well-being.[4]

Places can be "old" in only one generation. As I pondered why people were fighting to save Eastland Mall in Charlotte, invoking the same language of identity and memory I was using for places that were officially designated as historic, I realized that places may become "old" in only one generation. People develop relationships with places—place attachment and place identity—within their lifetimes. That's why we see people lament the passing of the malls, doctors' offices, schools, and other places that they knew growing up but that we may not yet think have architectural or historical significance. It seems to take only about thirty years for people to feel attached to places, which coincides with the time frame when places seem most vulnerable to demolition and loss. If we begin to think of how preservation can support a sense of continuity, stability, and memory, it may change the way we view the time periods for considering a place as historic, such as the National Register's fifty-year rule, and the idea of a period of significance that is tied to past events. The reality, as David Brown, chief preservation officer for the National Trust, frequently states is that the period of significance is *now*.

Old places can concurrently foster both much-needed stability and welcome change. Preservation is about managing change to keep the places that people value while still allowing for transitions that people also crave and need. My eyes have been opened to the role that preservation plays in facilitating change, from the way the revitalization of one important building in a disinvested community can improve the lives of everyone around, to how the preservation of a resource such as New York City's High Line can spur radical redevelopment and increased density, to the way the recognition of a previously unknown historic place can enfranchise an entire community of people who has felt unseen.[5]

The green benefits of building reuse are substantial and underrecognized. The sustainability rationale for retaining old buildings has the capacity to fundamentally change historic preservation practice. One of the reasons old places matter is because reusing old places is good for the planet: as the saying goes, "the greenest building is the one that's already built." If our society increasingly recognizes the inherent environmental benefits of reusing existing buildings and communities, we are likely to save many more buildings. Yet that may also challenge preservationists to embrace tools, such as ordinances that prohibit demolition, that don't impose current preservation standards.[6] My colleague Jim Lindberg, who heads the National Trust's Preservation Green Lab, frequently advocates for a changed paradigm—from an assumption of demolition to an assumption of reuse. If we simply continue to reuse buildings rather than heedlessly turning them into rubble, we satisfy many of the most fundamental reasons that old places matter to people.[7]

History and architecture remain vitally important but capture only some of the reasons that old places matter. Our existing preservation tools don't seem to fully capture all the reasons that old places matter to people. For example, the two primary reasons most often used to justify the preservation of places—architecture and history—albeit immensely important in their own right, support only some of the other fundamental reasons that old places matter to people as a secondary effect. If places are important to people because they provide a sense of continuity, memory, belonging, and identity, we may be failing to recognize countless other places that are not architecturally or historically significant but that are also vitally important for people's psychological and social well-being. Although many of our preservation tools already include the idea of culture as a criterion for recognizing and saving places, that concept has never been fully explored and incorporated into our practices. I urge the field to venture more deeply into the idea of culture—and similar concepts such as intangible heritage—to preserve more places for reasons of stability, continuity, memory, and identity.

Some reasons that we don't talk about as much today remain deeply important to people. Some of the reasons that old places matter to people aren't talked about as much as they used to be (perhaps because we feel forced to justify saving places for economic reasons), yet they remain important and deeply meaningful to people.

Beauty. Preservation regulation is sometimes referred to as aesthetic regulation, although rarely these days do we justify our work by talking about beauty. Yet encountering beauty remains a fundamental and positive experience for people, an idea that is increasingly supported by social science and neuroscience studies and may even deepen our sense of empathy with others.

Sacredness. Similarly, the idea of saving an old place because of its spiritual qualities and associations tends to be limited to certain situations in American preservation practice, such as the recognition of sites sacred to Native Americans. Yet the experience of sacredness found in old places is fundamentally positive for people and could be invoked more often.[8]

Ancestry. At one time the preservation movement openly advocated for the saving of places because we could find ties to our ancestors (or at least some people's ancestors) there. More recently, conducting genealogy research has become widely popular across a broad spectrum of the population, and people are interested in visiting places where their ancestors lived, worked, fought, worshiped, and were buried. In visiting these places, they find ties to identity and belonging that are important to their sense of who they are.

Old places inspire creativity and help the economy. Other purposes that we haven't fully developed, such as the way old places spur creativity, may have untapped capacity to demonstrate how they help people flourish. We've known for decades that there is a connection between old places and entrepreneurial activity. Jane Jacobs wrote about the need for cities to have smaller, older buildings to incubate and support new ideas.[9] Richard Florida has written about the way drivers of the creative economy are drawn to older places.[10] Recent work by the National Trust's Preservation Green lab further supports this notion with studies of the important role that older, smaller buildings play in bolstering the creative economy.[11] At the same time, we've all seen countless examples of old places providing inspiration for creativity. Creativity is an exciting and forward-looking reason to save and reuse old places.

Preservation is also about making old places good for people. Though I am passionate about the importance of old places, I readily acknowledge that old places are only part of what makes a place work for people. Safety, good food, accessible transportation, health care, jobs, education, recreation, and green space are all important components of a whole place as well. Some older communities do not include all these critical components, and people suffer as a result. All too often, the place is blamed. In my view, while helping old places play their many unique roles, preservationists should also foster the myriad other conditions that allow communities to flourish, whether by promoting safe streets, access to transportation, healthy food, or green space. Then the untapped potential of these old places can be fully realized.

Preservation may be about reconnecting people to place. The work of preservation should include both maintaining places and forging the connections between people and place, so that they are not alienated from one another. In some disinvested communities, people do not feel a connection to the old places around them. Sometimes this is because of the harsh reality of racial discrimination: because residents do not see themselves valued in their communities and feel disconnected from the old places surrounding them that represented an unjust system. Sometimes preservation work may require healing the connection among present-day residents, their identity, and the place around them. Perhaps this is what we have always done through new historical research and new information about historic districts—help people begin to see a connection to their communities through learning about them and valuing them.

One underused way to reconnect people to place is to facilitate opportunities for people to express what places matter to them. What are the places that residents value in their communities? The places chosen may not be those that would be identified from an architectural or historical perspective but may be significant culturally and deserve our attention.[12]

New research and new technologies will tell us more about people and old places. In considering how old places are good for people, there are plenty of innovative directions for research, from the mental health impacts of identification with place, to the innate preferences people may have for certain forms of architecture, to understanding how the brain perceives age and time in place. Many of these directions will be informed by the explosion of new research and writing about people and place. With new technologies, we are at the cusp of being able to measure people's reactions to actual places in real time, to measure their heart rate, respiration, and temperature as they experience different places. Some of this nascent research seems to confirm what preservationists have known intuitively for years—such as the close relationship between memory and place. Other recent studies suggest that people are hardwired to prefer premodern buildings, perhaps because their facades read as people and faces.[13] New neuroscience studies also seem to confirm the truth of Ruskin's thoughts about the hand of the maker being present in the materials; the brain reenacts the gestures and actions of the maker when it perceives the craft in the built environment, whether those signs of craft are the carpenter's plane marks on a plank or the mason's marks on stone.[14] I encourage preservationists to foster more of this groundbreaking research, recognizing that these findings may challenge many assumptions and current practices in preservation.

These ideas for further exploration are simply some of the directions suggested by the essays, and they reflect the wide spectrum of reasons old places matter to people. As these essays were always intended to start a conversation, I expect that you have many more and hope you take the time to share them.

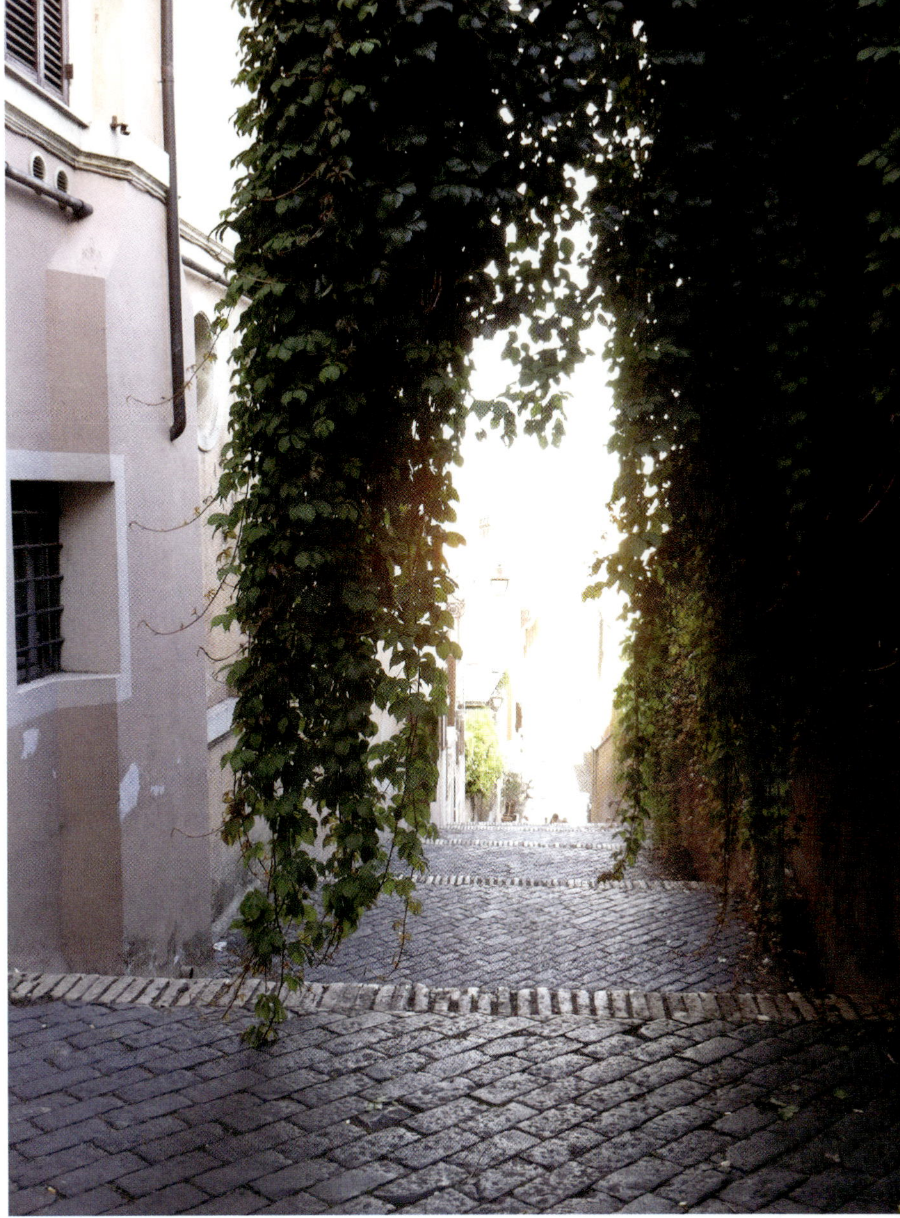

A stair street in Rome
TOM MAYES/NATIONAL TRUST FOR HISTORIC PRESERVATION

Along those lines, shortly after the initial essays were issued online, the National Trust's *Forum Journal* devoted an issue to why old places matter, with other writers and thinkers contributing articles.[15] Eric Nathan's musical composition *Why Old Places Matter*, commissioned by the Boston Symphony Chamber Players, premiered at Jordan Hall in Boston.[16] Max Page's *Why Preservation Matters* references the "why old places matter" essays in advocating for historic preservation to take a stronger role in social justice. Stephanie Meeks and Kevin Murphy's *The Past and Future City* advocates for historic preservation as a necessary tool to help make our communities better for all people and has already had a positive and powerful impact on the field.

I hope many others continue to explore why old places matter to them, and I look forward to continuing this journey. It's part of the magic and power of old places that we can't fully capture all the meanings they have for us. These meanings are so fully embedded in our lives that sometimes we barely recognize their influence. Writing these essays brought back visceral memories of the many old places that have mattered to me, from the smell of cedar trees on our family farm in North Carolina, to the warmth of sunlight on the brick facades of Washington, D.C.'s rowhouses, to the splash of the water in the fountains at the American Academy in Rome. These old places are part of who I am. I hope this book reminds people of places that matter to them and provides a glimpse of the ways old places help us live in the world.

During an interview at the American Academy in Rome with Juhani Pallasmaa, the Finnish architect and architectural theorist, Juhani used several phrases that struck me. He said, "the self doesn't end at the skin—the world is part of yourself." Then, "the real value of old places is the sense of self and the confidence in time." And finally, "if we can see the past, it makes us believe in the future."

I hope these essays help to make the invisible visible, help us to see the essential parts of ourselves that lie outside our skin in the old places around us, and in those places, to find a better, richer, and more meaningful future.

Now that this leg of the journey has concluded, why don't you start us off on the next one? Tell me, why do old places matter to you?[17]

NOTES

1. "The Accidental Preservationist: Artists, Artisans, Outliers and the Future of Historic Preservation," James Marston Fitch Foundation, accessed February 11, 2018, http://fitchfoundation.org/lecutres-symposia/the-accidental-preservationist-2014.
2. "Preservation for People: A Vision for the Future," National Trust for Historic Preservation, accessed December 27, 2017, http://forum.savingplaces.org/blogs/stephanie-k-meeks/2017/05/18/presenting-preservation-for-people-a-vision-for-the-future.
3. Tom Mayes, "A PastForward Reading List: Introduction to Health and Historic Preservation," National Trust for Historic Preservation, accessed February 17, 2018. http://forum.savingplaces.org/blogs/tom-mayes/2017/08/08/pastforward-reading-list-introduction-to-health-and-historic-preservation.
4. In collaboration with scholars including Jeremy Wells of the University of Maryland and Lynne Manzo of the University of Washington, the National Trust has been encouraging additional research in the connection between old places and human well-being. See "Show Me the Studies! Environmental Design Research and Historic Preservation," National Trust for Historic Preservation, July 21, 2017, accessed February 17, 2018. http://forum.savingplaces.org/blogs/tom-mayes/2017/07/21/show-me-the-studies-environmental-design-research-and-historic-preservation.
5. The recognition of historic places is deeply affirming, which is why the identification and designation of places representing previously discriminated against minorities are vitally important to people. The Movement for Black Lives includes in its claim for reparations additional resources for the identification and recognition of "cultural assets and sacred sites such as Black burial grounds; Black towns (e.g., Mound Bayou, Mississippi); houses of worship; meeting halls; one-room schools." "Reparations," Movement for Black Lives, accessed February 22, 2018, https://policy.m4bl.org/reparations/. In 2017, the National Trust created the African American Cultural Heritage Action Fund to "draw attention to the remarkable stories that evoke centuries of African American activism and achievement and to tell our nation's full history." "African American Cultural Heritage Action Fund," National Trust for

Historic Preservation, accessed February 22, 2018, https://savingplaces.org/african-american-cultural-heritage#.Wo7Tfkly7oo. See also "President Obama Designates Stonewall National Monument," Obama White House Archives, accessed February 22, 2018, https://obamawhitehouse.archives.gov/blog/2016/06/24/president-obama-designates-stonewall-national-monument.

6. Tom Mayes, "Changing the Paradigm from Demolition to Reuse—Building Reuse Ordinances," in *Bending the Future: 50 Ideas for the Next 50 Years of Historic Preservation in the United States*, ed. Max Page and Marla R. Miller (Amherst: University of Massachusetts Press, 2016), 162. See also Will Cook and Tom Mayes, "Shifting the Paradigm from Demolition to Reuse: New Tools," National Trust for Historic Preservation, accessed February 17, 2018. http://forum.savingplaces.org/blogs/special-contributor/2017/02/16/shifting-the-paradigm-from-demolition-to-reuse-new-tools.
7. "Preservation Green Lab," National Trust for Historic Preservation, accessed February 17, 2018. https://savingplaces.org/preservation-green-lab#.WohRqEly74g.
8. In 2015, Partners for Sacred Places, in collaboration with the National Trust, created the National Fund for Sacred Places, which provides training and capital grants for historic sacred places. "National Fund for Sacred Places/About," Partners for Sacred Places, accessed February 22, 2018, https://fundforsacredplaces.org.
9. Jane Jacobs, *The Death and Life of Great American Cities* (New York: Random House, 1961), 186–87.
10. Richard Florida, "What Draws Creative People? Quality of Place," UrbanLand, October 11, 2012, https://urbanland.uli.org/industry-sectors/what-draws-creative-people-quality-of-place.
11. National Trust Preservation Green Lab, "Older, Smaller, Better," National Trust for Historic Preservation, accessed February 18, 2018, https://savingplaces.org/stories/preservation-tips-tools-older-smaller-better-new-findings-preservation-green-lab#.WosvcUly7oo.
12. See, for example, Charles R. Wolfe, *Seeing the Better City* (Washington, DC: Island Press, 2016).
13. See, for example, Melody Warnick, *This Is Where You Belong* (New York: Viking 2016); Colin Ellard, *Places of the Heart: The Psychogeography of Everyday Life* (New York: Bellevue Literary Press, 2015); Justin Hollander and Ann Sussman, *Cognitive Architecture* (New York: Routledge Taylor & Francis Group, 2015); Sarah Robinson and Juhani Pallasmaa, eds., *Mind in Architecture: Neuroscience, Embodiment, and the Future of Design* (Cambridge, MA: MIT Press, 2015); Harry Francis Mallgrave, *The Architect's Brain: Neuroscience, Creativity, and Architecture* (Chichester, UK: Wiley-Blackwell, 2011); Nikos A. Salingaros, *A Theory of Architecture* (Kathmandu, Nepal: Vajra Books, 2013).
14. Vittorio Gallese and Alessandro Gattara, "Embodied Simulation, Aesthetics, and Architecture: An Experimental Aesthetic Approach," in *Mind in Architecture*, ed. Sarah Robinson and Juhani Pallasmaa, 171–72.
15. Stephanie Meeks, president of the National Trust, in the foreword shared the personal story of her family's homestead in Colorado and the deep sense of belonging it provides. Juhani Pallasmaa, the Finnish architect and architectural theorist, wrote about dwelling in time and the need for old places to help people domesticate time. Jeremy Wells, professor of historic preservation, wrote about what we either do or do not know from the body of scientific studies examining old places. Max Page, professor at the University of Massachusetts, Amherst, wrote about difficult places and the importance of memory. The musicians Ben Folds and Eric Nathan were interviewed talking about the importance of old places in inspiring music and creativity and transmitting artistic legacies. Ed McMahon wrote about the uniqueness provided by old places in our communities. Germonique Ulmer, the National Trust's vice president for communications, and her team developed a communications toolbox for how

the "why old places matter" essays can be used. "Why Do Old Places Matter?" *Forum Journal* 29, no. 3 (Spring 2015), http://forum.savingplaces.org/blogs/forum-online/2015/04/24/spring-2015-forum-journal-why-do-old-places-matter.

16. Eric Nathan, "Why Old Places Matter," https://youtu.be/dtc9gsrTWns.
17. This epilogue incorporates portions of an article originally published in the spring 2015 *Forum Journal* by the National Trust and has been edited and updated for *Why Old Places Matter*.

Bibliography

Akkurt, Humeyra Birol. "Reconstitution of the Place Identity within the Intervention Efforts in the Historic Built Environment." In *The Role of Place Identity in the Perception, Understanding, and Design of Built Environments*. Edited by Hernan Casakin and Fátima Bernardo. Bentham E-books. https://ebooks.benthamscience.com/book/9781608054l3.

Alexander, Christopher, Sara Ishikawa, and Murray Silverstein. *A Pattern Language: Towns, Buildings, Construction*. New York: Oxford University Press, 1977.

Alliance of Religions and Conservation. www.arcworld.org.

Alter, Lloyd. "Is There a 'Goldilocks Density'—Not Too High, Not Too Low, but Just Right?" Treehugger, November 1, 2011. www.treehugger.com/slideshows/urban-design/is-there-goldi-locks-density-not-too-high-not-too-low-just-right.

American Association for State and Local History. www.aaslh.org.

Ancestry.com. "Americans' Fascination with Family History Is Rapidly Growing." Ancestry.com. Accessed December 22, 2014. http://corporate.ancestry.com/press/press-releases/2005/06/americans-fascination-with-family-history-is-rapidly-growing.

Athill, Diana. *Beauty and a Love of Life*. London: Commission for Architecture and the Built Environment, 2010.

Australia ICOMOS. *The Burra Charter: The Australia ICOMOS Charter for Places of Cultural Significance*. 2013. VIC, Australia.

Bachelard, Gaston. *The Poetics of Space.* Translated by Maria Jolas. Boston: Beacon Press, 1969.

Bakhshi, Hasan. *Beauty: Value beyond Measure?* London: Commission for Architecture and the Built Environment, 2010.

Barthel, Diane. *Historic Preservation: Collective Memory and Historical Identity.* New Brunswick, NJ: Rutgers University Press, 1996.

Belsito, Hannah. "Building Community through Historic Preservation." Lecture, TEDxCLE, Cleveland, April 2011.

Benedict, Cynthia Buttery, and Erin Hudson. "Mt. Taylor Traditional Cultural Property Determination of Eligibility for the National Register of Historic Places." February 4, 2008.

Benfield, F. Kaid. *People Habitat.* Washington, DC: People Habitat Communications, 2014.

Benson, Susan Porter, Stephen Brier, and Roy Rosenzweig. *Presenting the Past: Essays on History and the Public.* Philadelphia: Temple University Press, 1986.

Berry, Wendell. *The Long-Legged House.* Berkeley, CA: Counterpoint Press, 2012. Google e-book.

Byrne, David. *How Music Works.* San Francisco: McSweeney's, 2012.

Carlino, Gerald A., and Albert Saiz. *City Beautiful.* Working paper no. 08-22. Research Department, Federal Reserve Bank of Philadelphia. 2008.

Casakin, Hernan, and Fátima Bernardo, eds. *The Role of Place Identity in the Perception, Understanding, and Design of Built Environments.* Bentham Science Publishers, 2012.

Chatfield-Taylor, Adele. Acceptance Speech. Vincent Scully Prize, National Building Museum, Washington, DC, 2010.

Cheong, Caroline, Donovan Rypkema, and Randall Mason. "Measuring the Economics of Preservation: Recent Findings." Advisory Council on Historic Preservation, June 2011.

Choay, Françoise. *The Invention of the Historic Monument.* Translated by Lauren M. O'Connell. Cambridge: Cambridge University Press, 2001.

Cicero. *The Treatises of M. T. Cicero.* Edited by C. D. Yonge. London: H. G. Bohn, 1853.

Civil War Trust. "FAQs: Battlefield Preservation." www.civilwar.org/about/faqs-battlefield-preservation.

———. "Trace Adkins Forges Links to the Past." *Hallowed Ground.* Summer 2013. Accessed December 22, 2014. www.civilwar.org/aboutus/heroes-of-preservation/trace-adkins-forges-links-to.html.

Claridge, Amanda. *Rome (Oxford Archaeological Guides).* New York: Oxford University Press, 2010.

Congress for the New Urbanism. "The Charter of the New Urbanism." Accessed February 8, 2018. www.cnu.org/who-we-are/charter-new-urbanism.

Cook, William, and Tom Mayes. "Shifting the Paradigm from Demolition to Reuse: New Tools." National Trust for Historic Preservation. Accessed February 17, 2018. http://forum.savingplaces.org/blogs/special-contributor/2017/02/16/shifting-the-paradigm-from-demolition-to-reuse-new-tools.

Cunningham, Sarah Bainter. "The Compass of Reason: Intellectual Interest in the Beautiful As a Mode of Orientation." PhD diss., Vanderbilt University, 2014. http://etd.library.vanderbilt.edu/available/etd-11272004-172937/unrestricted/SCunningham3.pdf.

Cuno, James. "Holy Site, Historic Site: The Challenge of Sarnath," *The Getty*, Spring 2014.

Daughters of the American Revolution. www.dar.org.

Davis, Ben. "Can Rem Koolhaas Save Architecture from Preservation?" *Artinfo.* May 24, 2011.

De Botton, Alain. *The Architecture of Happiness.* London: Penguin Books, 2006.

De la Torre, Marta, and Randall Mason, *Assessing the Values of Cultural Heritage.* Los Angeles: Getty Conservation Institute, 2002.

Dobbins, Hamlett. *Sant'Ivo: June 29th, 2014*. Memphis, TN: H. Dobbins, 2015.

Donofrio, Gregory. "Preservation by Adaptation: Is It Sustainable?" *Change over Time* 2, no. 2 (Fall 2012): 106–31.

Doyon, Scott. "Let's Get Metaphysical: Considering the Value of Soul in Redevelopment." Placemakers. Accessed October 28, 2014. www.placemakers.com/2014/08/11/lets-get-metaphysical.

Dwyer, Owen J. "Symbolic Accretion and Commemoration." *Social & Cultural Geography* 5, no. 3 (2004): 419–35.

Eco, Umberto, ed. *On Beauty*. London: Martin Secker & Warburg, 2004.

Elefante, Carl. "The Greenest Building Is . . . One That Is Already Built," *Forum Journal* 21, no. 4 (Summer 2007).

Ellard, Colin. *Places of the Heart: The Psychogeography of Everyday Life*. New York: Bellevue Literary Press, 2015.

Falkner, Gerhard, and Reynold Reynolds. *The Last Day of the Republic*. Nurnberg: Starfruit Publications, 2011.

Fitch, James Marston. *Historic Preservation: Curatorial Management of the Built World*. New York: McGraw-Hill, 1982.

Fivush, R, M. Duke, and J. Bohanek. "Do You Know . . . The Power of Family History in Adolescent Identity and Wellbeing." *Journal of Family Life* 2010. Accessed December 21, 2014. www.journalof familylife.org/ doyouknow.html#.

Florida, Richard. "What Draws Creative People? Quality of Place." UrbanLand. October 11, 2012. https://urbanland.uli.org/industry-sectors/what-draws-creative-people-quality-of-place.

Folds, Ben. Open Letter. In "Ben Folds' Open Letter: RCA Studio A to Be Sold." *Music Row*, June 24, 2014.

Frumkin, Howard. "Healthy Places: Exploring the Evidence." *American Journal of Public Health* 93, no. 9 (2003): 1451–456.

Gallese, Vittorio, and Alessandro Gattara. "Embodied Simulation, Aesthetics, and Architecture: An Experimental Aesthetic Approach." In *Mind in Architecture: Neuroscience, Embodiment, and the Future of Design*. Edited by Sarah Robinson and Juhani Pallasmaa, 161–79. Cambridge, Massachusetts: MIT Press, 2015.

Goldberger, Paul. "Cities, Time, and Architecture." Speech. Nelson-Atkins Museum, Kansas City, MO, 2007.

———. "Preservation Is Not Just about the Past." Speech. Salt Lake City, April 26, 2007.

———. *Why Architecture Matters*. New Haven, CT: Yale University Press, 2009.

Gray, Martin. "Sacred and Magical Places." *Sacred Sites*. Accessed February 7, 2018. www.sacredsites.com.

———. *Sacred Earth: Places of Peace and Power*. New York: Sterling, 2007.

Gray, Stewart. "Survey and Research Report on the Eastland Mall Signs." Report. Charlotte-Mecklenburg Historic Preservation Foundation, 2013.

Hanna, Stephen P., Vincent J. Del Casino Jr., Casey Selden, and Benjamin Hite. "Representation As Work in 'America's Most Historic City.'" *Social & Cultural Geography* 5, no. 3 (September 2004): 459–81.

Hatcher, William. "Building and Selling Community Identity." *PATimes*. Accessed March 2, 2015. https://patimes.org/building-selling-community-identity.

Hauge, Ashild Lappegard. "Identity and Place: A Critical Comparison of Three Identity Theories." *Architectural Science Review* 50, no. 1 (2007).

Hayden, Dolores. *The Power of Place: Urban Landscapes As Public History*. Cambridge, MA: MIT Press, 1995.

Heidegger, Martin. *Poetry, Language, Thought*. New York: Harper & Row, 1971.

Hersey, George L. *The Lost Meaning of Classical Architecture*. Cambridge, MA: MIT, 1988.

Herzog, Thomas R., and Theresa A. Gale. "Preference for Urban Buildings As a Function of Age and Nature Context." *Environment and Behavior* 28, no. 1 (January 1996): 44–72.

Herzog, Thomas R., and Ronda L. Shier. "Complexity, Age, and Building Preference." *Environment and Behavior* 32, no. 4 (July 2000): 557–75.

Hickey, Dave. *The Invisible Dragon: Four Essays on Beauty*. Los Angeles: Art Issues Press, 1993.

Hoelscher, Steven, and Derek H. Alderman. "Memory and Place: Geographies of a Critical Relationship." *Social & Cultural Geography* 5, no. 3 (September 2004).

Hollander, Justin, and Ann Sussman. *Cognitive Architecture*. New York: Routledge Taylor & Francis, 2015.

Jacobs, Jane. *The Death and Life of Great American Cities*. New York: Random House, 1961.

James Marston Fitch Foundation. "The Accidental Preservationist: Artists, Artisans, Outliers and the Future of Historic Preservation." Accessed February 11, 2018. http://fitchfoundation.org/lecutres-symposia/the-accidental-preservationist-2014.

Jokilehto, Jukka. *A History of Architectural Conservation*. Oxford: Butterworth-Heinemann 1999.

Kaufman, Ned. *Place, Race, and Story: Essays on the Past and Future of Historic Preservation*. New York: Routledge, 2009.

Kennedy, John F. "Remarks at Amherst College October 26, 1963." National Endowment for the Arts. www.arts.gov/about/kennedy-transcript.

Kennicott, Philip. "Mecanoo, Martinez + Johnson to Renovate MLK Library." *Washington Post*, February 18, 2014.

Khazbulatov, Andrey R., and Moldir Nurpeiis. "The Preservation of Cultural Heritage: Continuity and Memory." *International Journal of Social, Behavioral, Educational, Economic, Business and Industrial Engineering* 6, no. 6 (2012): 1026–28.

Kieran, Matthew. "The X Factor: Beauty in Planning." Report. London: Commission for Architecture and the Built Environment, 2010.

Kimmelman, Michael. "The Museum with a Bulldozer's Heart: MoMA's Plan to Demolish Folk Art Museum Lacks Vision." *New York Times*, January 13, 2014.

Koolhaas, Rem. "Cronocaos Preservation." Lecture on Vimeo. Accessed February 27, 2018. http://oma.eu/projects/venice-biennale-2010-cronocaos.

Ladd, Brian. *The Ghosts of Berlin: Confronting German History in the Urban Landscape*. Chicago: University of Chicago Press, 1997.

Lekagul, Apichoke. *Toward Preservation of the Traditional Marketplace: A Preference Study of Traditional and Modern Shopping Environments in Bangkok, Thailand*. Lambert Academic Publishing, 2010.

Levi, Daniel J. "Does History Matter? Perceptions and Attitudes toward Fake Historic Architecture and Historic Preservation." *Journal of Architectural and Planning Research* 22, no. 2 (Summer 2005).

———. "Perceived Authenticity of California Missions." *Focus* 9, no. 1 (2012).

Levi, Daniel J., and Sara Kocher. "Perception of Sacredness at Heritage Religious Sites." *Environment & Behavior* 45, no. 7 (May 23, 2012).

Lewicka, Maria. "Place Attachment: How Far Have We Come in the Last 40 Years?" *Journal of Environmental Psychology* 31 (2011).

———. "Place Attachment, Place Identity, and Place Memory: Restoring the Forgotten City Past." *Journal of Environmental Psychology* 28 (2008).

Licciardi, Guido, and Rana Amirtahmasebi, eds. *The Economics of Uniqueness*. Washington, DC: World Bank, 2012.

Lowenthal, David. *The Past Is a Foreign Country*. New York: Cambridge University Press, 1985.

Mallgrave, Harry Francis. *The Architect's Brain: Neuroscience, Creativity, and Architecture*. Chichester, UK: Wiley-Blackwell, 2011.

Marchand, Trevor H. J. "Process over Product: Case Studies of Traditional Building Practices in Djenné, Mali, and San'a', Yemen." In *Managing Change: Sustainable Approaches to the Conservation of the Built Environment*. Edited by Jeanne Marie Teutonico and Frank G. Matero, 137–59. Los Angeles: Getty Publications, 2003.

Mason, Randall. *Economics and Historic Preservation: A Guide and Review of the Literature*. Washington, DC: Brookings Institution, 2005. Accessed March 29, 2015. www.brookings.edu/research/reports/2005/09/metropolitanpolicy-mason.

Mason, Randall F. "The Future of Preservation." Lecture. Municipal Art Society's Summit for New York City. Lincoln Center, New York, October 2013.

Massachusetts Preservation Coalition and National Trust for Historic Preservation. *Preserving Historic Religious Properties*. June 2005.

Mayes, Tom. "Changing the Paradigm from Demolition to Reuse—Building Reuse Ordinances." In *Bending the Future: 50 Ideas for the Next 50 Years of Historic Preservation in the United States*. Edited by Max Page and Marla R. Miller, 162–65. Amherst: University of Massachusetts Press, 2016.

———. "A PastForward Reading List: Introduction to Health and Historic Preservation." National Trust for Historic Preservation. Accessed February 17, 2018. http://forum.savingplaces.org/blogs/tom-mayes/2017/08/08/pastforward-reading-list-introduction-to-health-and-historic-preservation.

———. "Show Me the Studies! Environmental Design Research and Historic Preservation." National Trust for Historic Preservation, July 21, 2017. Accessed February 17, 2018. http://forum.savingplaces.org/blogs/tom-mayes/2017/07/21/show-me-the-studies-environmental-design-research-and-historic-preservation.

Meeks, Stephanie. "Statement on Confederate Memorials: Confronting Difficult History." National Trust for Historic Preservation. June 19, 2017. https://savingplaces.org/press-center/media-resources/national-trust-statement-on-confederate-memorials#.WpLb8Ely74h.

———. "After Charlottesville: How to Approach Confederate Memorials in Your Community," National Trust for Historic Preservation. August 21, 2017. https://savingplaces.org/stories/after-charlottesville-confederate-memorials#.WpLbjkly74g.

Meeks, Stephanie, with Kevin C. Murphy. *The Past and Future City*. Washington, DC: Island Press, 2016.

Merleau-Ponty, Maurice. *Phenomenology of Perception*. Translated by Colin Smith. London: Routledge, 1962.

Milligan, Melinda J. "Buildings As History: The Place of Collective Memory in the Study of Historic Preservation." *Symbolic Interaction* 30, no. 1 (Winter 2007): 105–23.

Moe, Richard, and Carter Wilkie. *Changing Places: Rebuilding Community in the Age of Sprawl*. New York: Henry Holt, 1997.

Mok, Kimberly. "Cool but Endangered Conical Houses Get Preservation Treatment in Indonesia." Treehugger. May 9, 2013. www.treehugger.com/green-architecture/yori-antar-mbaru-niang-preservation-worok-flores-island-indonesia.html.

Montgomery, Nick. "Summary: Vibrant Matter by Jane Bennet." Cultivating Alternatives. November 28, 2013. http://cultivatingalternatives.com/2013/11/28/summary-vibrant-matter-by-jane-bennett.

Morris, William. *The Society for the Protection of Ancient Buildings Manifesto.* 1877.

———. *William Morris on Architecture.* Edited by Chris Miele. London: Sheffield Academic Press, 1996.

Morris Museum of Art. "The Charleston Renaissance." http://tfaoi.org/newsm1/n1m526.htm.

Movement for Black Lives. "Reparations." Accessed February 22, 2018. https://policy.m4bl.org/reparations.

Mumford, Lewis. *The Culture of Cities.* New York: Harcourt Brace, 1938.

Muschamp, Herbert. "The Secret History of 2 Columbus Circle." *The New York Times,* January 8, 2006.

Nathan, Eric. "Why Old Places Matter." https://youtube/dtc9gsrTWns. Eric Nathan Music. Accessed February 22, 2018. www.ericnathanmusic.com/news.

National Council on Public History. www.ncph.org.

National Main Street Center. "Reinvestment on the Rise." Accessed February 18, 2018. www.mainstreet.org/mainstreetimpact.

National Park Service. "Annual Report on the Economic Impact of the Federal Historic Tax Credit for FY 2016." Accessed February 25, 2018. www.nps.gov/tps/tax-incentives/taxdocs/economic-impact-2016.pdf.

———. "Personal Connections." Accessed February 8, 2018. www.nps.gov/pete/learn/historyculture/reserch.htm.

———. "Teaching with Historic Places." Accessed February 7, 2018. www.nps.gov/nr/twhp/wwwlps.

National Park Service and Rutgers University, Edward J. Bloustein School of Planning and Public Policy. "Annual Report on the Economic Impact of the Federal Historic Tax Credit for FY 2013." 2013. Accessed April 5, 2015. www.nps.gov/tps/tax-incentives/taxdocs/economic-impact-2013.pdf.

National Trust for Historic Preservation. "12 Economic Benefits of Historic Preservation." Accessed April 8, 2015. http://my.preservationnation.org/site/DocServer/Economic_Benefits_of_HP_April_2011.pdf?docID=9023.

———. "African American Cultural Heritage Action Fund." Accessed February 22, 2018. https://savingplaces.org/african-american-cultural-heritage#.Wo7Tfkly7oo.

———. *Forum Journal: Bridging Land Conservation and Historic Preservation* 25, no. 1 (Fall 2010).

———. *Forum Journal: Why Do Old Places Matter?* 29, no. 3 (Spring 2015). http://forum.savingplaces.org/blogs/forum-online/2015/04/24/spring-2015-forum-journal-why-do-old-places-matter.

———. *The Greenest Building: Quantifying the Environmental Value of Building Reuse.* 2011. Accessed June 11, 2018 https://forum. savingplaces.org/connect/communityhome/librarydocuments

———. "Nashville's Music Row," January 16, 2015. https://savingplaces.org/places/nashvilles-music-row/updates/national-treasure-designation-officially-announced-in-nashville#.WnxyPUly6Uk.

———. "Older, Smaller, Better." Accessed February 18, 2018. http://forum.savingplaces.org/connect/community-home/librarydocuments/viewdocument?DocumentKey=83ebde9b-8a23-458c-a70f-c66b46b6f714.

———. "Preservation for People: A Vision for the Future." Accessed December 27, 2017. http://forum.savingplaces.org/blogs/stephanie-k-meeks/2017/05/18/presenting-preservation-for-people-a-vision-for-the-future.

———. "Preservation Green Lab." Accessed February 17, 2018. https://savingplaces.org/preservation-green-lab#.WohRqEly74g.

———. "Welcome to HAHS: Witness Creativity." Historic Artists' Homes & Studio. Accessed February 8, 2018. https://artistshomes.org.

Nora, Pierre. "Between Memory and History: Les Lieux de Mémoire." *Representations* 26 (1989): 7–24.

North Carolina Historic Sites. "Somerset Homecomings." Accessed December 6, 2014. www.nchistorisites.org.

Obama White House Archives. "President Obama Designates Stonewall National Monument." Accessed February 22, 2018. https://obamawhitehouse.archives.gov/blog/2016/06/24/president-obama-designates-stonewall-national-monument.

Odum Institute for Research in Social Science, University of North Carolina at Chapel Hill. "Family History Research and Community Involvement." September 26, 2014. Accessed February 8, 2018. www.ancestrycdn.com/aa-k12/236/assets/Ancestry-Final-Report-Oct14.pdf.

Organization of American Historians. "Imperiled Promise: The State of History in the National Park Service." 2011. www.oah.org/site/assets/documents/Imperiled_Promise.pdf.

Oteros-Pailos, Jorge. Interview by Jo Byleveld and John Byleveld. *Radio Adelaide.* June 19, 2013. www.theplan.net.au/wp-content/uploads/2013/06/PLAN-Podcast-19th-June-2013.mp3.

Ouroussoff, Nicolai. "An Architect's Fear That Preservation Distorts." *New York Times*, May 23, 2011.

Page, Max. *Why Preservation Matters.* New Haven, CT: Yale University Press, 2016.

Page, Max, and Marla R. Miller, eds. *Bending the Future 50 Ideas for the Next 50 Years of Historic Preservation in the United States.* Amherst: University of Massachusetts Press, 2016.

Page, Max, and Randall Mason, eds. *Giving Preservation a History: Histories of Historic Preservation in the United States.* New York: Routledge, 2004.

Pallasmaa, Juhani. *Encounters 1: Architectural Essays.* Edited by Peter MacKeith. Helsinki, Finland: Rakennustieto Oy Publishing, 2012.

Parker, Patricia L., and Thomas F. King. "Guidelines for Evaluating and Documenting Traditional Cultural Properties." National Park Service, 1990; rev. 1992, 1998.

"Parkourplayhouse: Abandoned Stadium." YouTube video. June 27, 2012. www.youtube.com/watch?v=mebaCC3MxcY.

Partners for Sacred Places. "National Fund for Sacred Places/About." Accessed February 22, 2018. https://fundforsacredplaces.org.

Pee-Wee's Big Adventure. Movie Clip: The Alamo Tour (2005). YouTube, January 2, 2015. www.youtube.com/watch?v=0PdeHy_87OM.

Place Economics. www.placeeconomics.com.

Powers, Alan. *Beauty: A Short History.* London: Commission for Architecture and the Built Environment, 2010.

Quirk, Vanessa. "Glenn Lowry on American Folk Art Museum: The Decision Has Been Made." *Arc Daily*, January 29, 2014.

Redford, Dorothy Spruill. *Somerset Homecoming: Recovering a Lost Heritage.* New York: Doubleday, 1988.

Reisner, Yael, with Fleur Watson. *Architecture and Beauty: Conversations with Architects about a Troubled Relationship.* Chichester, UK: John Wiley & Sons, 2010.

Relph, Edward C. "Reflections on Place and Placelessness." *Environment & Architectural Phenomenology Newsletter.* 1996.

Reynolds, Reynold. http://artstudio reynolds.com/artworks/city-films.

Robinson, Sarah, and Juhani Pallasmaa, eds., *Mind in Architecture: Neuroscience, Embodiment, and the Future of Design*. Cambridge, MA: MIT Press, 2015.

Ruskin, John. "The Lamp of Memory." In *The Seven Lamps of Architecture*, 176–98. New York: Dover Publications, 1989.

———. *The Stones of Venice*. New York: Da Capo Press, 2003.

Rypkema, Donovan. "The Economics of Historic Preservation." Keynote Address. Alexandria Historic Preservation Conference and Town Meeting, May 5, 2007.

———. "Heritage Conservation and Property Values." In *The Economics of Uniqueness*. Edited by Guido Licciardi and Rana Amirtahmasebi, 107–42. Washington, DC: World Bank, 2012.

Said, Edward W. "Invention, Memory, and Place." *Critical Inquiry* 26, no. 2 (2000).

Salingaros, Nikos A. *A Theory of Architecture*. Kathmandu, Nepal: Vajra Books, 2013.

Save the Post Office. www.savethepostoffice.com.

Schama, Simon. *Landscape and Memory.* New York: Knopf, 1995.

Seamon, David. "Place, Place Identity, and Phenomenology: A Triadic Interpretation Based on J. G. Bennett's Systematics." In *The Role of Place Identity in the Perception, Understanding, and Design of Built Environments*. Edited by Hernan Casakin and Fátima Bernardo. Bentham E-books. https://ebooks.benthamscience.com/book/9781608054138.

Shannon, Sandra. "A Survey of the Public: Preference for Old and New Buildings, Attitudes about Historic Preservation, and Preservation-Related Engagement." Master's Thesis, University of Southern California, December 2014.

Siegler, Jeff. "Building Community through Historic Preservation: Sense of Place As an Economic Driver." Lecture, TEDxCLE, Cleveland, April 2011.

Sincavage, Rhonda. "Building Community through Historic Preservation: Not Your Grandmother's Preservation." Lecture, TEDxCLE, Cleveland, April 2011.

Smart Growth America. "Smart Growth Protects Natural Habitat." Accessed October 25, 2015. www.smart growthamerica.org/issues/environment/smart-growth-protects-natural-habitat.

Soule, Jeffrey. "Using the Historic Urban Landscape Approach: Context and Culture As a Framework." Sustaining Places. The American Planning Association. Accessed March 8, 2015. http://blogs.planning.org/sustainability/2014/11/20/using-the-historic-urban-landscape-approach-context-and-culture-as-a-framework/?utm_source=rss&utm_medium=rss&utm_campaign=using-the-historic-urban-landscape-approach-context-and-culture-as-a-framework.

Special Committee on Historic Preservation United States Conference of Mayors. *With Heritage So Rich*. Washington, DC: Preservation Books, 1999.

Sprague, Shaw. "Determined Advocacy Preserves the Historic Tax Credit." National Trust for Historic Preservation. December 20, 2017. https://savingplaces.org/stories/determined-advocacy-preserves-the-historic-tax-credit#.WpMThUly74g.

Starinsky, Thomas. "Building Community through Historic Preservation: Decisions on the Evolution of Cities." Lecture, TEDxCLE, Cleveland, April 2011.

Stearns, Peter N. "Why Study History?" American Historical Association. 1998. www.historians.org/about-aha-and-membership/aha-history-and-archives/archives/why-study-history-(1998).

Stipe, Robert E. *A Richer Heritage: Historic Preservation in the Twenty-First Century.* Chapel Hill: University of North Carolina Press, 2003.

Supple, Shannon. "Memory Slain: Recovering Cultural Heritage in Post-War Bosnia." *InterActions: UCLA Journal of Education and Information Studies* 1, no. 2 (2005).

Tuan, Yi Fu. *Space and Place: The Perspective of Experience.* Minneapolis: University of Minnesota Press, 1977.

Twigger-Ross, Clare L., and David L. Uzzell, "Place and Identity Processes." *Journal of Environmental Psychology* 16 (1996).

United States Green Building Council. "LEED Is Green Building." Accessed February 8, 2018. https://new.usgbc.org/leed.

Vitruvius. *Ten Books on Architecture.* Translated by Ingrid D. Rowland. Cambridge: Cambridge University Press, 1999.

Vowell, Sarah. *Assassination Vacation.* New York: Simon & Schuster, 2005.

Wanaselja, Leger. "Architecture." In *Sustainable Preservation Greening Existing Buildings.* Edited by Jean Carroon. Hoboken, NJ: John Wiley & Sons, 2010.

Warnick, Melody. *This Is Where You Belong.* New York: Viking 2016.

Wells, Jeremy C. "Authenticity in More Than One Dimension: Re-evaluating a Core Premise of Historic Preservation." *Forum Journal* 24, no. 3 (2010): 36–40.

Wells, Jeremy C., and Elizabeth D. Baldwin. "Historic Preservation, Significance and Age Value: A Comparative Phenomenology of Historic Charleston and the Nearby New-Urbanist Community of I'On." *Journal of Environmental Psychology* 32, no. 4 (2010): 384–400.

Weyeneth, Robert R. "Ancestral Architecture." In *Giving Preservation a History.* Edited by Max Page and Randall Mason, 257–81. New York: Routledge, 2004.

Williams, Michael Ann. "Vernacular Architecture and the Park Removals: Traditionalization As Justification and Resistance." *TDSR* 13, no. 1 (2001).

Wilson, Brian. "Milton Residents Fight to Keep Milton's Community Identity." Rutherford County Tennessee Historical Society. Accessed February 15, 2015. http://rutherfordtnhistory.org/milton-residents-fight-to-keep-miltons-community-identity.

Wolfe, Charles R. *Seeing the Better City.* Washington, DC: Island Press, 2016.

———. *Urbanism without Effort.* Washington, DC: Island Press E-ssentials, 2013.

Zumthor, Peter. *Atmospheres.* Basel, Switzerland: Birkhauser, 2006.

Index

About the Author

Thompson McCord Mayes, vice president and senior counsel at the National Trust for Historic Preservation, has spent his professional career preserving old places. In 2013, Tom was awarded the National Endowment for the Arts Rome Prize in Historic Preservation by the American Academy in Rome and subsequently spent a six-month residency in Rome as a fellow of the academy. The essays collected in this publication came about as a result of that experience. They were previously published in 2014 and 2015 as a series on the National Trust's preservation leadership forum blog, http://forum.savingplaces.org/connect/blogs.